Barbarous Play

Barbarous Play

Race on the English Renaissance Stage

LARA BOVILSKY

University of Minnesota Press

MINNEAPOLIS · LONDON

An earlier version of chapter 3 was previously published as "Black Beauties, White Devils: The English Italian in Milton and Webster," *English Literary History* 70 (2003): 625–51.

Published by the University of Minnesota Press
111 Third Avenue South, Suite 290
Minneapolis, MN 55401-2520
http://www.upress.umn.edu

Library of Congress Cataloging-in-Publication Data

Bovilsky, Lara, 1973–
    Barbarous play : race on the English Renaissance stage / Lara Bovilsky.
        p.   cm.
    Includes bibliographical references and index.
    ISBN 978-0-8166-4964-8 (alk. paper) — ISBN 978-0-8166-4965-5
(pbk. : alk. paper)
    1. Race in literature.   2. English drama—Early modern and Elizabethan,
1500–1600—History and criticism.   3. English drama—17th century—
History and criticism.   4. Theater—England—History—16th century.
5. Theater—England—History—17th century.   6. Race in the theater—
England—History.   I. Title.
    PR658.R34B68 2008
    822'.309355—dc22

                                                                            2008004242

Printed in the United States of America on acid-free paper

The University of Minnesota is an equal-opportunity educator and employer.

15 14 13 12 11 10 09 08   10 9 8 7 6 5 4 3 2 1

for my mother
and in memory of my father

Contents

Acknowledgments

❧❦❧

From my first sustained dialogue with him in a memorable class on Renaissance women writers, Jonathan Goldberg infused my graduate experience with the excitement, pleasure, and challenge that consistently elicited my best efforts. This book is deeply indebted to that exchange, and I offer him my most affectionate thanks for his teaching and friendship. Laurie Shannon's rigorous, clear-headed, and generous reading and advice likewise have been essential to this project and beyond it. Other former teachers also deserve thanks: I offer it to Leigh DeNeef, Joe Porter, and Maureen Quilligan for their encouragement, warmth, and the example of their own work.

Many of these arguments were refined in seminars at the Folger Shakespeare Library and at the annual meeting of the Shakespeare Association of America. I am grateful for the feedback I received; I wish to thank especially James Shapiro, Ian Smith, Natasha Korda, Carla Mazzio, Gail Kern Paster, Rebecca Totaro, and David Hillman for their thoughtful responses to early drafts. The two anonymous readers at the University of Minnesota Press offered invaluable criticisms and comments that improved this book enormously: I thank them for their time and care. I thank Richard Morrison, my editor, for his interest and advocacy; his suggestions and those of the Press's editorial board were invariably helpful and apt. I am grateful to Nancy Sauro and Lynn Walterick for their expert copyediting and to Brent Dawson for help with indexing.

Colleagues and friends at Washington University and elsewhere have contributed a great deal both to my writing and my life away from the computer. I am beholden to Joe Loewenstein for his generosity and for the openness and energy with which he approaches every problem. Joe, Steve Zwicker, Wolfram Schmidgen, Derek Hirst, and Christine Johnson make Washington University an exciting place to work in early modern studies. Marina Mackay is an inexhaustible intellectual and peripatetic resource. I owe warm thanks to her and to Angela Burns, Julie Paulson, Vin Nardizzi, Rebecca DeRoo, and Jami Ake for insightful readings of early drafts. Aaron Kunin gave much-appreciated encouragement and suggestions. Andrew Mattison deserves special thanks—more than I can provide here— for the brilliant attention he lavished on sentence after sentence.

I am grateful for my brother Adam's love and friendship. My parents, Jay and Deborah, have provided enduring love and support for all my endeavors; for these gifts, and many others, this book is dedicated to them.

Race on the Renaissance Stage

᭦᭦᭦

Yet what surface must an object have to appear black?

—Thomas Hobbes, *Physical Dialogue*

An Analogy: Salvini on the Nineteenth-Century Stage

In 1870, the Italian actor Tommaso Salvini began a North American tour in the United States. His first performances were as Othello, his signature role since he had popularized it in Italy in 1856. In New York, Salvini performed before a (primarily) English-speaking audience, but he himself spoke in Italian, with an Italian company. Despite the language barrier, Salvini felt Americans grasped his performance: "[it] mattered little; they understood me all the same, or, to put it better, they caught by intuition my ideas and my sentiments."[1] Still, by Salvini's own account, this acceptance and understanding were hardly instantaneous. In fact, the intensity of his performances disturbed many members of his audience. In an era that delighted in rich and even explosive theatrical depictions of emotional extremes, Salvini's portrayal went beyond American norms, particularly in his use of rage and physical violence; at various points he picked up and manhandled both Iago and Desdemona, expressing his character's fury through growling acts of violence that his character alternately restrained despairingly and indulged impulsively.[2] Especially shocking to Salvini's audience, where other period actors of Othello struck Desdemona using a letter Othello has received from Desdemona's kinsman (4.1.239), Salvini delivered "a backhanded blow" directly to Desdemona's "sweet lips."[3] According to Salvini, the American

I

public, though (as he said) intuitive, was only slowly won to the idea that such graphic portrayals of "excesses of fury were appropriate to the son of the desert, and that one of southern blood must be much better qualified to interpret them than a northerner" (157).

In Salvini's analysis, the stir excited by his vivid depictions of rage and jealousy was resolved into an appreciative understanding of his interpretation by means of a shared theory of regionally and environmentally determined psychology. As he saw it, American anxieties about the moral decorum of his theatrical violence were allayed when his performance was construed as accurately—and thereby decorously—depicting what were seen as relevant racial and national traits.[4] Salvini's success relied on standards of extradramatic verisimilitude, standards that accordingly tell us as much about nineteenth-century theories of race as they do about theories of acting. Salvini claimed to portray the passions of a North African "appropriately," an argument that derived force from eighteenth- and nineteenth-century conventions about Shakespeare's uncanny psychological insight and from older yet persistent conventions about national and racial temperament. Together, these beliefs implied that the precision of Shakespeare's psychological realism demanded a portrayal of the sort that Salvini provided.

My interest is not in the intellectual infrastructure of nineteenth-century Bardolatry, a decidedly post-Renaissance phenomenon. Rather, I begin with the example of Salvini because nineteenth-century reaction to Salvini's controversial performances reveals just the sort of racial content that critics and historians of the Renaissance and early modern period have generally assumed to occur only in pre-eighteenth-century racial formations. In this way, Salvini's cross-racial portrayal troubles the periodization of race that has been increasingly taken for granted among those who study race's early forms, a periodization that, this book will argue, has limited our ability to understand the history of race. As we will see, in describing what they saw as the racial components of his performance, Salvini's contemporaries do not focus on strict canons of bodily differences or scientific notions of racial variety. Rather, they dwell on impressions of differential systems of affect, psychology, and intellect, on racial analogy, and on racial fluidity—all sites of active racial signification in the early modern period. His example therefore illustrates an important consonance between Renaissance and modern racial logics, rooted in the very instability of racial identities usually taken to distinguish pre- from post-Enlightenment racial formations.

In fact, I will argue, early modern racial logics have much in common with modern and contemporary ones, including most of all those elements that make racial identities unstable and incoherent, elements long believed specific to the earlier period. These include changing categories of racial affiliation based on figurative, contradictory, and invisible group distinctions of temperament, genealogy, or "blood." Likewise, in both early modern and modern contexts, intransigent racial meanings and identities are often produced paradoxically through the very act of an individual crossing a racial boundary or changing an affiliation (as with Salvini performing a cross-racial impersonation). I will specify these elements further below, noting here that because they characterize racial experience transhistorically, they should be seen as central to the study of race—not as an impediment to substantive analysis as has often been assumed by early modern historicism. In describing how race is presented on the English Renaissance stage, this book will assume that narratives of fluidity and boundary crossing mark the characteristic sites for both the production and analysis of racial content, will trace their intriguing contours, and will use them to argue for a heightened sense of the relevance of the past to our present understanding of race.

The plays of the English Renaissance are particularly well suited to this sort of analysis, for in them racial experience appears almost routinely in myriad tales of interracial relationships and successful cross-racial disguises, facilitated by and entangled in proximate discourses of conversion, class transgression, troubled national boundaries, and narratives of physical and moral degeneracy. Such tales reveal the culture's conventional wisdom, as well as its anxieties and fantasies, about the stability, instability, and diffusion of racial identities in its midst. In examining several of these narratives found in plays by Shakespeare, Marlowe, Middleton, and Webster (and in some of Milton's poems), we will see that they tell a complicated story, one in which early modern racial difference is represented as both attractive and frightening; is both projected onto externalized groups (such as Moors, Jews, and Mediterranean peoples) and claimed as internal to English culture (for instance in "black" women, or people of low degree); and which depends for its expression upon interrelation with other key categories shaping group identities, such as gender, religion, and nationality.

The nineteenth-century example at hand will help illustrate how these elements—here race, nation, and psychology—can work together. Likewise, attending closely to how Salvini's performances were perceived will help us see how the early modern lasts into the modern. It is important to note in this context Salvini's claim that his own Italian identity was considered to be as relevant to the performance as the African identity of the character Othello. Salvini asserted a special faculty for what we might see as an early version of "method" acting by virtue of his origins, origins imagined as placing him in psychological proximity to African emotional "excesses." This posited similarity between Italian and African character may strike many twenty-first-century readers as surprising—yet I hope the connection will already resonate with the reader of English Renaissance drama, schooled to the special significance for the English of "Italian" settings as jumping-off places for narratives of emotional extremes, immorality, and "exotic" geographies and their inhabitants. I will have more to say about Italian settings in their Renaissance context in chapter 3, where I examine their cumulative impact in helping the English to imagine their own nationality as racially hybrid. Here it suffices that Salvini's argument about his Italianness proved convincing to nineteenth-century Americans: eventually his fury-fortified "southern blood" won out over American squeamishness, and his work enjoyed evident popularity in Boston, New York, Philadelphia, and "that pleasant city, Detroit" (157).

Ten years later, the Boston Globe Theater offered Salvini an innovative set of return performances that partly bridged the linguistic gap between the actor and his audience. This time, Salvini was to perform with an American troupe, responding in Italian to their English cues. The arrangement would be far easier on Americans, the theater-owner's factor explained to a skeptical Salvini, since it would lessen demands on the audience, which "[would] concern itself only with following you . . . and [would] not have to pay any attention to the others, whose words it will understand" (197). Despite this rather ominous view of the vagaries of the audience's regard, the linguistically hybrid performances were extremely popular, even though Salvini could not have been understood by the vast majority of playgoers.[5] Salvini played seasons in the United States in 1880 and 1883 and in London the following year. These performances have been largely responsible for Salvini's enduring Anglophone reputation, his reviewers again usually dwelling on the violence of his portrayal, especially the "terrible and almost excessive demonstration of fury of his last scene," with considerable ambivalence.[6] Whether approved or censured (and obviously haunting either way), Salvini's interpretation remained controversial, its extremes linked both to the Italian "nature" of the performer and the African "nature" of the character. For once Salvini was the only Italian speaker on stage, the spectacle of fictional Othello's arguably overindulged passions was still harder to separate from the spectacle of actual Italianness with which it shared corporeal space. Salvini represented to English speakers the unthinkable jealousies of an African partly by means of the incomprehensible language in which he uttered them, and he solicited the erosion of the barrier between fiction and reality when he claimed to draw on his own geographic and national origins for his dramatic insights into jealousy, rage, and revenge.[7]

Salvini's contention that his "southern blood" better suited him to channel the furies natural to a "son of the desert" was shared by one fan fluent in Italian, Henry James, who avidly attended Salvini's performances on both sides of the Atlantic, starstruck enough to declare he would "go every night" to see Salvini, "if he were to appear with a company of Hottentots."[8] James's comments are useful in concretizing the cultural associations that surrounded Salvini's performances. James disputed reviews of the performances as "ugly, repulsive, bestial" and "brutal and truculent,"[9] and, like Salvini, wished to convert critical accusations that the actor had overstepped into appreciation for the interpretation as a virtuoso inflection of the origins of performer and character: "Salvini's rendering of the part is the portrait of an African by an Italian, a fact which should give the judicious spectator, in advance, the pitch of the performance."[10] As assumptions about national temperaments have changed quite a bit since the 1880s, it is worth clarifying what judicious pitch, precisely, James intends the discriminating critic to hear.

For James as, presumably, for much of Salvini's audience, "the portrait of an African" entailed an irrational emotionalism. However, even given Salvini's "southern blood," this depiction might approach but was not to succumb utterly to the "bestial," that is, behavior that was unpleasantly unthinking, uncontrolled, and inhuman. To please, the actor could not simply indulge in an unsuitable portrayal of baseness associated with Africans.[11] For instance, James deplores the "bestial fury, which does much to sicken the English [English-language] reader of the play," in the Othello of another Italian actor, Ernesto Rossi. By contrast, even Salvini's wild gestural work displayed mitigating moral qualities:

> My remarks may suggest that Salvini's rage is too gross, too
> much that of a wounded animal; but in reality it does not
> fall into that excess. It is the rage of an African, but of a
> nature that remains generous to the end; and in spite of the
> tiger-paces and tiger-springs, there is through it all, to my
> sense at least, the tremor of a moral element.[12]

James's "but" and concessive use of animal imagery show that the audience did not wish to see portrayed a character conforming to their lowest expectations of an African. Salvini's Othello, tempered by the "moral element" that the nineteenth century read everywhere in Shakespeare, was reclaimed as suitable and authentically Shakespearean and no longer "sickened" the "English reader."

Less familiar to us is the tone of James's thoughts about Italians—which may surprise with their proximity to stereotypes about Africans: "[Salvini's characters] present themselves to him—as they naturally do to the Italian imagination—as embodiments of feeling, without intellectual complications; the creature to be represented appears a creature of passion, of quick susceptibility, of senses lying close to the surface."[13] The "Italian imagination," so free of "intellectual complications," "naturally" suggested the possibility of misreading: "Salvini reads [Shakespeare] with an Italian imagination, and it is equally natural to us to believe that in doing so he misses a large part of him."[14] Here, James broadens the range of effects thought to proceed "naturally" from Salvini's Italian psychology and intellect. Was it not possible that Salvini's Italian identity distorted his reception and representation of the play, much as his lines, translated, might be thought to do? (Imagination aside, he also read Shakespeare with an Italian *edition,* after all.) Or was Salvini's background, as he claimed, actually bringing him closer to the "African" character of Othello? If Othello's "susceptibility" to passion was a sign of his race, wasn't Salvini's analogous focus on overwhelming emotion in fact appropriate? And, given the condensation of Salvini's region of origin into his very blood, wasn't the nature of his performance a sign of his racial identity, over and above his national allegiance? Salvini's notorious blow to Desdemona seemed to some viewers to advertise his "taint of savage ancestry."[15] Just what was "Italian," that it can be seen to answer to a nineteenth-century sense of "African" in so many respects? Salvini's presence as a lone Italian among Englishmen might be read as recapitulating *Othello*'s own demographic scene, which presents "the," as the play's title has it, lone Moor among Venetians.[16] Playing Othello in this capacity, Salvini can be seen as representing a quality of Moorish "authenticity" to English-speaking audiences, using his "southern blood," his foreign tongue, and his impassioned, "unintellectual" responses to convey a Shakespearean vérité.

If the ingredients just mentioned evoked the Italian "race" for the nineteenth century, their genealogy had its roots in part in the Renaissance drama in which Salvini exhibited them. James's remarks rely on nineteenth-century beliefs that tied nation and race (the two virtually indistinguishable) to particular abilities in literary expression.[17] But the assumption that racial groups were defined by common blood, forged by common geographic origin (for example, in Salvini's words, "southern" or "desert"), and known for their common psychological makeup was far older. And this assumption, too, makes nation and race difficult to distinguish. Yet the discourse around Salvini's performances begins, I hope, to suggest ways in which the very interrelation of race with proximate, identity-forming categories such as nationality may be used to untangle racial content. Likewise, I would argue that Salvini's example suggests continuities between the racial experiences of the early modern and modern contexts in at least three respects. First, Salvini's example underlines some racist stereotypes that persist into modernity (for example, Iago's "these Moors are changeable in their wills").[18] More significantly, Salvini's reception provides a modern invocation of race that, as in the early modern period, in no way depends upon reified biological models—that, like many of the examples we will see from the Renaissance, *does not even require physical descriptions* of Othello or Salvini to construct them as racial subjects. And last, Salvini's reception shows that racial fluidity, as when the Italian stands in for the African, is a feature of racial representations that is not eliminated by the nineteenth century. But neither Renaissance nor nineteenth-century racial fluidity precludes generation of rich data or sure analysis about the specific content of the racial perceptions or operations that produce fluidity, even when those perceptions and operations are neither internally consistent nor entirely stable.

Terms for Reading Race

Salvini's incorporeal mapping of Italian onto African may have revealed a surprising or unexpected facet of nineteenth-century racial experience. Our first means of interpreting race, even as it existed in the past, remain the intuitive understandings we have come to possess over the course of our own lives. These understandings, shaped by the contingent rules of a particular time and place, make some instances of racialization seem obvious while they circumscribe the plausibility of others within unexamined categories learned individually. The growing body of work historicizing racial systems has therefore provided invaluable perspective on a form of social organization that can otherwise easily appear self-evident and incontestable.[19]

Yet even when successfully challenging the everyday orthodoxy of racial self-evidence, historicist work on race has proven enduringly uneasy about the very nature of the entity under study—the ontology, content, and parameters of past systems of race and racism. The difficulty of rigorous historicism has been compounded when applying theories generated in contemporary discussions of race, which may depend upon and imply their specific cultural moment, to a culture removed in time and/or place from our own. In this way, while discussions of race in earlier periods have proliferated and increased in theoretical sophistication, all too frequently they continue to rely on received notions of twentieth- or twenty-first-century racial formations. Yet definitions of race or racism attempting to bridge the ages may be unduly vague (or worse, may still imply specifically modern realities). Before looking at the Renaissance context, it will be useful therefore to consider the nature of race in the abstract.

Most frequently, definitions root race and racism primarily in biology, in phenotype, and in the fixity of racial identity.[20] In studies historicizing race, these elements are assumed to predominate as race takes its mature form, the fluidity of the early modern period giving way to fixed racial groupings based on scientific organization of physical characteristics.[21] This book will argue that these assumptions are false: first, that race is not now, and indeed has never been, a matter merely of biological categories, phenotypes, or fixed identities; second, that the past is neither as fluid as has been nearly universally assumed, nor the present as rigid.

As a start, we can observe that neither biology, phenotype, nor fixity explains the connection made by nineteenth-century theater critics between Salvini's Italian identity and the African "savagery" he portrayed onstage. The critics' beliefs about Salvini show that often more is involved in the cultural productions of racism than theories about biology and physical differences. Racist theories encompass specific beliefs about nationality, language, psychology, intellect, religion, morality, vocation, class, gender, and sexuality, to name some significant and interrelated categories. Belief in races relates members of a group to each other in ways not always strictly accounted for by biological theory or physical essentialism. Moreover, theories of biology have altered greatly over time: Renaissance humoral theory, a way of understanding human physiology and psychology, and thus the version of "biology" most relevant to the present study, is not the same as Victorian or modern understandings of biology. The racism of any historical period or place will reflect the beliefs about race, as well as the beliefs about other fields of knowledge deemed relevant by the culture, specific to that context.

In the chapters that follow, I trace racist logics that are based in physical differences and ideas about the body, but also racist logics that arise from beliefs about culture, nation, ancestry, gender, religion, class, and other categories under whose rubrics group identities are forged. My argument reflects the understanding that racialist discourse is inconsistent but will nonetheless tend to have content of predictable types. Necessarily, each type of racialist content will possess a substantial fictive element centering on the belief that the membership, origin, and/or cohesiveness of human groups is determinate. For instance, group membership may be selectively or circularly determined; likewise, the diversity or hybridity of groups may be ignored or denied.[22] Though fictive notions about the determinacy of groups unite them, the ideas and representative tropes that produce racial meaning are varied in their scope, imagery, mechanisms, and implications. I provide the following list of the chief types of racialist content in order to indicate their range, limitations, overlap, and disjunctions and to present the most fundamental components of belief in races, components hardly requiring a complex biological theory for their articulation.[23]

First, racialist discourses predictably include content about the corporate inheritance of particular physical and moral traits and abilities. Belief in corporate inheritance persists even when individuals within the group are not directly related to one another or when individuals lack the posited traits and abilities. We might call this a troubled *genetic* theory of group identity.

Second, racialist discourses predictably assert a relation between offspring and forebears guaranteed by their metaphorical sharing of physical substance, especially "blood." The metaphors associated with this relation, though materialist, can also figure the sharing of immaterial traits and abilities, thus blood may figure moral resemblance. Via the claim of bodily material held in common, one member of a group can assert rights over the body or behavior of another member (particularly a relative), rights akin to the property rights held over one's own body. People do not ever actually share blood, yet the belief that they do possesses tenacious and widespread appeal. We might call this a troubled theory of *substantial similarity* within groups.

Similarly, racialist discourses may assert a relation between multiple sets of offspring and forebears guaranteed by their metaphorical sharing of values and history, in which "common" history circularly defines just who is considered to be offspring or forebears. Thus even a close relation may be considered not to share history and may be excluded from group membership. This presents a troubled theory of *historical identity* and *moral similarities* within groups.[24]

Next, racialist discourses may speculate about the causes of human variation, attributing variation to climate or human adaptation in a broader form. This might include ascribing physical and moral variations to cultural and environmental variations. We might call this a *nongenetic* theory of group identity.[25]

Racialist discourses may assert the difference of some people from others, concretizing difference in derogatory or distancing tropes, such as comparisons to animals, children, objects, or intermediate beings, such as "savages." This is the rhetorical strategy most baldly directed at emphasizing clear-cut racial boundaries (through hyperbole and distortion). Such assertions present a theory of *ontological* differences between groups.[26]

Last, racialist discourses may assert the difference of some people from others, exaggerating variations in human phenotypes or behavior in tropes that order and measure difference—particularly tropes that assign *relational meanings* to difference, such as antithesis and hierarchy. These exaggerations theorize that the facts of difference are intrinsically subject to *comparative measurement and symbolic interpretation.*

The last form of racial content is less frequently remarked as an objectionable logic, though we will see it is as much at the root of racialist meaning as the others. Put more simply, I mean that the move from the observation of differences, say, in stature or hair texture, to the creation of an organizing scheme to map these variations in relation to each other is a contingent move. For example, if skin color differences are perceived metaphorically as "opposites" (antithesis), as when we distinguish a "white" person from a "black" one, both colors are only figuratively perceived (no one has skin of either color), and the color terms are in fact being used to evoke an opposition that does not exist. Every time color terms are used in this way, the damaging suggestion of an opposition between people assigned to each category is intensified. If bone structure or hair texture is perceived as belonging to a hierarchic ordering, as routinely used to happen in older (but recent) anthropology charts or sociological explanations of racial "development," this too is a specious distortion used just to create a fallacious relation of physical attributes to each other, a relation intended to figure a moral or ontological hierarchy.[27] Such ordering of physical characteristics is more dangerous when combined with the fallacious group logics given above. That is, hierarchic or oppositional ordering of groups or group characteristics depends upon greater distortions and inflicts greater damage than hierarchic or oppositional ordering of individuals.

In examining the different types of racialist content, we should note that they do not tell the same story: some refer primarily to a group identity as constituted by its (selectively identified) ancestors; some refer primarily to physical differences among people; and others are concerned with the relation of nonphysical attributes of people to physical ones (as in the Renaissance theory of humors, which correlated individual psychologies with the variety and proportion of individual bodily fluids).[28] Some racialist discourses center on searching for causes of human difference (as with the topoi in Renaissance writing that dwell on the causes of Moorish dark skin, for which both genetic and nongenetic explanations were advanced, or on the causes of New World Indian "innocence"). Others are more concerned with the effects of difference (as when Las Casas and Sepúlveda debated the human status of Indians, to determine whether they might be converted and what forms of control/abuse were legitimately applied to them, or when, as we will see, dramatic characters like Iago and Brabantio worry about the implications of interracial marriage).[29] Still others are most concerned with establishing the membership of the group, through physical or nonphysical attributes or, as with the important, much-used trope of shared "blood," through a metaphorical attribute masquerading as a physical one. In addition, we should note that not all of these forms of racial discourse refer to human physical difference. Some refer instead primarily to the "spirit" or values associated with different races. In many cases during both the Renaissance and the present, the maintenance of group identities based on beliefs in heritable membership, in common history and values, or in a metaphorically shared physical substance (that does not require obvious bodily manifestations) is sufficient for an ascription of racialization, one that does not necessarily depend on physical signs or that is able to overlook physical diversity within a group.

The range and variety of discourses contributing to any culture's understandings of race are therefore broad, perhaps broader than is usually acknowledged. Yet all are involved in the production of racial experience and important for its analysis, as we will see in the following chapters. Even bearing this discursive variety and range in mind is salutary; I believe it helps clarify the nature both of differences that distinguish Renaissance from later racial systems and also of the elements they have in common, that is, the types of discourses themselves. For as cultural and literary historians have made clear, racial experience in the Renaissance, not yet thoroughly marked by the history of race-based slavery and not yet decisively associated with the discourses and classificatory logics of modern scientific thought, was quite different from race in our own time. Nevertheless, as will be seen, these differences may also be overestimated.

Race in the Renaissance: A Critical History

Some of the difficulties of reading race in the Renaissance are immediately obvious. Renaissance racial vocabulary presents interpretive difficulties, first of all, because names and categories of racial groups are unstable. For instance, Anthony Barthelemy notes uses of the word "Moor" to describe both light- and dark-skinned Africans, Muslims and non-Muslims, as well as Asians, Arabs, Native Americans, and Jews.[30] Likewise, James Shapiro finds shifting and intertwined definitions of both Englishness and Jewishness.[31] Such referential variety and drift should be taken seriously, indicating that membership in racial groups is less discrete and indelible during the Renaissance than we take it to be now. Not necessarily organized into stable or discrete identity categories, period markers of racial difference encompass distinctions of nationality, religion, geographic and climatic origin, humors, skin color, body type, cultural variation, and "degree."[32] Many of these categories impact one another. As Mary Floyd-Wilson has shown, early modern ethnology posited a relation between climate and bodily humors to explain and map regionally characteristic body types and psychologies.[33] Meanwhile, understandings of degree justified the boundaries between highborn and lowborn with beliefs about heritable differences between the two groups in skin color, feature and body type, psychology, and quality of blood. Similar physical and psychical distinctions made between men and women suggest deep connections between Renaissance ideologies of gender and race.

In some places, race may be invoked as an obscure symbol or trope when least expected, as in *The Winter's Tale,* when Florizel represents his Sicilian wife as the Princess of Libya to her own father in order to disguise her identity.[34] Such moments—in which a family member is represented in some way as a member of an external group—testify to central English fantasies and anxieties about an *internalized* racialization, a narrative we will see repeatedly in the plays discussed throughout this book. But of course, Florizel's imposture with Perdita also has something to say about English understandings of racialized resemblances between and among different foreign groups, especially Mediterranean ones; I discuss some of these understandings in chapters 3 and 4.

Yet at the same time, in drama and other Renaissance texts, racialized vocabulary may be absent where we have come most to expect it. For instance, there are few early modern English descriptions of Jewish hooked noses—so few that it has been possible to suggest an English conceptual separation between matters of theology and ethnicity or race for Jews, Turks, and Muslims, though more recent work has demonstrated to the contrary, showing that racial concerns exist even without their modern physiological signifiers.[35] These differences from modern organizations of racial experience imply that we have something to learn about and from race in the Renaissance and indicate moments where research can begin.

Nonetheless, as the field of race studies emerged within English Renaissance literary criticism, the first large-scale investigations did not generally begin with the assumption of a radically altered conceptual landscape for race, nor did they consider the implications of unstable or different identity categories or of different understandings of human variation. Instead, the most frequent (and well-motivated) strategy was to collate imagery in Renaissance texts that seemed to reflect racist or tolerant views of groups understood in our own time to be coherent racial or ethnic communities.[36] These studies admirably directed critical attention to a range of representations of race, and the best of them feature intricate, particularized readings. But their reliance on preexisting identity categories and groupings implied a different array and a greater coherence of racial identities than in fact exists in the period. The premise of stable, recognizable Renaissance racial groups distorted the conclusions to be made about Renaissance attitudes toward race. In particular, the choice to study a single group limited the information to be derived from analogies and shifts between groups and between individual characters—analogies and shifts more representative of Renaissance racial logics than is the presence of coherent groups.[37] Barthelemy's survey of the representation of "black" characters in English Renaissance drama, for instance, notes the period's seemingly loose application of the term "Moor," the varied complexions and temperaments of African characters, and the conflations of black with Native American and Mexican characters in pageants and plays. This evident diversity is still fused in his book's title and its central argument into a claim that Renaissance drama as a whole adopts a negative attitude toward "black" characters and *the* (that is, singular) "black race."[38]

Still, where scholars had once assumed that the imagery of race in Renaissance literature was infrequent and derived primarily from textual sources, this group of researchers found a wealth of material, evidence that the early modern English were deeply invested in representing African, Moorish, and Jewish characters—and that these characterizations reflected the experience of substantial interaction with non-English people, both outside and inside England. Building on this work, the most important contribution to English Renaissance studies of race, Kim Hall's *Things of Darkness,* expanded the recognized sites of racial signification still more vastly. In discussions both of texts and objects, Hall's book illustrated the centrality of discourses and images of blackness to English culture, their importance in shoring up authorial ambitions, codes of aristocracy, and gender hierarchy, and their ability to provide omnipresent material reminders, in the forms of miniatures, portraits, or earrings, of optimistic English mercantile and colonialist ambitions.

Things of Darkness moved race studies to the forefront of Renaissance literary criticism, presiding over what Peter Erickson has memorably called "the moment of race in Renaissance studies," a moment that saw "the emergence of systematic, intensive investigation of race" in the field.[39] After Hall delineated an expanded field of study, researchers recognized, discovered, and made use of further historical and textual materials with increasing command over their meaning and interconnections, exploring, for instance, how race affected early English passes at colonialism or how beliefs about the humors affected English understandings of racialized bodies.[40] Critical accounts of race and racial identity that were worked out in this period (the mid-1990s) have proven lastingly influential and generative. It is worth noting, therefore, that these accounts often continued to rely on present-day terminology and definitions in their analyses of race, particularly in framing theories used to govern the approach to race studies itself—those theories, as I put it earlier, concerning the ontology, content, and parameters of historical racial systems. I turn now to these theories and the continuing impact they have had on the field.

The meaning and reference of period racial terminology, particularly the word "black," remained an interpretive problem, as did the relation of such terminology to its modern successors. Like the word "Moor," which Barthelemy had first showed to be surprisingly flexible in its application to diverse individuals and groups, "black" seemed to possess broad, unpredictable applicability. While "black" often clearly signaled racial content, critics were both intrigued and discomfited when that content attached to individuals and groups not called black today. Some readers, such as Hall, saw continuity between modern and early modern racial color logics, asserting that even when "black" was applied to the Irish, the Spanish, or to Native Americans, "in these instances it still draws its power from England's ongoing negotiations of African difference and from the implied color comparison therein."[41]

Much turns on the question of what "black" means in its various Renaissance usages. The word is always applied metaphorically (to selective parts of the body and populace) as an intensifier. We know, for instance, that it was routinely applied to people, especially women, with dark eyes or hair, a usage that merits close attention and that I will explore at greater length in chapter 1. The word was also applied to people of diverse national, religious, ethnic, and geographic origins. It is my view that deciding in advance what relates these different uses of the word by subsuming them all under a settled definition in which skin color and Africa are the perfectly aligned master tropes threatens to simplify our understanding of the parameters of race in the early modern period and, as Hall herself worries, to "reify the very binarism I am trying to deconstruct."[42]

Modern American terminology, it is true, refers only to people of African descent as black (regardless of the color of their skin). Yet of course the interpretive problem itself is motivated by Renaissance English uses of "black" that do not follow this practice. In trying to analyze the meaning of this term during the Renaissance, it may be helpful to note that the conflation of geography, genealogy, and color in the American usage of "black" is not even a modern universal. For instance, a difference in modern usage between the United States and England is worth emphasizing here and elsewhere: in the United States, race's color predicates invariably reflect the history of Africanized slavery, while in England the more explicitly interwoven histories of slavery and colonialism extend the number and origins of racialized groups and correspondingly broaden the application of "black," especially to people of South Asian and Arab descent.[43] As I will discuss further, such variability in terminology indicates that even racial identifications that seem based on objective, visual evidence (as is suggested by the term "black") may in fact be determined by the contexts of their observation. Racial meanings that now seem empirical and unalterable may be shown to result from historical contingencies; in this regard, the early modern context differs from modernity in certain crucial respects.

The period on which I will be focusing predates the rise of profitable, slave-based plantation economies that led to the consequent expansion, consolidation, and definitive Africanization and racialization of the slave trade. At this time, dark-skinned people were not only imagined as slaves, slaves were not only Africans, and many

Englishmen were themselves enslaved in North Africa and within the Ottoman Empire—so many, in fact, that "slave" was more likely to connote a captive Englishman than an African laborer.[44] Nor was it inevitable that the English would systematically enslave Africans. Sujata Iyengar has provided a vital account of the diversity of responses with which the English greeted the prospect of enslaving fellow human beings—reluctance and repugnance alongside cupidity and cruelty.[45] Mary Floyd-Wilson notes that prior geohumoral beliefs—according to which Africans were presumed to be quick-witted, pious, and noble—were in fact incompatible with the racist stereotypes that accompanied the slave trade. Indeed, according to these prior beliefs, often enough it was the English, Northern body that appeared vulnerable or inferior.[46] Similarly, as Richmond Barbour, among others, has shown, English feelings of inferiority themselves contributed to xenophobic or chauvinistic posturing: in many cases the English wrote or staged self-glorifying fictions precisely to contest their political and material weakness in their encounters with other cultures. We are mistaken, Barbour reminds us, when we "suppose that the unexplored world was . . . supine."[47]

Iyengar's and Floyd-Wilson's narratives remind us that generating the institutions and ideologies that facilitated racialized slavery took enormous cultural effort. Many early components of that effort may be found in the logics traced in this book, but these are entangled with other beliefs that reveal English attitudes toward race as complex and conflicted, as, in Daniel Vitkus's words, both "xenophobic and xenophilic."[48] Such complexity (and not simply taxonomic instability) is also reflected in part in the period's inconsistent terminology. This book will address topics that become visible when we allow for broader definitions of blackness and of race: English involvement with racialized non-African cultures, whether or not they are called "black"; other forms of racialized representation besides tropes of darkness; other forms of English relations to images of racial darkness besides successful or failed dominance; and the repeated shifts in English and non-English and partially English racial identities and identifications that we see during (and after) the period within English texts.

We should not assume that Renaissance understandings of race mirror ours. But the differences between them need not prove interpretively daunting or render the past meaningless for us. One of the great virtues of Hall's study is its proofs of the thoroughness and urgency with which representations of darkness were woven into the material and literary texts of the English imaginary. The vast archive assembled in her book presents a corrective to the tentative and not infrequently skeptical tone of much of both the prior and subsequent criticism on race in the Renaissance. Indeed, to produce critical meditations on the experience of race during the Renaissance is to become fully aware of the irony according to which those critics most sensitive to the difficulties of describing race in an unavailable culture are prone to overemphasizing the impossibility of their (self-chosen) theoretical task. The tone was set early on. For example, in an especially fruitful exploration of the interrelations of race, gender, and class in Aphra Behn's *Oroonoko,* Margaret Ferguson raises the difficulties of analyzing concepts subject to great temporal and geographic ideological variability and provides "my personal solution: a plea to scholars to suspend their own assumptions about what a category like race means or meant to members of a different culture . . . without assuming that we have any a priori understanding of what they mean even in our own by no means homogenous academic subculture."[49] To be sure, suspending critical assumptions and avoiding the specious comfort of a priori expectations is sound advice for performing research, but Ferguson's warning against generating sustained conclusions about race in Renaissance England and in contemporary academia alike tends to discourage or disallow scholarship that would provide more substantive understandings of race in both cultures, even the ones that her study ably generates.

As my own project implies, I view pursuing such understandings as essential in order to add to the history of an ideological category that has been immensely powerful partly because it has usually been seen as intuitive, obvious, and ahistorical. It's been said before but bears repeating: stripping race of these associations can most easily be begun by understanding race's historical contingency and contesting its continuing prescriptive and punitive force.[50] Indeed, Ferguson's very observation that the ideological content of race has varied over time and space seems to me most valuable inasmuch as it asserts the changing forms of racialized experience and challenges the cultural historian to put a diachronic, human, complicated history in place of what has so often been characterized as an unchanging, natural, simple, and "obvious" fact. To note that criteria for racial identification, for instance, vary over time and space is to disprove their supposed simplicity and algorithmic precision. To note that the content of racist ideologies about the same group varies according to the economic, political, and personal situations of their believers is to deprive racist beliefs of their supposedly empirical authority.[51] Racist ideology is further deflated when its contradictory content is foregrounded. All told, Ferguson's insight about the cultural variation of race suggests possibilities for the historicization and dismantling of the ascendancy of prescriptive racializations taken for logic or fact. The variability of racial ideology and experience may mean that no stable or simple account of race is available for casual theoretical application, hence Ferguson's caveat. However, recognizing this variability proves valuable since the recognition prevents marshaling just such a casual racial theory in the service of an actively racist application or a passively racialist essentialism.

Though I hope to argue against Ferguson's advocacy of suspended judgment by providing contextualized readings in place of the protracted "juggling" her essay's title endorses with its indefinite participle, I find Ferguson's insistence on the conceptual difficulty of race within present academic cultures heartening (if, again, a bit too forbidding). As the above comments indicate, I believe the most valuable research into the history of race will emphasize the contingency and specificity of racial experience in all periods. However, often and invidiously enough, the significance of race in a contemporary or modern context is taken by historians to be far simpler than in earlier periods, especially in discussion of the contested discursive racial matrix of the Renaissance. This belief in the comparative simplicity and self-evidence of modern race has proven surprisingly durable.

A number of preconceptions about modernity can contribute to the problems that Renaissance specialists in particular face when investigating racial experience in their fields. Critics trained to engage the whimsical and unstable logics of Renaissance science and anthropology may expect that modern and contemporary racial settlements, in contrast, provide systematic and logical racial categorizations. Post-Foucauldian scholars working in early periods, used to the Enlightenment as a conceptual *terminus ad quem,* may presume that racial logics existing after the eighteenth century are all very similar but do not resemble those in their own fields. Finally, race theorists working with the diverse categories producing racial identifications in early modern Europe may assume that modern and contemporary racial identifications are made much more simply. In short, for a reader of early modern texts, unexamined assumptions about twentieth- and twenty-first-century racializations and their relation to the past may pose as large a theoretical impediment as the temporal and cultural distance of the texts under discussion.

Together, these misconceptions disable the critic's ability to make definitive statements about race in the past: they produce an indefinite juggling similar to that Ferguson recommends, though for a less considered reason. They bring into question the possibility that race has a recognizable history before the eighteenth century at all and muddy the relation of that history to its modern successors. Characterized in this way, the still-voiced objection (or worry) that reading race in the Renaissance is anachronistic may be seen to depend as much on an incomplete examination of racial ideology and experience in the present as on historicizing that shows us the concept in its past specificity.

Such a theoretical bar happens when, for instance, Juliana Schiesari interrupts her nuanced analysis of early physiognomy with a disclaimer seemingly meant to qualify her argument's intuitive claims of significance for the study of the history of race. Schiesari notes physiognomy's move from observations of physical differences to "prejudicial moral judgments" associated with those differences, but then she writes, "It is hard to argue that early modern physiognomy is *per se* racist in the sense that nineteenth-century phrenology or the writings of Gobineau incontestably are."[52] Importantly, Schiesari does not provide the basis for phrenology's or Gobineau's incontestable racism at this point, as she has for the physiognomic texts; beyond the suggestion of the development of modern science, the nineteenth-century texts' relevance to an obvious claim to racism is left implicit. Later, after explaining the ways in which the humanist Giovan Battista Della Porta physiognomically classifies human beings according to physical types, Schiesari offers a second, longer qualification:

> Nevertheless, there is a certain *ad hoc* quality to the physiognomic analysis that makes it much less systematized and categorical than modern racist ideology . . . its construction through compilation, typical of much Renaissance thought, favors the listing of particulars, no matter how contradictory, over the conceptual rigor of the logic of noncontradiction. (66)

We may certainly sympathize with Schiesari's notes of reluctant apology as she draws her distinctions. It is, as she says, "hard to argue" that what she is working on is racist "in the sense" of a later racism, and Schiesari is uneasy that her seventeenth-century text does not precisely illustrate a racism of the sort flourishing in the nineteenth century (phrenology or Gobineau) or afterward (the less specified "modern racist ideology"). Note that Schiesari assimilates the three: she assumes that "modern racist ideology" is sufficiently similar to earlier phrenology and the anthropology of Gobineau as to warrant the use of each as an equivalent contrasting example. The divide she sets up between the early and late racisms emphasizes the epistemological developments common to the later disciplines. These later racisms are "incontestably" the *real thing,* because they are logical, "systematized and categorical," never, one assumes, *"ad hoc"* in the scattered manner of earlier periods—the manner of Della Porta, who classifies women, men, and animals in varying, contradictory schema full of inconsistent analogies, manufactured data, and pre-determined conclusions (57–66). In its double assumptions, first, that the definitive feature of contemporary racism is its consistent, systematic application and, next, that Renaissance discourses, lacking this consistency, are only doubtfully said to be racist at all, Schiesari's text is entirely typical.

These assumptions have not disappeared since Schiesari published her essay; if anything, they have become orthodoxy. Generally, even the most brilliant and original scholarly treatments of race in the early modern period that engage the question tend to accept this periodization, in which early modern racial forms are seen as effectively irrelevant to later developments because unsystematic.[53] A recent example may be found in Floyd-Wilson's *English Ethnicity,* which provides a history of the geohumoral theory and ethnic lore of the early modern period. Floyd-Wilson's work offers the first careful consideration of the medico-philosophical-historical views of race that prevailed in Europe before the eighteenth century. Yet, permeated by the association of modern racial systems with fixity, biological transmissibility, and hierarchically arranged, discrete identificatory categories, her book disputes the relevance of its own findings to later racialisms. Floyd-Wilson insists that "early modern ethnology is *not* racialism" and contrasts the early modern geo-humoral regime she describes so richly with "modern racial binaries, [in which] the white 'self' derives an assumed sense of stability and superiority from fixed, hierarchical categories of difference."[54] Here, Floyd-Wilson echoes Schiesari's characterizations of modern racial systems. In fact, as I will demonstrate more fully below, modern racial systems do not feature the fixed categories that both writers assume differentiate modern and early modern.

A related difficulty in reading race in Renaissance texts is found in Lynda Boose's influential inquiries into the boundaries of Renaissance racial discourse.[55] Boose wishes to develop an understanding of the significance of racializations as they were experienced during the Renaissance, to historicize the early meanings of race, which means recognizing differences of racial signification between the twentieth and sixteenth centuries. One way of conceptualizing these differences is to identify and distinguish the "determining factors" of race in the two periods. In this matter, the Renaissance, bursting with relevant but ambiguous national, religious, physical, and colonial identity categories and language, seems to Boose difficult for modern readers to penetrate; by contrast, "the twentieth century has generally presumed that skin color is [racial discourse's] determining factor" (35).[56]

As a result of this contrast, Boose first questions the validity of the reader's twentieth-century-determined responses to period color references, such as Brabantio's nasty remark that Desdemona could not love Othello's "sooty bosom" (1.2.70): should this comment be seen as different in kind from, say, Portia's snide generalizations about her suitors, based on national stereotypes (35)?[57] Further, because according to her implicit history of racism, modernity has a straightforward method of racial identification (skin color), and the Renaissance does not, Boose feels, like Schiesari, that Renaissance discourses of difference are hard to categorize: "that [black Africans] had darker skins was clearly recognized: but exactly what significance was attached to that fact?" (36). Boose questions whether these recognitions are simple prejudice, observation, or stereotype and whether period discourses of difference are primarily centered in culture, theology, politics, or biology. She finds it difficult to assimilate them to racism, which "can legitimately be defined as a systemic form of prejudice" (36) associated with "biologically empirical" (36) and "incontrovertible" (39) differences.

For Boose, the Renaissance would be "legitimately" racist only given particular, systemic meanings associated with the skin color of Africans. That is, as in the critical desire for the term "black" to be used in Renaissance England as it is in the modern United States, ideas about Africans not centered on their skin color are not clearly racialized ideas to Boose, while all Africans are presumed to be dark. Boose also assumes that systematic racial prejudice must arise in reaction to actual physical differences—dark skin. Predictably, her reliance on the equation of modern racism with attitudes about skin color affects her choices of the textual moments she perceives to attest most fully to a nascent racism—moments in which skin color differences seem to arise—and also her sense of those that raise the most difficult and provocative questions for historicism—moments in which people or groups the late (American) twentieth century identifies as white, such as Jews, Spaniards, or the Irish, are analogized to people of color (36–40). Boose invokes both types of racial discourse to indicate the early development of a modern racist preoccupation with skin color. Nonetheless, she notes that the latter sort of analogies fracture the expected color preoccupation in their figural links between the presumptively white and nonwhite. For example, Boose writes, "Yet if we assume a rudimentary racial theory based on skin color, how and where does Shylock's category of 'Jewishness' fit?" (39–40). Though she notes that "Jewishness" also poses a problem for *modern* racism (when that is conceived to be determined by skin color), a problem she is unable to resolve, Boose ultimately does not extend the range of attributes she imagines to signal racial divisions. Instead, the interpretive difficulties posed by the analogies significantly lead to a rhetorical withdrawal of analytic ambition, possibly one akin to that advocated by Ferguson: "it is the questions rather than the answers that are important" (39). Like the assumption that modern racisms differ from early modern ones in their fixed categories, the assumption that skin color trumps other forms of racial distinction (as it does in the United States) has persisted, even in the most carefully historicized work and even when, as in Boose's essay, counterexamples to this assumption are included in critical analysis.[58]

The frustrations expressed by Boose and Schiesari, along with the assumptions about racial periodization they share with most later historians of race, result directly, as I have been suggesting, from an expectation of historical drift that proves theoretically disabling for their projects, though all the above critics make substantial contributions in spite of it. Ironically, their interpretive difficulties emerge partly because they acknowledge historical difference and take pains to think about racialized meanings specific to the cultures they study—that is, because they try to practice a judicious historicism. But their acknowledgment of the differences of earlier periods, *in combination with* their beliefs that modern racisms, understood to be static and systematic, are the real ones, undermines their historicism. Before turning at long last to case studies in the Renaissance, therefore, I will examine the logics of modern racism more closely, with an eye to its significance for historians working in early periods.

Modern Race and Racism

Like Schiesari, Boose measures the racism she detects against the evocation of a modern racial ideology and assumes that a resemblance between the two is necessary for the earlier form to register as racism at all. Both authors associate modern racism with systematic application and scientific epistemology and therefore assume that modern racial categories are simple to delineate (the emphasis on skin color). Yet these assumptions merit scrutiny. "Modern racist ideology" (Schiesari, "The Face of Domestication," 66) is hardly "scientific." By virtue of lacking the rigor and systematicity with which it is persistently associated, it possesses such inconsistent classificatory analogies as intrigue Boose in English drama and such predetermined conclusions, supported by arbitrary, manufactured data, as vex Schiesari in early Italian physiognomy. Renaissance representations of racialized human beings may be only partially informed by nascent anthropological and scientific expressive styles, which eventually claimed an exhaustive, "objective" racial classification. But this should not obscure the fact that the protocols and expressions of racial "knowledge" vary in every culture, including our own, whose own racial divisions and commonplaces have shifted over the last century and even in recent decades.[59]

Indeed, to speak of "modern racist ideology" as though it is a single, integrated belief system is already problematic. The abbreviated phrase mystifies just the broad variation among recent racist formations that would help to indicate their fantastic, incoherent character—and, incidentally, that would allow the Renaissance critic to perceive the relevance of the illogics and multiplicities she encounters in her own research. Distinguishing between early and modern racisms on the basis of the supposed rigor and simple taxonomies of the latter not only misrepresents the actual state of affairs but in so doing also contributes to the myth of racialist legitimacy that modern racism's scientific associations have played no small part in sustaining.

This dynamic prompts Kim Hall to voice concern "that much of the seeming anxiety over the propriety of the use of the term 'race' in the Renaissance works to exclude an antiracist politics,"[60] because it prevents the critic or teacher from marking historical continuities that might bear on her position in contemporary struggles as well as her disposition toward early modern texts. For this reason, Hall notes, she does not use scare quotes around the term "race," since "the easy association of race with modern science ignores the fact that language itself creates differences within social organization and that race was then (as it is now) a social construct."[61] I would extend Hall's reasoning here. Race is a social construct precisely because discourses other than scientific ones are involved in generating racial classifications and racial hierarchies, making the association of science and race obfuscatory in at least two ways.[62] Belief that the racism one knows, "modern racism," is a single, scientifically precise entity invests identifiable racist foundations with respectability. Belief that the racism one knows is racism's developed, "real," or "mature" form endows it with inevitability and masks its continuing changes and its many, contradictory forms.

The impact of these beliefs becomes clearer when we reexamine the claim that the taxonomies of modern racial classification are generated by a single, objective determinant, in contemporary critical articles, virtually always the "criterion" that Boose, among many others, identifies with the system as a whole: skin color.[63] The expectation that racial groups are reliably individuated by phenotypes such as skin color is an artifact of theories of racial typology, the belief that race membership invariably entails the possession of traits that no member of a different race shares.[64] Were this true, one might assign a human being to a racial category based on the color of her skin, since any given skin color would belong only to one group. Put this way, the theory is obviously grossly flawed, since there is in fact a broad range of skin colors among the members of contemporary racial groups. Because the United States has emphasized ancestry over appearance in many racial identifications, individual "white" Americans, for instance, often have darker skin than individual African Americans, and the comparisons among individuals of these two groups could be extended to encompass individuals from all groups.[65] Indeed, for this reason, racial typology has proved neither the most recent racialist theory nor the most sustainable (again, there are many modern racisms), though the widespread assumption that "race is based on skin color" and, more obviously, the practice of referring to racial groups by colors attest to its persistence in the form of residual beliefs.[66]

These beliefs derive part of their strength from the intensity with which racial ascriptions often appear to be unmediated perceptions, in this case, of color differences, what Marvin Harris, in his entry for "Race" in the *International Encyclopedia of Social Sciences,* has called "the apparent adequacy of phenotypical cues for the establishment of unambiguous identity."[67] Sense perceptions of this kind often suppress awareness that other beliefs help structure racial identifications. But the cognitive work performed by racial ideology means that perceptions are shunted into available cultural categories and often follow the terms of the prevailing ideology, so that it is possible at some times in some places to see and refer to Jews, Irish, Italians, or Pakistanis as "black" (and at others to be utterly unable to) depending on one's racial context.[68] The distortions of perception by ideology also account for the nonrecognition of the ambiguities of skin color itself.

Further, the emphasis on a single taxonomy of color obscures the degree to which the "traits" identifying members of racial groups remain a heterogeneous lot, including supposedly "common" physical features (skin color among many others) but also cultural, geographic, and linguistic affiliations as well as, importantly, the criterion of "descent"—selectively or spuriously identified "common" ancestors. Sociological work has long provided diverse examples of racial classification systems. Harris notes that "the term race . . . is applied in vernacular contexts to human populations organized along an astonishing variety of principles. Nation-states . . . tribes . . . language families . . . minorities . . . and phenotypically distinct but genetically hybrid aggregates such as whites, Negroes, yellows, and Coloureds are cognitively equivalent in many ethnosemantic contexts."[69] Within a given historical moment, however, people participating in a given system of racial organization are typically unaware of other organizational possibilities. Or, as when the Renaissance critics cited above (and many others) persistently associate racial classifications with skin color, people may be unaware that racial ascriptions may follow more than one pattern of organization within a given system.

That is, Harris's point may be extended; it is important to realize that even within a single cultural context—whether Renaissance England or the millennial United States—there is not a single determinant according to which all people are matched with a racial identity. In fact, membership of different groups is routinely constituted by quite different criteria, many falling outside the expected norm of somatic or phenotypic cue. The range of these criteria alone can begin to dispel the myth that racial classifications result from rigorously applied, biologically derived distinctions. For instance, there is, obviously enough, no biologically consistent theory to account for the American practice of determining some racial affiliations through unreflective (and inconsistent) applications of criteria of phenotype (as in the usual classification of African Americans), others by descent (as in the usual classification of Jews), and still others primarily by national and/or geographic origin (as with many Asian populations, such as Japanese or South Asian) or linguistic affiliation (as in the usual classification of Latinos). Note that many groups are associated with a number of identificatory categories, though usually not all of them, and usually one or two central ones.

In addition, some people may be subject to different identifications based on different criteria. Phenotype groupings, for example, may divide some populations (East from South "Asians"; "black" from "white" Latinos). Though Harris offers the criterion of descent as a more stable social mapping of race, he notes that descent logics involve their own "powerful fictions," as revealed by multiracial children, who are generally identified with a single race, "the racial group of the lower-ranking parent."[70] Such capricious logics, again, give the lie to the myth that racial categorization reflects rigorous scientific principles.

Similarly, although discourses of race in the late eighteenth century through the twentieth were often saturated with precise measurements, exhaustive lists, and gradated rankings, it must be remembered, first, that the interpretation and generation of these data were universally flawed both methodologically and theoretically,[71] and second, that scientific productions coexisted with philosophical, aesthetic, religious, political, and economic discourses that offered the primary justifications and motivations for racial distinctions and rankings. The latter discourses, of course, provided the framework in which the implications of racial data, whose conclusions they foreordained, might be understood. In short, though a significant part of the means of articulation of racial difference in the eighteenth century and after was given by the new techniques and philosophies of scientific production, science provided neither the motives for nor the conclusions about racial rankings; nor were the various resultant policies and campaigns (colonialism, slavery, and denial of human and political rights among them) in any sense determined by science.

Precise, scientifically derived divisions, then, are not so much characteristic of racial classifications, and by extension racial discourses, as are the persistence of racial groupings *despite* the incoherent logic of large-scale racial classificatory schema. Racial groups are maintained by the widespread belief in stable classifications of group differences, a belief that overrides awareness of significant variation within groups or overlap between them. Such a mechanism has

long been perceived to structure ethnic divisions—themselves distinguished from racial divisions only with difficulty—at least since
Fredrik Barth's theories of ethnic boundaries rethought the prem-
ises of ethnic studies.[72] Barth argued that distinct ethnic groups did
not result, as had been virtually universally assumed, from the relative isolation of one culture or ethnicity from another but rather out
of "social processes of exclusion and incorporation" that delineate
discrete groups in pointed contrast to the fact of "a flow of person-
nel" among them in the form of "changing participation and membership in the course of individual life histories."[73] Barth's model
usefully highlights the discursive content of ethnic (and by extension, I would argue, racial) divisions, since divisions are no longer
imagined to reflect innate or unalterable or empirical differences but
rather relational, cultural productions of difference. When boundaries between ethnic groups are perceived as stable, the qualitative
"cultural stuff that [the boundaries] enclose" need not be the focus
of attention.[74] Emphasizing the boundary between groups, that is,
the belief in their difference, particularly through tropes of exag-
geration or distortion, is sufficient to perpetuate group divisions by
suppressing awareness of commonalities.

Redirecting Barth's analytic from ethnicity to race proves especially useful in thinking about racial divisions in contexts where racial
identifications are especially fluid, as in the Renaissance, since any
marked boundary-supporting language will point critical attention
to culturally significant classifications. The critic need not have limited herself beforehand to commentary on just a few relevant criteria
thought to signal racial difference (such as skin color). Conversely,
Barth's theory allows us to predict that the most dynamic sites of
racial production will occur at moments when racial boundaries
are permeated or indistinct, since especially exercised discursive
effort will result in order to reinforce blurry boundaries—or else,
and as interestingly, boundaries between groups will be redefined
to accommodate the pressures of unclear distinctions. With this
framework in mind, analogies between incompletely distinguished
groups, such as the analogies that trouble Boose between Irish or

Jews and Africans, or the analogy between African and Italian with which I began, become fruitful sites for interpretation rather than signs of an incoherent and impenetrable past social order.

Barbarous Play

Barth's insight that individual racial identification can change over the course of a life history is central to this project. In this book, I focus on the shifts in individual identity depicted in Renaissance drama—among national, religious, or class affiliations, for example, or resulting from prohibited relationships and desires—that prove especially likely to precipitate racial signification. I attend closely to the boundary-marking language that signals these shifts, particularly to the movements of certain keywords—"black," "fair," "blood," "gentle," "gross," and "nature" among them. With intricate, compulsive, eager, reluctant, repetitive, rigid, and innovative play on such words, drama registers, works through, and revises the operating conditions of race, telling us how race works in the culture.

Dramatic representations of racial identity are no less important, no less powerful—both compelling and punitive—for being fluid, variable, and often contradictory. I have employed drama in part because drama is a fruitful locus for the depiction of such shifts, emphasizing and putting pressure on changes in interpersonal relationships and individual identities over time. As noted above, Renaissance drama provides narratives of racial fluidity in profusion. Moreover, drama is free to channel and transmute influences from throughout the culture, allowing for the productive and representative intermingling of discourses from multiple disciplines and subject positions. But drama is also important because, as an element of Renaissance popular culture, its interest in and insistence on depictions of fluid racialization highlight the commonplace, entertaining, and seductive quality of these representations. While racialization of a character is often accompanied by derogatory rhetoric, narratives of interracial desire also figure racial difference as attractive and internal to English culture.[75]

To underscore the attractions of these stories, I have chosen plays that are, for the most part, both familiar to us and popular in the Renaissance. In some cases, my readings of these plays articulate racial meanings where they have not usually been seen, as in chapter 3, which examines the racial content of Jacobean notions of national difference—specifically, the implications of an Italian identification for English subjects, and the physical and moral blackness structuring Webster's depictions of Italians. In others, I emphasize fluidity as a characteristic feature of racial signification to complicate racial meanings where they have seemed obvious and static. For instance, racial fluidity governs even the drama's most familiar representation of an African character: my reading of *Othello* in chapter 1 emphasizes that Othello's racialization alters as it is seen in relation to his marriage or to his service for the state. Surprisingly, though, much of *Othello*'s most exercised racial abjection results when Desdemona exerts sexual and dynastic agency at the expense of her father's and husband's wishes. Her transition from "fair" daughter to "begrimed and black" wife signals deep parallels between the period's ideologies of race and gender. Throughout this book, I attend to these parallels, often manifested in similar "blackening" of unruly women—the racial language that attempts to discipline and eroticize the agency of female characters such as Shylock's daughter Jessica or *The White Devil*'s Vittoria, discussed in chapters 2 and 3, respectively.

However, as these last examples suggest, gender is not the only Renaissance concept dependent on constitutive racial meanings. My chapters are organized around the interrelation of race with the other categories that underpin and call out racial identity, particularly in narratives of boundary crossing. In this way, reading for the racial and class components of religious identity in chapter 2, we see how the racialist Venetian ideology of "gentility" functions to exclude those seen as outsiders, including Shylock and, finally, Jessica, from the advantages held by the gentle, gentile folk of Venice and Belmont, themselves enabled by Jewish wealth. While chapter 3 explores Renaissance English ideas about Italians, chapter 4 extends this discussion to Jacobean racialization of other Mediterranean nations and, in a reading of Middleton and Rowley's *The Changeling*, considers the role of metaphors of blood in representing genealogy, differences of rank, and humoral physiology and psychology.

The determinants of early modern racial identity are multiple and tangled, and the legacy of their interaction extends well beyond the seventeenth century. My book ends by engaging the epistemological component of this legacy, asking why science came to be so important in modern understandings of racial difference. I examine a longing for objectivity expressed by many of *The Changeling*'s characters, a longing to ratify subjective hatred, suspicion, and desires with objective data and explanation. In such personal desires, we find the roots of the emphasis on science as prescriptive and descriptive agent that will come to embody the system of racialism as a whole and to sustain perceptions of racial distinctions, distinctions whose effects have been no less real than their grounds, like the literature that represents them, are metaphorical, contradictory, and imagined.

ONE

Desdemona's Blackness

❦

So will I turn her virtue into pitch.

—William Shakespeare, *Othello*

The Uses of Fairness

Waiting for Othello to arrive at the Cyprian harbor, Iago and
Desdemona pass the time by trading bawdy quips. In rhymed couplets provoking appreciative groans from Desdemona, Iago serially
pokes fun at wise and foolish, "fair" and "black" women. According
to Iago, all these women scheme for sexual encounters. Rife with
chiasmus and antithesis, the tropes that heighten oppositional
logics—social as well as rhetorical ones—Iago's generalizing couplets
draw attention to pairings of complexion and sexuality. Surprising
parallels between the continuums of chastity and color emerge in his
banter as his epigrams run through all the possible combinations of
female attributes Desdemona suggests to him, for Iago uses "black"
to signify both female darkness and female promiscuity:

If she be black, and thereto have a wit,
She'll find a white that shall her blackness fit.   (2.1.132–33)

Iago's pun on "white"/"wight" (man) implies the sexual nature of
female blackness. More obviously, his couplet suggests the inevitability of a miscegenistic sexuality, that whiteness and blackness "fit."
This "fit" echoes the logic of Desdemona's marriage, while inverting its terms. At the same time, the white/black "fit" serves as an

emblem for a disturbing pairing of female "fairness" and sexuality, embodied, for instance, in Desdemona herself. Iago's couplet praising her attributes concludes ominously: "fairness and wit / The one's for use, the other useth it" (2.1.129–30). While ambiguous about who (or what) is using what, Iago's couplet suggests that female wit uses fairness so that fairness may be used sexually. As we will see, such uses of fairness are imagined as damaging and, through the Renaissance association of promiscuity with blackness, darkening to fairness. Iago here imagines that female fairness is intended to be damaged in this way ("for use"), setting out, witty or foolish, to undo itself.

Far from simply representing his own villainous or jealous tendencies, or even the early modern obsession with female chastity, Iago's contempt for female sexuality is echoed in punitive commentators on this scene from Thomas Rymer through the twentieth century.[1] All too predictably, Desdemona's eager participation in Iago's rhetorical game has proved disturbing to the play's readers: the interchange is omitted in every production of which I am aware, and critical opinion has been overwhelmingly negative. Epitomizing the negative view, M. R. Ridley notes:

> This is to many readers, and I think rightly, one of the most
> unsatisfactory passages in Shakespeare. To begin with it is
> unnatural . . . then, it is distasteful to watch her engaged in
> a long piece of cheap backchat with Iago, and so adept at it
> that one wonders how much time on the voyage was spent
> in the same way.[2]

Ridley's concerns about Desdemona's "adeptness" at "cheap" repartee all too quickly set him on a jealous train of thought, wondering, like Othello, what she does when she's not in front of him and echoing Iago's conclusions about the prurient ambitions of the dangerous female combination of "fairness and wit" (2.1.129).[3] Critics worry that Desdemona's racy joking with Iago undercuts viewer/reader sympathy for her, as she must be utterly "innocent" for her murder to fully outrage the audience (as her servant Emilia's hardly ever does).[4] She must have no whisper of extramural sexual experience, which the Renaissance sometimes called "blackness," about her.

Early modern moralizing on chastity may seem a strange place to look for prevailing racialist doctrine. The equation between figurative darkening and the transgression of female chastity may be so familiar to the reader of Shakespeare as to pass without comment. After all, female "blackness" is metaphorical; although critics have noted the terminological overlap, Desdemona's "blackness" and Othello's "blackness" have generally been regarded as two quite different phenomena. This chapter will explore the coincidence of the two meanings in a single word more carefully, attending closely to Desdemona's racialization in order to argue that discourses of race and gender are not fully separable in the early modern period and indeed possess numerous identical features.

Gender's similarity to race is particularly dramatized by marriage plots, in which attention to sexual difference, concern over the boundary between exogamy and endogamy, and application of the color logics associated with female sexual activity intersect with and amplify one another. These elements are present throughout Renaissance drama; their interaction is especially notable in *Othello,* whose tensions they power. Yet continuing anxiety about female chastity has paradoxically made traffic between gender and race harder to detect. When productions of *Othello* eliminate the bawdy dialogue between Iago and Desdemona, for example, they suppress Desdemona's agency as a sexual subject and thereby also suppress important elements of the play's racial logic, which simultaneously insists on Desdemona's flawless "fairness" and disturbing "blackness." For, as Iago's couplet on blackness and wit implies in reverse, Desdemona's whiteness is instrumental in producing the negative connotations of Othello's blackness. At the same time, however, Desdemona's agency, in defiance of her father's and husband's expectations, leads directly to her progressive and virulent racialization in the play.

Othello's Marriage

From its very first scene, *Othello* is saturated with the imagery and concerns that make it the most familiar example of an English Renaissance play interested and invested in race. In that scene, in dialogue with Roderigo and Desdemona's father, Brabantio, Iago employs varied elements of an apparently vast manipulative repertoire of racist barbs, innuendo, stereotypes, and threats. Combining these, Iago presents ideas about Desdemona's and Othello's marriage as a mixture of kinds whose participants possess a disturbing animality; he hints at an accompanying inheritance of undesirable traits. His depictions rely on additional ideologies of gender, nation, religion, and a materialist understanding of familial integrity for their application to Othello and Desdemona. In response, Roderigo and Brabantio are quick to make their own contributions, referring to Othello in language that insults his appearance and interprets his behavior as reflecting malign alien origins. As we will see, they refer to Desdemona in similarly charged racial language, describing her as physically compromised by her alliance and as compromising Brabantio as well, through her betrayal of their shared "blood."

Collectively, then, this scene presents racial content of nearly every kind outlined in my Introduction. Strikingly, even the racial insults that most exaggerate Othello's perceived racial difference—those that compare him to animals—are applied to him mainly in the context of his relationship with Desdemona, in ways that have not been fully explored.[5] Iago's famous lines, "even now, now, very now, an old black ram / Is tupping your white ewe" (1.1.87–88), exemplify such bestial imagery. Intending to outrage Brabantio, Iago arranges a set of recognizable antitheticals (black/white, ram/ewe) that heighten a perceived opposition between Othello and Desdemona in order to dramatize its breach. Color predicates cast the pair as contraries, and the implication of a mixture of kinds is further advanced through the trans-species imagery, which emphasizes both the raw physicality of the claimed sexual relationship and the violation of parental property rights.

The immediate effect of this on a sleepy or confused Brabantio is unclear (he replies only "what, have you lost your wits?" [1.1.91]). But by critics, the explicit, animalistic sexual imagery of the speech is generally taken as a hateful extreme with which Iago, or the play, racially characterizes Othello. "In the 'old black ram,'" Michael Neill writes, is "projected Iago's own loathing and fear of Othello as sexual rival."[6] For Ania Loomba, the lines reveal "the black man . . . identified as . . . animal," and the pairing of Othello and Desdemona as "just as unnatural as the supposed lust between animals and people in Africa."[7] These critics are certainly correct to point out the racist significance and charge of Iago's description of Othello as an animal. As I wrote in my Introduction, such tropes, implying an ontological distance between people, are those that most insistently (and most falsely) cultivate clear-cut boundaries between groups. Still, lost in these critical accounts, which assume that Othello is the sole object of Iago's racism, is the additional effect of the lines on Desdemona's figuration, closely tied to Othello's, and the definitional nature of Iago's links between gender, sexuality, and race.

Like Iago's sexually themed couplets on Cyprus, his inflammatory rhetoric here starts to suggest the complementarity of opposites, partly through the very symmetry of his antitheses (which are, after all, pairs), and partly through their blurring of gender and race. If Othello is compared to an animal, Iago's antithesis figures Desdemona as one of the same kind, a sameness that complicates her status as someone imperiled by the threat of exogamy. Rather, because ram and ewe are an antithesis properly matched, Iago's image can imply a likeness between Desdemona and Othello revealed by their matched bestial labels and sexual compatibility.

The ram-ewe pairing complicates Iago's color logic as well. When ram and ewe no longer figure an obvious mutual repulsion, Iago's color terms can align with the gender differentiation of the animals to suggest that racial difference is coded and produced by sexual difference. Alternately, guided still further by his color troping, we might suppose that Iago imagines ram and ewe—male and female— as of fundamentally different kinds (restoring the difference between

Othello and Desdemona). In this reading, gender difference itself again figures or reflects racial differentiation, a possibility I will explore further below. Either way, with gender difference and sexual contact catalyzing racial meaning, we may begin to understand how on Cyprus the opposition of "white" and "blackness" will likewise suggest a sexual "fit" to Iago. As in his still more compressed image of a sexual "beast with two backs" (1.1.115), the disturbing consequences of Iago's animal analogies are not confined to Othello. It is important to acknowledge that Desdemona and Othello are racialized differently.[8] Nonetheless, however dehumanizing the effect of Iago's sexual rhetoric, that effect is felt by both Othello and Desdemona.

Conversely, outside of the context of his relation to Desdemona, language demeaning Othello or even emphasizing him as a racialized subject is initially absent. The senate is chiefly occupied with the threat posed by "the Turk," who, as the "general enemy" (1.3.49) with an alien religion, culture, and competing imperialism, monopolizes senatorial defensive and xenophobic energies.[9] The Duke and senators are sufficiently invested in Othello to send three parties searching for him (1.2.46), and the Duke greets "valiant Othello" before Senator Brabantio (1.3.49) when the two enter the council chamber together, though the presence of both has been remarked (1.3.48).[10] Sent to Cyprus, Othello replaces the governor, Montano, whose experiences with Othello do not dispose him to resent the dispossession. Rather, Montano exhibits relief: "I am glad on't, 'tis a worthy governor . . . for I have served him, and the man commands like a full soldier" (2.1.30, 35–36) and, like the senators, unlike Iago or Roderigo, calls his governor by name: "brave Othello" (2.1.38).

Othello's praise echoes through the first two acts—at least, his praise by those involved with him through state business. This praise has often been taken as exposition meant to highlight the pathos of Othello's decline into slavish and irrational murderousness, but it can also be seen as demarking an unproblematic context for Othello's presence in Venetian society, a zone in which racial differences are irrelevant, to be compared with the racialized hostility attending Othello's marriage that is also present from the beginning.[11] The contrast is most spectacularly seen in Brabantio, who invited Othello over "oft" before the marriage (1.3.129), presumably to curry favor with the senate's rising military star, but who is sufficiently outraged by Othello's marriage to spew a litany of accusations that center on Othello's foreignness and the disruption of Venetian bloodlines. Likewise, Othello's status as rival to Roderigo, and, later, Roderigo's wishful and projective thinking about Othello as a cuckold and rejected lover, are produced by Othello's relation to Desdemona; it is Othello's connection to Desdemona that unleashes in Roderigo the string of physical slurs and inappropriately familiar speech that mark Othello as a racialized outsider.[12] As a result, the racial tension experienced around Othello is generated by his union with Desdemona, not only in the compressed racial logics of Iago's vicious attacks (which are, in fact, echoed by these other characters) but also through the tensions of more dilated social narrative.

As Kim Hall notes, the term "miscegenation" was not used during the early modern period.[13] Given that "miscegenation" and similar terms were unavailable to the English, it follows that critics must be careful in recovering the connotations interracial relationships possessed as a potential class.[14] Cautioning against anachronistic application of twentieth-century concerns, Leslie Fiedler, for instance, argues against reading *Othello* as centered on a tale of racial mixing: "the whole notion of miscegenation had not yet been invented."[15] Upping the ante, Karen Newman has argued that as a narrative or discursive element, miscegenation is so unpalatable as to be unavailable to the early modern English as an actual or even cognitive possibility. The interracial marriage in *Othello,* she writes, is one "all the other characters view as unthinkable . . . The play is structured around a cultural aporia, miscegenation."[16] Unlike Fiedler, Newman asserts that the notion of miscegenation is contemporary yet positions miscegenation as a Renaissance impossibility topos, bespeaking an obsessive impasse in the cultural imaginary, characterized by an inchoate logic. Yet Newman's own essay works brilliantly to qualify the aporia of miscegenation, offering a plausible set of historical associations, including hyperbolically phobic cultural myths of monstrous black sexuality and monstrous female desire, through which early modern subjects, she argues, would interpret Desdemona's and Othello's marriage.[17] Given Newman's descriptions of the bent of early modern sexual fantasies about women and black men, one might expect that depictions of interracial relationships and marriage in Renaissance popular culture would be frequent, rather than "unthinkable."

Indeed, erotic interracial relationships are readily, in fact frequently, thematized in English Renaissance texts—so much so, that their proliferation would seem to satisfy a deeper desire for and pleasure in the ostensibly disturbing representations of miscegenation themselves. Miscegenation provides extensive material for Shakespeare. Iago's representation of sexuality and gender difference as a matrix of race provides one theoretically important instance and explanation for this extensive use. As topic and trope, miscegenation's figuration may reach an apotheosis in its fantastic amplification in *Othello,* but it is repeatedly used elsewhere, from Aaron's sexual involvement with Tamora in *Titus Andronicus,* to Antony's with Cleopatra in *Antony and Cleopatra,* to Claribel's wedding in Tunis in *The Tempest.* Shakespeare often associates racially exogamous marriage with the guilty pleasures of illicit unions and filial defiance, as when Florizel "disguises" Perdita as the Princess of Libya in *The Winter's Tale,* or when Lorenzo elopes with Jessica, freighted with the valuable signs of her father's alien religion, his "Jewels," even as she flees his control in *The Merchant of Venice.*[18] Such narratives are not confined to Shakespeare. Indeed, as the surveys of Moorish characters in Renaissance drama amply show, nearly every such character is erotically linked with a non-Moor.[19] Further, in these depictions, as with Othello and Desdemona, the conjunction of "fair" and "dark" plays a crucial role in establishing and intensifying the racial figuration of both members of interracial couples.

By the end of the seventeenth century, Thomas Rymer, in Newman's words, "a kind of critical Iago," was able to generalize on the topic, reading *Othello* as "a caution to all Maidens of Quality how, without their parents consent, they run away with Blackamoors."[20] Rymer's warning is pointedly directed at the female member of the couple, who is assumed to be both fairer and richer than the "blackamoor" she is so drawn to when unhindered by parental controls. As we will see, such an elopement carries a price. While one may object to an argument that employs Rymer as a representative reader of *Othello* (his book presents a rabid critique of the play), his interpretation is indeed anticipated by Iago, who contrasts the fact that Desdemona consents to miscegenate with her earlier resistance to desirable matches, in order to suggest to Othello her inevitable errancy:

> Not to affect many proposed matches
> Of her own clime, complexion and degree,
> Whereto we see, in all things, nature tends—
> Foh! one may smell in such a will most rank,
> Foul disproportion, thoughts unnatural. (3.3.233–37)

Stippling the narrative of Desdemona's interracial desires with factors of geography and, importantly, class, Iago (and before him Roderigo and Brabantio) is able to isolate conceptually a willingness to miscegenate and to place it within a causal chain in which interracial marriage mediates between Desdemona's unnatural chastity and unnatural promiscuity. All are instances of "disproportion." Her father had invoked Desdemona's compulsive chastity in strikingly similar terms, emphasizing her resistance to proportionate money and beauty: "so opposite to marriage that she shunned / The wealthy, curled darlings of our nation" (1.2.67–68). Iago extends the principle, arguing that such resistance is "opposite to marriage" in every sense, implying a "rank" and "foul" sexuality. That extreme chastity and breeding, unable to bestow itself on a suitable mate, is always an ominous sign of its own undoing is reinforced by Iago as he encourages Othello to avenge himself: when Othello mourns that Desdemona was "of so gentle a condition," Iago responds with the flat paranoiac tones of a film noir narrator: "Ay, too gentle" (4.1.190–91).

Iago's insinuations that Desdemona's extreme gentleness is itself a precursor to miscegenation and promiscuity attest to the way
in which Desdemona's chastity and her marriage to Othello raise
racial anxieties that dog both characters, anxieties I will return to
more fully later. But to assess the play's total range of such anxieties, it is important to note that the causes and results of the interracial marriage are not imputed to Desdemona's psychology alone,
nor are the repercussions of the marriage confined to her "sacrifice"
(5.2.65) at the altar of Othello's jealousy. Iago's racial ideology is invested in pathologizing Othello and his descendants as well, often
independently of Desdemona. When Iago threatens Brabantio that
"the devil will make a grandsire of you" (1.1.90), he appeals to medieval traditions of religious iconography that represented devils
with black skin.[21] Significantly, however, Iago links this reference
to a threat of inherited blackness that will reflect back on Brabantio
through his "blood" connection to his grandchild, that is, to an ideology of genealogical relation that is not simply theological. Iago's
threat reveals the use to which religious color iconographies can be
put, for even if one were to argue that the representation of devils in
blackface need not be racist,[22] Iago's link of such representations to
genealogy shows that they may be made to signify in a highly racialist and racist way.

Where he might have been thought to be technically unnecessary,
Brabantio's own involvement in the production of Desdemona's and
Othello's children is concretized in Iago's description that presents
reproduction as something Othello is doing in part *to* Brabantio.
Like cuckoldry, the act of "making a grandsire" is here imagined
as a sexual act one man does to another.[23] Through the genealogical tie, Brabantio himself is implicated by whatever occurs between
his daughter and Othello. Iago emphasizes Brabantio's responsibility for a new family characterized by an animality originating
with Othello. Pointedly, in the image emphasizing the genealogical threat, unlike the image of ram and ewe, Othello's sexuality is
imagined as less than human in contrast to Desdemona's: "you'll
have your daughter covered with a Barbary horse; you'll have your

nephews neigh to you, you'll have coursers for cousins and jennets for germans!" (1.1.109–12). Brabantio's daughter's elopement is imagined as immediately and almost parodically fertile, surrounding its patriarch with an alien, preverbal clan, derided as not even belonging to the same species as Brabantio.

Brabantio echoes and expands this logic when musing on the fellow-feeling he thinks his predicament is sure to produce in his peers in the senate:

> Mine's not an idle cause, the duke himself,
> Or any of my brothers of the state,
> Cannot but feel this wrong as 'twere their own.
> For if such actions may have passage free,
> Bond-slaves and pagans shall our statesmen be.   (1.2.95–99)

Brabantio makes a crucial leap here, from the subject position of an individual trapped by genealogical ambition gone awry to the creation of a group identity and a plural first-person subject position made of nobles and Venetian statesmen, whose similarities to himself are such as to stimulate, he believes, a common disciplinary impulse against Othello. These Venetians are now also integrated into Brabantio's imaginary family as "brothers"; the threat to Brabantio is thus figured as a genealogical threat to them as well. One may debate whether this represents an evolved class-consciousness responding with versatility to a race threat, or a nascent race-consciousness dependent on class identity to be set in motion; both ingredients are necessary here, combined in the threat of a contagious "slavery."

Whichever the domains of Venetian privilege and group identity being made vulnerable, however, the mechanism of the threat is a racial one: Brabantio, assuming that Othello is pagan and slave material, claims that these qualities will be disseminated throughout Venice, inherited by Othello's offspring. It is important to note that Brabantio imagines broad politically apocalyptic repercussions from the match between Othello and Desdemona, and these repercussions are declared to result specifically from offspring that will, unavoidably it seems, be tainted by Othello's racial legacy. Accordingly, Brabantio finds it possible here to ignore the fact that Othello is an important leader of the Venetian military, not a slave, and by all appearances identifies with Venetian religious and political values.[24] To make his prediction, Brabantio assumes that Desdemona's Christianity and "Venetian" propensity to avoid slavery will not prevail in her own children; that is, he assumes that his grandchildren will be identifiable as Othello's, reproducing Othello's relevant traits, not hers.[25]

Brabantio's erasure of Desdemona's genetic legacy in his story of Venetian degeneration does not merely result from patriarchal logics that characterize his (and Shakespeare's) worldview. Patriarchal logics, after all, as frequently take the form of overemphasizing the mother's responsibilities in guaranteeing the reputation and moral inheritance of her children as with common ideologies that attribute a presumed and unalterable immorality of children conceived or born outside of "wedlock" to their mother's faults, as is implied, for instance, by the equation of Edmund's villainy and illegitimacy in *King Lear*.[26] In either case, the assumption is that the more corrosive parental element is passed down.[27]

At times, then, Othello's race is represented as dominant and menacing, constituting an external threat to the Venetian polity itself. His status as racial and national outsider—a "wheeling stranger" or "erring Barbarian" (1.1.134, 1.3.356)—with an exotic past is seen as static and unassimilable in Venice. This is precisely the view expressed in Brabantio's characterization of Othello's genealogical threat to Venetian "statesmen," a view that depends upon erasing Desdemona's role in contributing to that legacy or, for that matter, in pursuing Othello as husband (and so finding him assimilable). Yet as we have already seen, Othello's racial identity is also presented differently, as emerging through the marriage itself in ways that neither ignore Desdemona nor leave her immune from the play's racial content. In this view, which we will now explore more fully, racial difference echoes the logic of sexual difference and is dramatized by marriage itself, in which the ideal of a union of likenesses (clime, complexion, degree) cannot fully accommodate period beliefs about gender difference. Desdemona's failure to contract herself with the appropriate degree of likeness in marriage underscores the difference in kind between men and women, that is, the exogamous potential of *all* heterosexual marriage. Her agency in marriage also stimulates processes of racialization not only for Othello but also for her in response to her own violations of normative femininity.

Desdemona's Race

Earlier I argued that Iago, warning Othello that Desdemona is "too gentle," threatens that Desdemona's concentrated gentility is itself suspicious. To tease out the nature of Iago's threat, which reflects the play's general treatment of the agency of women in marriage, including the racial implications of this agency, we must further explore the contours of cultural imagery around chastity, and chastity's ties to racial and color tropes. Discussing interlinked early modern rhetorics of gender and race, Kim Hall notes that since " 'white' is attached to values—purity, virginity, and innocence—represented by (or notably absent in) women . . . this means that the polarity of dark and light is most often worked out in representations of black men and white women."[28] The association of feminine virtue with whiteness accounts for a seeming lack of black female characters in period texts. But Hall's parenthetical qualification, "(or notably absent in)," troubles the particular gendered polarity she argues for. The period's obsessive engagement with actual, imminent, or potential states of "impurity" (generally meaning sexual activity) in women is sufficiently persistent and disturbing that, like as not, the female half of the equation is associated with literalistic[29] or figurative racialized imagery of darkness and blackness. Hall's explanation of the likely representation of the polarity of light and dark, referenced by frequency, ignores this blackened woman in favor of the "black woman" understood according to modern American nomenclature, a woman whose representational status is especially problematic, as Lynda Boose, among others, has argued.[30]

While Hall and Boose perform valuable analyses of dominant

gendered figurations of race in Renaissance England, their overriding interest in the absence of dark-skinned women allows them to bracket the presence of women whose hair, eyes, and skin tones (rather than skin color), or whose violations of norms of chastity, leads to their being labeled "dark" or "black." But it is precisely the overlapping terminology of these various discursive fields that identifies the parameters within which racial meanings are being generated, meanings special to the time and culture in which they signify. To cordon off these representations, to create separate taxonomies of sexually willful, dark-skinned, and raven-eyed women, is to obscure their racialized interdependency.[31] Emphasis on the dark-skinned woman as a representational limit case leads to a misrecognition of the pervasiveness of the trope of the black woman, where in fact Renaissance insistence on an ideal equation of female virtue, female beauty, and female lightness/whiteness ensures innumerable representations of female darkness. I do not mean to deny the significance of Boose's and Hall's observations about the surprising infrequency with which dark-skinned women appear in period texts. At the same time, the relation between these women and women who are regularly described with "dark" imagery, a relation central to early modern understandings of race and gender, has gone unexplored.

It is with this in mind that I want to consider Desdemona. Desdemona's status as racial foil to Othello, that is, white to his black, is generally taken as obvious. There is much in the play to support this, from Iago's early introduction of Desdemona's whiteness, which, as we have already seen, he contrasts with Othello's blackness in simple antitheticals, to Othello's much later images for Desdemona's sleeping body, with its "whiter skin . . . than snow / And smooth as monumental alabaster" (5.2.4–5). Yet there is much in the play also that complicates this monolithic depiction. When not being directly contrasted with or idealized by Othello, Desdemona's racial identity is less static and less easily classified (just as Othello can appear less starkly or simply racialized outside the context of his marriage). Punitive enforcement of the equation of virtuous femininity and fairness that, as Hall shows, represents a period wish (and code) is brought to bear on Desdemona's actions, both real and slandered. The play consistently represents Iago's attacks on and Othello's suspicions of Desdemona's chastity, as well as her own exertions of agency, as compromising the whiteness she at other times embodies or symbolizes. These representations of darkness indicate the links between ideologies of race and gender operating on the early modern English stage and elsewhere, links far more literal and materialist than has been generally believed. According to these ideologies, as we will see, women ought to be categorically purer, more virtuous, and fairer than men; shown or suspected not to be, they are represented as concealing or figuring forth a compromising blackness.

In Desdemona's case, suspicions of her virtue and fairness begin with her exertions of agency in selecting Othello as husband. Desdemona is first called upon to give an account of her role in the illicit love affair between herself and Othello by her father at the meeting of the Venetian senate. Brabantio does not ask Desdemona for an extended explanatory narrative, which her husband has already provided to the senate, but merely for an articulation of her consent to the marriage. Or rather, Desdemona's consent is the ostensible object of her father's interest. He avows, "If she confess that she was half the wooer, /Destruction on my head if my bad blame / Light on the man" (1.3.176–78), but his actual subsequent question to her concerns not her wooing but her sense of the location of authority: "Do you perceive, in all this noble company, / Where most you owe obedience?" (1.3.179–80).

In redirecting attention away from Desdemona's agency and back (so he hopes) to himself, Brabantio restates the problem of his daughter's elopement in terms readily recognizable to any Renaissance theater audience. Those terms work to define marriage as a conflict between generations: willful children who settle their affections with little regard for dynastic or economic interests; unsympathetic and intractable fathers or guardians with little regard for anything else.[32] Arguably, marriage is the primary site of discord between generations; in other issues, at least in drama, the child's and the parent's interests are generally presumed to be consonant. In any case, Brabantio is in good company: one thinks of Capulet and Juliet, Polixenes and Florizel, of Shylock and Jessica, or their literary forebears, Marlowe's Barabas and Abigail.

When the conflict between Brabantio and Desdemona is described as a familiar and familial one, a contest over authority indexed primarily along the axis of age (even more than gender), however, the previously significant fact of Othello's blackness drops out of analysis. Brabantio doesn't mention it here; as we have seen, it outrages him earlier. Before examining Desdemona's answer to her father's question about authority, I want to consider the nature of Brabantio's outrage in detail. How does miscegenation figure in Brabantio's thinking, and more generally, in Renaissance dramatic representations of the relationship between fathers and daughters and of the problematic transformation of virtuous virgins into virtuous wives?

Desdemona's willfulness evokes in both father and husband the threat of her racial contamination, as we will see, yet the very fluidity and symmetry of these associations—from miscegenation to sexual impurity, and from sexual impurity back to racial contamination—threatens the presumed discreteness of the original categories. In this way, the play hints that category contamination, like racial contamination, is predicated on the agency (always fearfully imagined as disobedience) of the female subject, whose choice of sexual partner/s starts all the trouble. If generational conflicts primarily occur over the placement of the child in marriage, when the daughter is most likely to assert desires contrary to her father's, and when in any case his most direct power over her is soon to elapse, then her transition from daughter to wife, from virgin to sexual partner is predictably fraught with anxieties for the father, especially when the daughter moves to exert control over the outcome. My gendering of the participants in this family/dynastic drama is specific to the situation in *Othello*. As Stephen Orgel points out, struggles over marriage are also likely to be bitter when the child is a son, whose marriage was equally likely to be arranged—witness the example of Florizel.[33] One might add to this that wives and mothers in English households frequently participated in or controlled the marriages of children. However, the specific nature of anxieties over filial rebellion and of the language generated in response are conditioned by period beliefs about the gender of the child.

In this way, Brabantio's sense of how Desdemona ought plausibly to relate to Othello is utterly permeated by Renaissance tropes of idealized female mildness and timidity:

> A maiden never bold,
> Of spirit so still and quiet that her motion
> Blushed at herself; and she, in spite of nature,
> Of years, of country, credit, everything,
> To fall in love with what she feared to look on? (1.3.95–99)

In his argument, on the one hand, Desdemona's timorousness is so pervasive that Othello's blackness is practically beside the point; "what she feared to look on" appears to be a category so broad as to exclude every possible object of her affections: the formulation seems to encompass both Italian men and African men and also, surprisingly, Desdemona herself. Yet at the same time, the fearfulness of Othello's blackness *to someone like Desdemona* is obviously what Brabantio naturalizes. He claims that a phobic response to racial difference is built into the mechanics of perfect womanhood, that is, that gender already has knowledge about race.

Brabantio's argument is virtually syllogistic: to a certain kind of woman, Othello, as a black man, is fearful to look on; Desdemona is such a woman; we do not love what we fear to look on; ergo, Desdemona could not love Othello/a black man. In this version of the argument, Desdemona's general timorousness, though perhaps ideologically desirable, is logically irrelevant. The important thing is that she fear what Brabantio knows is properly feared. Brabantio is convinced she must fear Othello's blackness: "Would [she] ever have, t'incur a general mock / Run from her guardage to the sooty bosom / Of such a thing as thou? *to fear not to delight*" (1.2.69–71; emphasis added). Therefore, he concludes, Othello must have "abused her deli-cate youth with drugs or minerals / That weakens motion" (1.2.74–75), "motion" being desire, instinct, or inward prompting, that is, the fear that ought to possess her.

Brabantio's worries about Desdemona's artificially perverted "motion" anticipate his striking description of her "motion [that] / blushed at herself" caused by her "still and quiet" spirit. Since the means by which Desdemona's impulses and desires might blush at herself are obscure, I take the meaning of this remarkable passage to be inverted: Desdemona is so mild that her very desires shame her. As we saw, the female phobic response is a window into (Brabantio's) gender ideology; disturbingly, Desdemona's own desires manifest (through shame) a self-alienating fracture within female perfection itself. But what could these desires be?

To answer this question, I will return to Brabantio's interest in Desdemona's understanding of the location of authority, his request that she indicate to the senate "where most [she] owe[s] obedience." Desdemona's response depicts what she calls a "divided duty": obli-gations of "life and education" have always impelled her to obey her father, "the lord of duty," but, she observes deictically,

> But here's my husband
> And so much duty as my mother showed
> To you, preferring you before her father,
> So much I challenge that I may profess
> Due to the Moor my lord.   (1.3.185–89)

Desdemona's evocation of dutiful division appears neatly to define an operation of patriarchy, her progress from the hands of father to hus-band, which she defines in terms of a transfer of obedience. According to one theory of kinship relations, no self-interested lord of duty could expect more satisfying (verbal) results from his program of filial edu-cation than Desdemona's endorsement of the "traffic in women."[34]

But Desdemona calls attention to a figure frequently occluded in theorizations of this trafficking: her mother. Using her mother as precedent, Desdemona depicts her transfer of obedience from father to husband as a pattern imagined as transgressive of restrictions imposed on daughters by fathers. Desdemona implies that the authority of the husband's claims on obedience from his wife is *constituted* by her voluntary withdrawal of submission to her father's like claims. Inasmuch as the husband's power expands, it is conferred on him by his wife, who, with a feudal flourish, "prefer[s him] before her father." The scene evoked by the imagery of preference, whose period meaning of ritual enhancement of class or status by a superior I emphasize, echoes the drama enacted in the Venetian senate. In it, the suitor's rank is publicly elevated "before her father," that is, by a pun, both above and in the very presence of the previous favorite, now displaced in order to indulge a new partiality.

In Othello's case, the elevation of status in Desdemona's maternal analogy pointedly accommodates Brabantio's abjected category of race: despite Othello's blackness, he is preferred to a position of domestic command correlate with his military rank. Rhetorically, the analogy is devastating, reminding Brabantio of previously enjoyed benefits that implicate him in a system of filial agency he now, as father, attempts to derail. Finally, while Brabantio's account of Desdemona's decorous fearfulness inserted information about race into the ideology of gender (even as it hinted at filial desires that exceeded the bounds of acceptable womanhood), Desdemona's analysis of female agency in marriage negotiation contests the assumption of feminine racial panic. Brabantio claims that certain women are alienated from racial others; Desdemona claims that a defining operation of female agency is the preferment of suitors whose inadequacies are accordingly refigured. She implies a generalized, if temporary, unequal status between bride and suitor, and her analogy, by relating Brabantio to Othello (as similarly lowly in status prior to their preferment, as similarly deserving of obedience afterward), finds no real difference between the interracial couple and the (presumed) intraracial one. Brabantio takes up the analogy in his warning to Othello that implies their utter equivalence: "she has deceived her father, and may thee" (1.3.294).

Curiously, if not surprisingly, the narrative of male "preferment" and the purity of female "perfection" (1.3.101—Brabantio's word) imply male defects, not least among which is a conventional depiction of men as darker and coarser than women. This commonplace of theatrical and literary convention maps gender by color.[35] Belief in a gender-differentiating fairness underlies the Renaissance theatrical practice, for example, of boy actors representing women in part through whiteface, as well as the real-world practice of aristocratic women (who did not need to labor outside) supporting the ideal of fairness by wearing masks to prevent tanning.[36] Such practices intersect in *The Two Gentlemen of Verona,* when Julia passes as a man in part by discarding her sun-blocking mask and subsequently describes herself as "black."[37] The color contrast between men and women will recall Iago's pairing of the "black ram" and "white ewe," which likewise presented sexual differentiation within and across species as including the physical difference of color. Yet of course, as Brabantio feared, in this system, male darkness does not always repel female fairness: in the blushes of virtue there are tinges of desire.[38] Speaking to Othello, Iago makes the connection Brabantio leaves implicit: "when she seemed to shake, and fear your looks / She loved them most" (3.3.210–11). The statement equivocates between a discourse of race and one of sexuality: it hardly matters whether Desdemona seemed to fear Othello's appearance or his gaze (both are "looks"), whether she rejects clime, complexion, or degree. Chastity loves most the racial and sexual possibilities it should "seem . . . to fear." In Desdemona's schema, marriage is always "mixing."

Brabantio's angry response to Desdemona, "I had rather adopt a child than get it" (1.3.192), might seem peculiar. If, as seems likely, Brabantio is dismayed by his loss of control over his heirs—specifically, over their heredity—adoption only compounds his problem. On the face of it, too, adoption hardly guards against the possibility of a rebellious daughter. In fact, Brabantio is expressing a wish to control his own behavior, not his child's. Cutting his losses, displacing his impulse to regulate his daughter's desires—a project gone hideously awry—

Brabantio retrospectively, even poignantly, turns to self-discipline. As though the original facts of Desdemona's conception were to blame, he changes from husband to parent by removing his arena of choice from whom to marry, to whom to father. That is, Brabantio erases the wife, whose erotic agency, Desdemona has taught him, enabled his current predicament.

In denying the value of his sexual relationship with his wife, now compromised by its affinity, established through analogy, with Desdemona's interracial one, Brabantio anticipates Othello's bitter obsession. The problem is wives. The chain of associations Desdemona has made available to Brabantio suggests that as women become adults, they arrange their marriages that are always adulterations— and it is only a short leap from here to adultery (another goad to adoption?).[39] Conversely, as Othello will later see it, adultery signifies adulteration of a standard of purity inevitably imagined as whiteness:

> Her name, that was as fresh
> As Dian's visage, is now begrimed and black
> As mine own face. (3.3.389–91)[40]

Again, Othello's imagery implies that not simply adulterous marriage but all marriage is suspect. For if "Dian's visage" signifies an unblemished reputation for chastity, can that white virgin's face easily serve as emblem for the honor of the married woman?[41] The lines suggest the degree to which the prescriptive cultural emphasis on the virtue of wives may be unrealizable, compromised by equally prohibitive and knowing discourses about the nature of female sexuality. The indictment of female virtue is definitively tied to racist imagery of moral darkness. Othello's image of Desdemona's moral and racial pollution trades on these associations in endorsing Iago's and Brabantio's reasoning: Desdemona was chastest and also whitest when she refused all marriages proposed to her. Her shamefast blushes, masking sexual response, figured forth the racial darkening that was her fate as soon as she agreed to marry.[42]

As we saw with Iago's joking couplets, female sexual behavior is often characterized in this way as darkness or more processually as darkening or dirtying. The striking materialism of the association between gendered morality and color often goes unremarked, though its thoroughly widespread use ought instead to suggest the centrality of racial concepts in policing chastity. Surprisingly physicalist and graduated terms elaborate the transition from "fair" virgin—whose prior virtues, as we saw, were necessary to elevate the defects, also imagined as darknesses, of a prospective male spouse— to abjected sexual subject, a morally "black" woman in the ubiquitous terms of Renaissance texts.[43] The vocabulary here points to the intensely racialist content in descriptions of women gone wrong, a racialism rooted in images of the female body, as when the progress of Desdemona's "name" is illustrated by being sandwiched between images of white (virginal) and black (sexual) faces. Though far from indifferent to lineage, such a discourse doesn't theorize genealogical apocalypse (as Brabantio had before the senate) so much as it complements that narrative with one of individual bodily degeneration.[44]

Iago notes the role of slander and malice in effecting such transformations, when he emblematizes them: "I'll pour this pestilence into his ear . . . So will I turn her virtue into pitch" (2.3.351, 355).[45] Iago imagines both his poisonously persuasive force and Desdemona's corrupted virtue as actual fluid substances, and virtue in particular, once "fair" and possessed of all "delighted beauty" (1.3.290), has become dark, warm, and viscous "pitch."[46] The blackening of Desdemona's name imagined by Othello was a transformation of surface, but Iago evokes a transformation of substance.[47] The two metaphors represent different ways of measuring the extent of racialization, but in both, Desdemona is imagined, through visual metaphors, to be physically altered. Both associate the origins of this change with adultery, emphasizing the period's dense coarticulation of gendered sexual morality and racist metaphysics.[48]

Desdemona's case is particularly overdetermined, of course, since, as I have argued, her marriage to Othello points up the racialization of both characters. The asymmetry of Renaissance gender theory racializes the characters differently. While Brabantio perceived Othello qua son-in-law as the source of a lineal contagion in the Venetian state, the consequences of racial degeneration associated with Desdemona's sexuality are limited to her. Interestingly, the racialized associations of marriage and adultery that accrue to her do not require that Othello be racially different from her, but these associations are occasionally intensified with remarks about Othello's background or appearance, remarks seemingly generated for that purpose alone. The descriptions of Desdemona's racial transformation reference both her alleged adultery and her willful marriage, suggesting that both licit and illicit forms of female sexuality are sufficient to precipitate racial degeneration.

For an example of the imagery of Desdemona's degeneration amplified by reference to Othello's race, recall the play on "fair" and "gross" in Roderigo's initial conceptualization of the affair, framed to provoke Brabantio: "If 't be your pleasure and most wise consent, / As partly I find it is, that your fair daughter / . . . [Be] transported . . . with a knave of common hire, a gondolier, / To the gross clasps of a lascivious Moor" (1.1.119–24). "Fair" Desdemona's passage from the lower-class hands of a gondolier—available for anyone's service—to Othello's "gross clasps" evokes a metaphysical dissolution depicted in the period's derogatory physicalist vocabulary. "Gross" represents the corpulence, coarseness, or rankness of matter *(OED),* matter in its most unappetizingly Aristotelian formulation, and by extension, the unrefined, dull, or egregiously malicious element in morality or intellect. Clasped in a Moorish and "gross" embrace, Desdemona's fairness is encircled by a rank, dense, unrefined—and let's not forget "lascivious," for "gross" is the play's name for the materiality of sexuality as well as of race—physicality that threatens to incorporate her into its own unpleasant material, an association that echoes and modulates throughout the play. Iago uses the same word to suggest a deeply repugnant adultery, both apparently trying to calm Othello down—"I am to pray you not to strain my speech / To grosser issues" (3.3.223)—and to spur him on—"would you, the supervisor, grossly gape on? / Behold her topped?" (3.3.398–99).[49] Both the comparative "grosser" and the counterfactual "would you . . . grossly gape" link the word to a transformational and degenerative logic. The word marks inferential shifts in the onlooker/discussant, hinting that he is implicated and altered by things seen or thought of. Renouncing just this immoral and transformative physicality, Desdemona enters denial: "there be women do abuse their husbands / In such gross kind?" (4.3.61–62).

But when Roderigo twists the knife, he transfers the powerful adjective from Othello's "clasp" to Desdemona and points to a compound metaphorics of politicized corporeality: "Your daughter . . . / I say again, hath made a gross revolt" (1.1.131–32). An outrageous and material revolt: this is the revolt that Brabantio presumably refers to when, before Desdemona has confronted him with the valorizing precedent of her mother's agency, he initially names his injury, a violation of his control over his daughter in which genealogical anxiety is analogized to a betrayal of the state: "O heaven, how got she out? O treason of the blood!" (1.1.166).[50] By metonymizing Desdemona through the important blood trope, Brabantio gestures fictively toward father and daughter's supposedly common substance, an effort to exaggerate the scope of her betrayal, to exclude the foreign blood of her husband, and to extend Brabantio's controlling presence through such common substance, into Desdemona's very veins.

Michel Foucault has remarked the usefulness and importance of the blood metaphor in establishing systems of alliance, which trade on blood's ability to serve as a sign, its "reality with a symbolic function."[51] But the extent to which the metaphor is seriously pursued marks also the gravity of its consequences. If, taking Brabantio's lament literally, Desdemona's treason is not seen as merely structurally filial, if she represents Brabantio's actual blood violating its proper course, that blood is ominously inadequately programmed to its supposed best interests (for example, combining only with other blood imagined to be suitably similar). The rebellion of Desdemona's blood implies its potential foreignness, abrupt reversals, and vulnerability to alterations of substance, or "gross revolt."

As we have seen, Brabantio prefers to displace the causes for such rebellion onto the nature of femininity, either onto the evident guilt requiring blushing (blood "naturally" marking its own immodesty), or else onto the female perfection that consigns all daughters to mixed marriages and resultant contamination as wives. The latter narrative also shows up flaws in the system of metaphors around blood as kinship guarantor, since a gender ideology that marks female difference so extremely can only result in female blood unable to match itself in marriage.[52] The result is what J. M. Coetzee has called a "tragedy of blood," meaning a human drama whose pathos is claimed to result inevitably from the physical nature of the participants, a tragedy in which dictates of the body leave no room for exertions of will (as when Othello's failings are seen to arise from his aroused and pathological "blood").[53] Such a tragedy adopts the prototypical logic of racial typology, since typology claims that racial difference entails narrative in the form of significant and unavoidable abilities and behaviors, often using the blood trope as its chief narratological device.

In *Othello,* the overdetermined tragedy results when Othello registers the cultural belief that Desdemona's nature will be unable to assimilate him—to transform to the degree originally suggested in Roderigo's insulting "gross revolt." As usual, Iago explains the mechanics:

> Her eye must be fed, and what delight shall she have to look
> on the devil? When the blood is made dull with the act of
> sport, there should be, again to inflame it, and to give satiety a
> fresh appetite, loveliness in favour, sympathy in years, manners
> and beauties, all which the Moor is defective in.   (2.1.223–28)

The process Iago portrays for Roderigo has Desdemona undergoing another physical change from her sexual activity, her "blood" becoming "dull" from indulgence and exhausted sexual appetite. "Blood," like grossness, bridges the play's sexual and racial themes. Here the blood that at the play's start committed "treason" encounters the results, as it begins to starve. Iago posits that the cure, in an ideal marriage, would be "delightful" similarity of appearance, custom, and age, which "the Moor" (Othello, as always, not named in such descriptions) is not made ("defective") to provide. (This is the same logic that prompts Brabantio's disbelief in Desdemona's desire for Othello to begin with, "For nature so preposterously to err / Being not deficient . . . Sans witchcraft could not" [1.3.63–65], and that incites Othello's suspicions, "And yet how nature, erring from itself . . ." [3.3.231].) The results?

> . . . her delicate tenderness will find itself abused, begin to
> heave the gorge, disrelish and abhor the Moor—very nature
> will instruct her in it.   (2.1.229–32)

Desdemona's "gross revolt" against her father is repeated against Othello, or rather, her "delicate tenderness" attempts to repel the opposed grossness associated with her husband and their sexual life. Her starving, dulled blood induces a nausea that takes Othello as an object to be expelled, as if he dwells in Desdemona's own body. Just as Roderigo's evocation of fairness clasped by grossness propelled a marital imagery with materialist implications, here the combination of "Moor" and "delicacy" engenders a "natural" physic(s) according to whose principles Desdemona becomes dull and nauseated upon contact with Othello. Her body, it is supposed, must reject him even as it is altered by the contact and internalizes Othello.

This view, when taken to be valorized by the ultimate events of the narrative (in which the marriage proves mortal to both), is increasingly adopted by other characters. Emilia, for example, characterizes heterosexuality in strikingly similar incorporative metaphors, emphasizing the cost to women of men's apparently superior digestions: "[Men] are all but stomachs, and we all but food: / They eat us hungerly, and when they are full / They belch us" (3.4.105–7).[54] Likewise, Othello's threats against Desdemona register his desire to assimilate her to his control by disassembling her and making her more palatable: "I'll tear her all to pieces!" and "I'll chop her into messes! Cuckold me!" (3.3.434; 4.1.197).[55] Desdemona's promiscuity is imagined as part of the tragedy of blood: a matter of her substance, which even though disturbing to Othello, he continues to see as properly his subsistence.

The characters' tendency to voice interpretations of events as a matter of racial destiny grows more intense by the end of the play. After Desdemona's death, the racializing energies that had begun to equate her blackness with Othello's are progressively reversed, leaving her "pale as thy smock . . . Cold, cold, my girl, even like thy chastity" (5.2.270–74).[56] At this point, Brabantio's resistance to the marriage is invoked and refigured by his brother Gratiano: "Poor Desdemona, I am glad thy father's dead; / Thy match was mortal to him" (5.2.202–3). The line is insidious; Gratiano's melodrama rewrites Brabantio's objections to the marriage as concern for Desdemona's safety, rather than patriarchal frustration and genealogical anxiety, and attempts to blame the marriage for the murder as well as for Brabantio's collateral death. Similarly, sounding like Brabantio, in an extended exchange with Othello, Emilia exaggerates his imagined racial distance from Desdemona with tropes of ontological and chromatic antithesis aligned with accusations of wickedness:

EMILIA: O the more angel she,
And you the blacker devil!

OTHELLO: She turned to folly, and she was a whore.

EMILIA: Thou dost belie her, and thou art a devil.

OTHELLO: She was false as water.

EMILIA: Thou art rash as fire to say
That she was false. O, she was heavenly true!
(5.2.128–33)

The use of such antitheses in the service of racist scapegoating is the most extreme in the play after Iago's initial bestial antitheses, in which Desdemona and Othello figure as both complementary and opposed farm animals, an "old black ram" and "your white ewe." The characters trade accusations of moral "blackness" tied to cultural associations with devils and promiscuous women. Neither questions the underlying iconography, and perhaps no one is surprised when Othello chooses to write his own epitaph in self-comparisons to a tribal and "base Indian/Judean" who undervalued a (white? black?) pearl, and to a "malignant and a turbanned Turk," a "circumcised dog" (5.2.345–53), the chief racial and religious enemy of the Venetian empire. Faced with his own self-pitying and self-degrading imagery, he stabs himself in the name of serving the state, trying to excise these figurations that exist uneasily both inside and outside of the Venetian self-conception.

The characters prove unable to extricate themselves from a racializing and racist interpretation of events, even responding to the revelation of Iago's orchestration of the tragedy by extending racializing explanations to his behavior—he gets called "inhuman dog!," "viper," "devil," and "damned slave" (5.1.62; 5.2.282, 284, 241) in close succession.[57] The play seems equally confined by a worldview in which bodies write their own inescapable tragedies, and in which the more people attract one another, the more they are seen to be "opposites." As long as female desire is identified with "gross" transformation and female chastity with unmatchable purity, all the possibilities imagined for marriage in *Othello* are interracial or racially compromising ones.

In a sense, the most radical attempt to rewrite the code through which kinship and alliance are inevitably evaluated in terms of ontologies of likeness and difference is Brabantio's move in the Venetian senate to eschew the liabilities of blood and lineage, instead advocating ideological reproduction by adoption: "I had rather adopt a child than get it." Brabantio tries to find likeness and kinship solely by election. Yet Brabantio's bitter gambit is motivated by a desire less for reconciliation than for dissociation from Desdemona. Brabantio longs for the abstract and reversible, though impossible, relation to his daughter of an adoptive parent. Built into this plot of fatherly repudiation is the insight that the alienable strongly resembles the alien. We will examine such fantasies of familial negation and disowning further as they appear in narratives of Jewish conversion and transformation in chapter 2. In *Othello,* interest in miscegenation, imagined as the result of filial or spousal agency, leads to startling imagery of gendered racial transformation within the home. But the rueful response of attempted separation from racial contamination by means of a proposed reorganization of alliance such as adoption can only be expressed as an unrealizable fiction, a denial of the interracial structures that are already there. *Othello* thus fantasizes miscegenation as an artifact of fear but also as the architecture of its cultural moment, a narrative permeating and bonding husbands and wives, families and strangers.

TWO

Exemplary Jews and the
Logic of Gentility

⌒⚜⌒

Tush, who amongst 'em knows not Barabas?

—Christopher Marlowe, *The Jew of Malta*

Gentle Lady . . .
I freely told you all the wealth I had
Ran in my veins.

—William Shakespeare, *The Merchant of Venice*

The Stock of Barabas

Shylock and his Jewishness have occupied an increasingly privileged place in the criticism of *The Merchant of Venice*. At times, the bulk of critical writing on *Merchant* can read like an extended referendum on Shylock's character, and consequently on the existence of a Shakespearean bias against Jews.[1] Shakespeare is excoriated or exculpated in due proportion as Shylock comes to figure a quasi-demonic (or simply anti-Christian) vengefulness, a harassed and sympathetic humanist universalism, a villain not thoroughly let off the hook by being partly formed by social intolerance, or even, as in one study, a Jew who doesn't live up to Judaism's highest ideals.[2]

As if this weren't enough of an interpretive burden to bear, most readers have assumed that Shylock remains a—perhaps *the*—central imaginary figure in perpetual reaction to whom the English produce their collective fantasies about Jews and the Jewish relation to

Englishness more generally. To take a prominent example outside the field of Renaissance or Shakespeare studies, Michael Ragussis's study of projects for Jewish conversion and the formation of English national identity argues for Shylock's overarching influence over all English representation of Jews and Jewishness: "Shakespeare's text invades the novel from *Harrington* to *Ulysses* . . . a sign of the play's indisputable authority; *no portrait of a Jew can exist in English without reference to it.*"[3] Though Ragussis's own readings are nuanced and thoughtful, his hyperbole partakes of a basic element of *Merchant* criticism: conflating the representation of Shylock with English attitudes toward Jewishness as a whole. In this criticism, Shylock becomes both individual and type, both origin and determinant of English Jewish discourse, both "the worst" and the most paradigmatic representation of a Jew.

Such a stance oversimplifies English constructions of Jewishness; it buys into, instead of analyzing, the play's intermittent, typologizing equation of Shylock and "the Jew."[4] In this chapter, in order to explore the intersection of period notions of religion, race, and class, I will discuss Shylock's role in signifying Jewishness in relation to other Jewish characters, such as Marlowe's Barabas and Shylock's own daughter, Jessica. This will entail analysis of the differences present in the dramatic representation of different Jewish characters—as we will see, Barabas's Jewishness is not like Shylock's. More importantly, examining multiple characters in dynamic relation to one another will allow us to see that Jewishness does not stand alone as a static entity: the meaning of Shylock's Jewishness is shaped by representations of Barabas and of Jessica; Jessica's Jewishness in turn is affected by her father's Jewishness and by the representation of the gentile and gentle identities she is trying to claim; and gentile identity itself depends on those elements of Jewishness that it either excludes or absorbs. The result is a range of English dramatic projections of Jewishness, according to which Jewishness is differently and variably racialized.

Amid these options, a literary history in which the icon of Shylock predominates may be recognized as evolving less from Shylock's inherent power to determine the shape of an English Jewish imaginary than from changing popular and critical attitudes toward Jewishness, race, and Englishness that have converged on Shakespeare.[5] The present sense that the intersection of the three former terms is best accessed through the figure of Shylock is partly achieved by occluding other Jewish representations and the representations of Englishness, Christianity, and Islam against which Jewish representation is formulated. The question of exemplarity, then, is central to evaluating Renaissance notions of Jewishness; as we will see, assessments of Jewishness often proceed by reading over or reading out some Jewish characters as inadequately or partially Jewish. This reading over is in turn strongly anticipated in the Renaissance plays' own treatment of the—multiple—characters in question.

For it may be worth noting—and a habitué of Renaissance drama will scarce need reminding—that there are a few exceptions to Ragussis's "no portrait" rule. Strangely, in *The Merchant of Venice,* Shylock himself invokes a different stage Jew, Marlowe's Barabas, as possessing just the cult status of originary religious and racial instantiation that later criticism has primarily identified with Shylock. The invocation comes at a critical moment during Antonio's trial, when his friends Bassanio and Gratiano, disgusted with the seeming impotence of the legal expert (the heroine Portia, in disguise) and with Antonio's increasingly hopeless bleats of submissiveness, burst out with descriptions of the sacrifices they wish they might make on his behalf. Addressing a deep tension in the play, the two vie with one another for the honor of sufficiently valuing masculine friendship above "companionate" marriage, each bragging that he would be pleased for his wife to die should her death (inexplicably) deliver Antonio. Shylock is momentarily distracted from his vengeance against Antonio by this show of male exclusivist rhetoric (which eclipses even the display of Christian exclusivist rhetoric elsewhere characterizing the trial). He scornfully comments in an aside: "these be the Christian husbands! I have a daughter— / Would any of the stock of Barrabas / Had been her husband, rather than a Christian" (4.1.291–93).[6]

Barabas is, of course, the protagonist of a different play, Marlowe's *The Jew of Malta*. Shylock's allusion to him capitalizes on *Malta*'s extraordinary popularity among Elizabethan theatergoers, functioning both to confirm Shylock's own literary pedigree and to affirm his religious identification with a larger (but similarly fictive) Jewish commonality.[7] The allusion is agreeable for the purposes of this chapter because it immediately broadens and complicates the scope of Jewish signification present in *Merchant* and therefore available to its author, audience, and readers. Shylock's allusion provides a small hint at Shakespeare's notion of Shylock's own understanding of Jewishness. Then, too (or to rephrase the point), the invocation of another fictive Jew reminds us that "Shylock" is a set of speeches and conventions whose "Jewish" behavior and characterization are partly indebted to and scripted by preexisting Jewish intertexts.[8] Consequently, Shylock's line implies that for all Gratiano's and Antonio's cause to hate him, their gleeful antipathy does not arise from their personal history with him alone (as his critical status as the origin of Jewish signification for the English would have it) but depends on larger cultural beliefs about Jewishness as well.

Shylock's own wish that he might be Barabas's, not Lorenzo's, father-in-law invites his perception as Jew rather than individual bondholder, no less than does Portia's final judgment. Yet his reason for contrasting Gratiano's and Bassanio's fickleness with an imaginary descendant of Barabas as son-in-law would seem to be not simply that he can spare one last regret that daughter Jessica has eloped with a gentile but that, from his point of view, "Christian husbands" per se are unworthy husbands, whose investments lie outside of the family proper. Shylock decries the sanctimony of the Venetians' wife-sacrificing rhetoric. Interestingly, it is at this point that Shylock's analysis of the situation fleetingly intersects with Portia's, who, overhearing, ironically remarks at Bassanio's willingness to forfeit her in favor of Antonio: "your wife would give you little thanks for that" (4.1.284). Nor, as we will see, is this the only moment in the play in which "Jewish" values approach a species of "Christian" ones. Is it coincidence that Portia replies to Shylock's critique of Bassanio's offer with her own most abrupt and clear-cut award of the judgment he desires?: "A pound of that same merchant's flesh is thine, / The court awards it, and the law doth give it" (4.1.295–96).

Still, the momentary alignment between Shylock and Portia, predicated on mutual disidentification with male homosociality, is shortly to be decisively reversed. And, indeed, the basis for this harmony is vexed, since Shylock's invocation of "the stock of Barrabas" makes a strange opening for a critique of Christian domestic feeling. Barabas himself is hardly a family man—which the audience of *The Jew of Malta* knows from the moment he compares his feeling for his daughter Abigail to Agamemnon's for "his Iphigen" (1.1.136). Indeed, for an audience, part of the punch of Shylock's allusion comes from its implicit endorsement of Barabas's stagy and indiscriminate viciousness—his overlap with Shylock's own villainous tendencies. Inasmuch as Barabas is just the sort of profit- and mayhem-seeking "Machevil" that some have imagined Shylock as desiring to be, Shylock's invocation of Barabas assimilates the two, reading their shared Jewishness as shared villainy, both figurative and literal "kinship."[9] To this end, Shylock makes Barabas figure the genealogical view of Jewishness to be found, as we will see, primarily in Venice and Belmont.

But it is not clear that the genealogical view is sustainable. Perhaps the oddest feature of Shylock's wish to have his family marry into the "stock of Barrabas" is that by the end of Marlowe's play, Barabas has poisoned his daughter as well as his adoptive replacement for her and spends his final moments ensnared by his own stratagem, having fallen into a cauldron within a pit below the stage (5.5.76–88). That is, there is no surviving "stock of Barrabas" for Jessica to marry.[10] Why, then, does Shylock use this idiom?

Shylock's manner of referring to a possible Jewish son-in-law as "any of the stock of Barrabas" employs a lineal metaphor. His reference works by implying that Jews are an extended family, that their supposed shared identity and resemblance results in part from actual consanguinity, from something like shared genetic stock. The implications of consanguinity are twofold: according to this definition, Jews represent a closed bloodline and are (1) all related to one another, and (2) never related to the Venetians (or the Maltese, or the English, or to Christians in aggregate). Shylock's allusion to Barabas therefore serves as a synecdoche of an unpolluted and non-polluting Jewishness even while, through the incoherence of its referent (Barabas has no descendants), the phrase reminds us that such familial definitions of religious or racial groups are metaphorical, tenuous, and illogical.

A definition of Jewishness implied by a trope of consanguinity is just one example of a logic that racializes Jews in Renaissance drama. Other key tropes and logics assert Jewish ontological inferiority in derogatory epithets such as "dog" or "devil," while still others detail an inflexible Jewish cultural or moral specificity, including proliferating tropes of wealth (especially gold and jewels) and pathological malevolence, concretized in supposed acts of virtually motiveless murder, compulsive deceit, or fathomless greed. Jews are variously identified by these tropes as possessing common morality, common history, common blood, common ancestors, and uncommon wealth and greed. The associations of Jews with hostility, "practice," and murder support their construction as "the very antithesis of Englishness."[11] The alien status of Jews serves as both explanation and motivation for the characters' villainous impulses; such circular logics are intensified when either alien status or villainy needs clarification. Yet, importantly, Jewish characters also elicit audience identification, compelled by their fabulous wealth and intricate, competent machinations—even their villainy may possess its own attractions.

Not all tropes are in operation at all times. Though Barabas himself occasionally resorts to definitions of Jewishness that rely on embodied genealogical continuity, referring to Jews as the "tribe that I descended of" (1.2.113) and as male and patriarchal "sons of Israel . . . Abraham's offspring" (2.1.13–14), such definitions of Jewish affiliation are in fact far more representative of *Merchant*'s Jewish logics than of *Malta*'s, which rarely employ them. In this way, Shakespeare's own use of "Barrabas" reads (and misreads) *Malta* selectively and, invoking a genealogical relation between the two Jews, stacks the deck in favor of the critical fixation on Shylock.

It will be useful to present Marlowe's own Jewish logic before going on to consider Shakespeare's, in order to see an earlier, different framing of the problems of Jewish exemplarity and morality, of group membership and exclusion, and of conversion that are of interest in Shakespeare's *Merchant* and to its reader. Both Marlowe's and Shakespeare's plays are interested in definitions both of Jewishness and the Christian or Muslim identities presented alongside Jewish ones. *Merchant* considers both cultural and racial definitions of Jewishness, doggedly preferring the latter as a means of shoring up an equally racialized gentile identity. Yet despite the fact that Barabas is as villainous as possible, Marlowe characteristically presents Jewish identity differently—as more compelling, more dazzling, and less inflexibly defined.

The typical formulations of Marlowe's play present Jewish identification as an attribute less of genealogical continuity than as something between performative allegiance and occupation. In *Malta*'s language, Jewishness and Christianity are "professions," as when the Maltese governor, Ferneze, rebukes Barabas's early attempts to hold onto his commandeered property: "justify thyself as if we knew not thy profession?" (1.2.119–20). With this single word, Ferneze seemingly refers to Barabas's Jewishness, to any prior avowals of his Jewishness (in the speech-act sense of "profession"), and to his proficient and (hence) cutthroat mercantilism.[12]

"Profession" does not connote Jewishness alone and is applied also to Malta's Christian and Muslim characters—especially to their cynical religious fluidity and opportunism, as when Turkish Ithamore, Barabas's new slave, describes himself to his master: "my birth is but mean, my name's Ithamore, my profession what you please" (2.3.166–67).[13] The exchange between Ithamore and Barabas amply indicates the degree to which Marlowe associates "profession" with fluidity. To this point, "profession" has been used half a dozen times in explicit connection with religious faith. The audience has been taught to expect that Ithamore's answer, "my profession what you please," and the prior question that elicited it, "Now let me know thy . . . profession" (2.3.165), concern his faith. Yet Barabas responds to Ithamore's flexibility blithely: "Hast thou no *trade?*" (2.3.168; emphasis added). In a further Marlovian irony, Barabas then twists the word further by enjoining Ithamore to learn a trade of "smil[ing] when the Christians moan" (2.3.173) and launching into his own notorious curriculum vitae of Jewish-specific villainies ("as for myself, I walk abroad a' nights / And kill sick people . . . " [2.3.175–76]). In short, in these lines, Jewishness becomes something of a trade, which Barabas offers to Ithamore, turned apprentice, with its attendant skills and products—poisoning, perverted medicine, treason, stratagems.

The Jewish trade also comes with wages. For Barabas further defines Jewishness predominantly as he is defined by those around him, as constituted by fantastic wealth. No matter how often deprived of money, goods, and home, Barabas springs back unaffected, always possessing more, seemingly, than before. In *The Jew of Malta,* this resiliency is identified with Barabas's Jewish "profession," linking *what he does* to *what he is.* He sees his fortune as the sum of divine prophecy and religious destiny: "these are the blessings promis'd to the Jews." Wealth is also the chief cause of Christian antagonism: "Who hateth me but for my happiness? . . . Rather had I, a Jew, be hated thus, / Than pitied in a Christian poverty" (1.1.103, 110–13). Barabas views the Jewish diaspora as creating a map of the world with capital points of bright Jewish wealth:

> They say we are a scatter'd nation:
> I cannot tell, but we have scambled up
> More wealth by far than those that brag of faith.
> There's Kirriah Jairim, the great Jew of Greece,
> Obed in Bairseth, Nones in Portugal,
> Myself in Malta, some in Italy,
> Many in France, and *wealthy every one:*
> Ay, *wealthier far than any Christian.*
>   (1.1.119–26; emphasis added)

In Barabas's catalog, riches are not just a possession or attribute but an exclusive sign of Jewishness, definitionally unattainable by Christians. Though the belief that Jews are "wealthy every one" is untenable, even in the limited context of the play, the point for Marlowe's audience is that the wealthiest and most diabolical Jews serve as the relevant exemplars of Jewishness, defined less by faith than by a metonymic fraternalism endorsed by and embodied in the play's title character, namely, "the Jew" in Malta. Barabas's slogan, "wealthy every one," is an acceptable one, as contradictory evidence is easily overlooked. Like the Maltese, who levy an enormous penalty on all Jews in Malta to pay the Turkish tribute while aiming to "take particularly" Barabas's fortune (1.2.96), Barabas mistakes his exceptional census for a representative one. When half of all Jewish possessions is demanded, one unnamed Jew laments, "Alas, my lord, the most of us are poor" (1.2.57), belying Barabas's previous world survey.

Yet if Barabas's intense self-interest detaches him from concern for or even awareness of his coreligionists, the play endorses the equation of Jewishness and hyperbolic wealth in his case. Along with his villainy, his involvement with money is the hallmark of his character, one that seems the more telling in that, for all the plots hatched to restore or avenge the loss of his fortune, Barabas's interest in money seems more acquisitive and possessive than instrumental. For Barabas, money serves virtually an atmospheric or aesthetic function. His wealth is often characterized as abstract, recursive, regenerative plenitude, as in the play's most celebrated, opening trope, when Barabas extols the quality and quantity of his possessions, recommending that "men of judgment" should, "as their wealth increaseth, so enclose / Infinite riches in a little room" (1.1.34–37).

The fantasy of confining and compressing the infinite, reconstituted in comparisons that freely and delightedly collapse orders of magnitude, reappears throughout the play and several times in this first speech, always in relation to value. Barabas wishes to condense his silver holdings into gold, so that "a man may easily in a day / Tell that which may maintain him all his life" (1.1.10–11), and fantasizes about "the wealthy Moor" who possesses casual piles of jewels of such quality that a single one, "indifferently rated . . . may serve . . . to ransom great kings from captivity" (1.1.29–32).[14] Such descriptions locate Jewish wealth's allure in recursion, density, and withheld power. They might productively be compared to Barabas's own facility for reversals of fortune, executed when he is most defeated.[15]

As in other Marlovian dramas, in which the protagonists' temporary omnipotence appears to be both premise and subject of the play, Barabas is constituted by his endless *resourcefulness*. Like Faustus's magic and agnostic verve or Tamburlaine's self-conception as *imperium sui generis*, Barabas's "bags" and the matchless if callous ingenuity that keeps them full are the pretext for staging Marlovian tragicomic inexorability, the momentum unleashed by boundless appetite capably pursued. Marlowe's heroes are invariably outsiders, and their difference is integral to their appeal. The images of fluency and power converging in Barabas effectively become signals to the reader or audience of his Jewishness, as much as his occasional references to Abraham or the Maccabees, or his boasts of poison and murder, if only because his wealth and schemes are more efficacious, distinct, and densely layered than those of his Christian or Turkish counterparts—and because efficacy, schemes, wealth, power, and fluency are how Barabas understands his own Jewish "profession."

Shakespeare's Shylock obviously lacks Barabas's ability to triumph and flourish in adversity. Criticism focusing on Shylock exaggerates just that distinction; in the modern cultural imagination, Shakespearean ascendancy over Marlowe has entailed and permitted a greater role for early modern Jewish haplessness.[16] Likewise, in the context of Shakespeare's cultural centrality, Shakespeare's greater interest than Marlowe in lineal definitions of Jewishness attests, benefits from, and invigorates desires for such definitions. To belabor the point, in a Marlovian *Merchant of Venice*, Shylock would without question obtain the flesh of his bond and, further, become the Duke before Portia's final triumph, just as Barabas is allowed to conquer Malta and replace its governor, a position in which he proves utterly uninterested.

Instead of reanimating authentically Marlovian energies, Shylock's invocation of Barabas as Jew focuses on his role within a Jewish genealogy—though he forgets that Barabas chooses to forgo that role, in *Merchant*'s strategic rewriting of *Malta*'s Jewish metaphorics. Shylock's stress on genealogical Judaism reflects his play's preferred signifiers of Jewishness. *Merchant*'s racial logic elects blood and genealogy as determinants of racial identity, in contrast to *Malta,* whose Jewish characters barely have elaborated blood or bodies at all. Shylock's misreading of Barabas, however, participates in *Merchant*'s attempt, where possible, to maximize the racialized alignment of blood, genealogy, morality, theology, nation, and class. Shylock's invocation of Marlowe's play therefore shows that as early as *Merchant,* a lineal construction of Jewishness begins to function as *Malta*'s subverted literary and cultural inheritance. The persistence of this lineal vision of Jewishness is a further way we might gloss "the stock of Barabas."

Still, from another point of view, Shylock's reference to Barabas's "stock" in the specific context of Venetian fantasies of wife sacrifice is not entirely erratic when it stimulates analysis of Barabas's self-engineered childlessness. Barabas's violence against his daughter, executed after she has attempted to marry a Christian, renounced her father's villainy, and converted to Catholicism, is hardly capricious. In effect, Barabas literalizes and externalizes a disciplinary impulse that we have seen before, formulated more usually and conflictingly in wistful or frustrated metaphors or counterfactuals, or otherwise muted by being directed against the self. Just as Brabantio responded to Desdemona's assertions of filial agency in marriage with the angry, yet ultimately self-disciplining desire that he "had rather adopt a child than get it" (*Othello* 1.3.192),[17] the Jewish families in *Merchant* and *Malta* likewise express numerous fantasies of destroying or disowning their kin, as well as (most interestingly) fantasies denying their actual relations of kinship itself. As in Brabantio's case, their denials are typically provoked by the threat or reality of exogamous alliance. Shylock's wish that his "daughter were dead at my foot, and the jewels in her ear: would she were hears'd at my foot, and the ducats in her coffin" (3.1.80–82) is thus in a sense a more representative reaction to daughterly defection than his wish that she had married into the stock of Barabas.

These metaphors and counterfactuals mark the contested racial territory that is the focus of this book. By erasing family members who attempt to affiliate themselves with an external ethnicity, religion, or other group, the figurative language of Jewish characters expresses emotional resistance to the crossing of racial and religious boundaries. Yet at the same time, this language acknowledges, and even facilitates, such transformations. Strikingly, as with Desdemona, the Jewish daughters' attempts to change their family, racial, and religious affiliations are partly furthered by their fathers' repudiations. Jessica's conversion plot in particular relies upon repeated variations on the theme of her secret or obvious dissimilarity from her father. Still, imagery that erases familial relationships may propose and yet not ultimately enable passage between groups. We will see that *Merchant* investigates Jewish identity largely by assessing tropes of lineal sameness and difference, settling on bloodlines themselves as the relevant criterion. Parallel exploration of the boundaries of gentile identity defines blood as its crucial determinant. To analyze these dynamics more closely, we turn now to the middle of Jessica's story, at a moment when she is (almost literally) poised between gentile and Jewish identities.

A Gentle and No Jew

Descending from the windows of her father Shylock's distasteful home to the welcoming arms of her Christian suitor Lorenzo, Jessica does not allow the demands of haste to prevent her from appropriating some of her father's wealth. Lorenzo and she turn out to have different ideas about the nature of the disguise she will employ in her escape—dressed as a boy, she'd prefer secrecy and the cover of darkness, while he has her masquerading as his torchbearer in the company of his Venetian friends. They wrangle about how desirable her disguise, or display, "in the lovely garnish of a boy"

(2.6.45) makes her. Nonetheless, the two have agreed about the assets Jessica will bring to her marriage, assets that offset the loss of the dowry she has forfeited through elopement. In an earlier letter to Lorenzo, Jessica has carefully specified "what gold and jewels she is furnish'd with" (2.4.31) along with matters of rendezvous and disguise. Still, during the elopement, after tossing Lorenzo a casket of valuables, Jessica delays her descent from the stage's gallery space in order to supplement these, to "gild myself / With some moe ducats" (2.6.49–50). This prudent act immediately precedes a hearty welcome below from Lorenzo's friend Gratiano, whom the extra provisioning of gold, perhaps, encourages: "now (by my hood) a gentle, and no Jew" (2.6.51).

The episode is, on the surface, light-hearted and playful. Against the backdrop of bloodthirsty and vengeful contract negotiation that elsewhere propels the play, Gratiano offers what may seem to be a more hopeful and flexible framework for interaction between members of different religions in Venice, while Jessica and Lorenzo provide a marriage plot more representative of the comedy the Folio promises in its version of the title. Gratiano's mock award of non-Jewish status is remarkable for its emphatic immediacy, as though Jessica's transformation from Jew to "gentle" can occur in the space of a moment, simply by exiting her Jewish home, as she has hoped. Amid the play's conflicts and contests between religions, ethnicities, and genders, Gratiano seems to support a pragmatically expansive model for self-fashioning through conversion. That is, Gratiano's welcome seems to suggest conversion is gratifyingly absolute—bestowing a new identity and group membership given new circumstances of time, place, and intent. As we will see, Jessica herself has employed this very model of conversion as she imagines her own future.

But at the same time, the sequence here—the proffered dowry, and the enthusiastic welcome by the Christians below—may appear to tell an overdetermined story. In this story, assimilationist Jewish insecurity literally makes a bid for acceptance by Christians whose open-mindedness is proportional to the extent of their prospect of gain. In this more cynical reading, the very abruptness of Gratiano's claim for Jessica's transformation signals the provisional, phatic, or disingenuous nature of his acceptance and, therefore, the provisional, performative, or tenuous status of Jessica's acceptability.

As I will argue, this possibility is made more likely by Gratiano's significant choice of approving name for Jessica—to which I will return at length—given by the first quarto's and Folio's "gentle," second quarto's "gentile." Modern readers expect the latter word, "gentile," as antonym to "Jew," and modern editions generally provide it. The play's Arden editor assumes the first spelling is an archaic variant of the second—distinct—word; his note tells us the two words were "not completely distinguished in spelling at this time" (2.4.34n).[18] Yet the overlap between these two terms is not limited, in my opinion, to the orthographic. Later, I will consider the extent of their mutual conceptual indebtedness—and, at the narrative level, their cumulative saturation of one another. I argue that *Merchant*'s presentation of the boundary between Jewishness and Christianity trades on an equation of Christianity and gentility, the latter term as vital to the play as the former. Gentility's meanings, force, and exclusions unite the Shylock-Antonio, Portia, and Jessica plots and subplots of *Merchant*. The word "gentle" itself echoes through the play, nearly always marking or strengthening divisions between characters and serving to encode the values the play endorses. These values permit the absorption of Jewish qualities considered desirable, such as wealth. At the same time, "gentleness" is far more leery of sharing its privileges, or bloodlines, with outsiders. Jessica's initial success in conversion and intermarriage therefore provides an important exception and test case, though her means of achieving a new identity, differentiation from her father, may have dire consequences for him. Yet the limits of Jessica's success grow increasingly evident as her example is linked and contrasted over the course of the play with the unique conditions surrounding Portia's own courtship, nuptials, and postmarital behavior. Portia's drama of husband selection indicates the degree of difference that gentile identity is willing to accommodate in marriage, providing intradramatic commentary on Jessica's efforts at conversion.

Bringing Home the Bacon

At first glance, Jessica appears to escape entirely the negative associations with Jewishness that many readers and critics of the play have seen manifested liberally in its representation of Shylock. Both her virtue and her femininity make her a likely candidate for Christian recuperation in a play that represents Jewishness, primarily in her father, as malign, self-interested, scheming, and vengeful. Yet Jessica's status as simultaneously Jewish and virtuous, like Shylock's and Jessica's lack of familial resemblance—both much remarked by the play's characters—may paradoxically both broaden and limit the play's field of Jewish representation. For in practice, once being Jewish becomes coextensive with possessing qualities of deceitfulness and malice, a character lacking those traits, even if Jewish by other criteria such as descent, may escape not just the stigma of Jewishness, as that has become identified with Judaism's distinctively malign psychology, but also the identification as Jew. Just as the familiar "present company excepted" tag confers local absolution of racial stigmas, especially ethical or psychological stigmas, the "exceptional" morality of virtuous Jewish characters can provide them with access to complimentary Christian identity. Likewise, it may govern the attitudes of other characters (and critics), who view them as less Jewish than more marked or malicious Jews.[19] In this way, an individual's rise in status may be unlikely to broaden audience expectations about other members of the individual's racial group, since status is nearly always perceived as resemblance to the dominant, discursively "neutral" population. In Renaissance drama, because religiously or racially exceptional characters are depicted with a virtuous disposition, and virtue is defined by the theology and culture of Christianity, the plays may partially refigure them as Christians.[20] Christian identity may become a narrative endpoint, when virtue results in conversion to Christianity. In the case of Jewish daughters,

Christian status is provisionally obtained through conversion or, as with Jessica, through marriage to a Christian.

The impetus for such transformations, individual virtue, interestingly subverts any prima facie inauspicious resemblance of Jewish daughters to their closest historical counterparts in Elizabethan and Jacobean London: resident Marranos, that is, Spanish and Portuguese Jews who had been required in their home lands to convert (or be exiled).[21] The Marrano possessed an orthodox exterior, characterized by outward adherence to Protestant ritual and participation in commerce beneficial to English national interests (providing ready capital and connections to Mediterranean and Levantine trade infrastructure). Marranos provoked fears, however, of a hidden, treasonous interiority: of heretical Jewish rituals confirmed in private and, worse, of secret political loyalties to Catholic nations and religious organizations sustained through participation in murderous, even regicidal, plots.[22] According to the intricate fear, Marranos were both secretly Jews and secretly anti-English Catholics. In contrast, in the entertaining world of popular drama, seductively virtuous (and entrancingly moneyed) Jewish daughters present a transcendent (i.e., Christian) ethics and beauty "trapped within" the body, habitus, family structure, and dwelling of Jew.[23]

But because Jessica is a female character, her fate is not solely determined by a purely religious notion of virtue. Indeed, a growing critical interest in Jessica reflects the need to account for the ways in which gender impacts the forms of racial and religious identity and to consider both male and female representatives of Judaism.[24] Yet, like her virtue, Jessica's gender renders her status as a Jewish "representative" ambiguous and contentious, because she, like Abigail and other female non-Christian characters in drama, appears primarily in religious transition, desiring to convert and marry out of her faith. The extent to which her transition from Jew to Christian is possible therefore provides an important window into the play's representation of both Jewish and gentile identity. Some critics have read Jessica as capable of leaving her Jewishness behind, suggesting that religious and racial fluidity is gendered female, and Jewishness primarily male. For instance, James Shapiro connects the trope of female conversion to his sense that "the religious difference of Jewish women is not usually imagined as physically inscribed in their flesh," as circumcision is, rendering easier female transition between Jewish and Christian identities.[25] Implicitly, according to Shapiro and others, Jessica is able to make this transition because she is seen as less Jewish than her father.[26]

By contrast, my reading of Jessica's conversion will suggest that her passage into Christian wifehood is not as easily attained as Shapiro and others imply, largely because the presence of physical marking is not necessary for the ascription of categorical difference, though it is one of the easiest means by which such difference may be perceived and/or generated. In Jessica's case, as often with racialized groups, an emphasis on genealogical continuity, with its tropes of flesh, blood, and spirit shared between parents and children, is sufficient for the ascription of Jewishness she is at pains to leave behind. Jessica's conversion and marriage do not leave her Jewishness diluted or quantitatively less than her father's. Rather, the opposition between father and daughter leads to their mutual construction of Jewish otherness, in which attraction and repulsion each lend charge to the other, two sides of the same coin.

Jessica herself is represented as resisting assimilation both to the version of Jewishness Shylock represents and to Jewishness generally. To further the distinction she courts, she attempts to sift ethical or cultural Jewishness from genealogical Jewishness. Jessica claims that the cultural breach between herself and Shylock defines her own identity and therefore makes genealogy less relevant: "though I am a daughter to his blood, / I am not to his manners" (2.3.17–18). Jessica's distinction between lineage and manners complicates the presumed monolithic identity of what may be called a racial group by pointing to a boundary between two distinct components of the discourse defining Jews in the play. The blood metaphor constructs Jewishness as a matter of literal substance and of genealogical inheritance, a "genetic" legacy in the etymological sense, while the question of "manners" points to a concept of distinctively Jewish culture, ethics, and group psychology. According to a strongly racialist logic, Jews would be a discrete, self-similar population, and Jewish blood and manners would delimit one, not two, groups of people, in which bloodlines disseminate Jewish ethics and culture. However, Jessica imagines herself occupying a corner of what sounds more like a Venn diagram: she is Jewish by blood but does not share Shylock's Jewish "manners"—that is, his deceit, greed, and vengefulness.

The vocabulary of "manners" is highly adaptable, signifying in Jessica's deployment not only the regulation of ethical behavior by religious stricture but also the regulation of mannerism and social intercourse by the discourses of etiquette, an equal concern for the folk of Venice and Belmont. In addition to these primary meanings, "manners" or "manner" can signify more generally "species" or "kind" (as in the interrogative "what manner of . . . ?"). The proximity of the two fields of meaning hints at the word's uses for social and ontological classification. Significantly, as with Gratiano's "gentle" welcome of Jessica, the term "manners" functions as a code for in-group acceptability elsewhere in the play. This occurs at Belmont, as part of the contrasting plot of spousal selection, when Portia is at last excited about her messenger's description of a prospect come to woo her: "come, come Nerissa, for I long to see / Quick Cupid's post that comes so mannerly" (2.9.99–100). The "mannerly" youth is, pointedly, a "young Venetian" sent by Bassanio, who fares far better than the prior suitors who are mocked for peculiarities imagined at once as determined by their nationality (the German is a drunkard, the Englishman is an incoherent ape of fashion, and so on) and as rendering them unsuitable for marriage to Portia.[27] In contrast, Bassanio's proxy's "mannerly" suitability, making him "so likely an ambassador of love" (2.9.92), consists wholly in his bringing "gifts of rich value." His rhetorical skill is glancingly referred to in a parenthetical aside, the better to point out his pricey offerings:

> . . . he bringeth sensible regreets;
> To wit, besides commends and courteous breath,
> Gifts of rich value. (2.9.89–91)

Perhaps it would be more accurate to say that the skill praised here *is* rhetorical, namely, Bassanio's rhetoric of materiality, his knowledge that the most acceptable "regreets" will be those that are "sensible" (tangible). Bassanio's messenger is compared to an "April day" that forecasts the imminence of "costly summer" (2.9.94–95)—a seasonal lavishness here strangely, and characteristically, literalized. The tangible is obviously preferable to the evanescent "courteous breath" that other suitors will have provided in tedious abundance. It appears that the foreign suitors are disqualified both for their national predispositions (manners) and their ignorance of the proper displays of competitive generosity required (lack of manners), that nature and culture conspire to define foreignness as unacceptable "ambassador" material for Cupid. The overdetermined call for endogamy, rendered in the very idiom Jessica uses to legitimate her exogamous refashioning, should sound an ominous enough note for her project.

For the success of Jessica's conversion and marriage relies on the persuasiveness of her separation of nature and culture. She claims, in effect, that her laudable performance of Christian values proves she is uncompromised by any genetic residue of religious inheritance—that Shylock's "blood" entails simply a familial relation. In her account, the "strife" between her manners and blood, between cultural style and filial identity, may be resolved by their very lack of resemblance. This underlies Jessica's professed desires that her ethical dissimilarity from Shylock will enable a smooth transition into Christianity and wifehood, untrammeled as she is by Jewish manners:

> But though I am a daughter to his blood,
> I am not to his manners. O Lorenzo
> If thou keep promise I shall end this strife,
> Become a Christian and thy loving wife! (2.3.17–20)

Her purpose is not least to leave the stigma her father represents behind; apostrophizing Shylock, she hopes "if fortune be not crost, / I have a father, you a daughter, lost" (2.5.55–56). That is, Jessica hopes— shockingly—literally to cancel out their blood relation.

In this way, the ramifications of Jessica's lack of ethical resemblance to her father are immediately subsumed into her conversion plot. She at once raises the specter that not all Jews are immoral and allays the doubts such a premise might stir up by aligning herself with Christianity and a Christian lover.[28] In the past, the maneuver to disarm such a character of whatever threats she poses by reading her as essentially a Christian maiden with a rough start has been echoed in criticism that either tends to ignore such characters as representations of Jews or that, more recently, reads conversion as ultimately "successful" integration.[29] Noting the prior omission in Jessica's case, Mary Janell Metzger takes critics to task for reading Shylock alone as the play's representation of Jewishness and thereby replicating a certain trend in the play itself to settle on him as the exemplary Jew.[30] In contrast, Metzger sees Jessica and Shylock as embodying "competing notions of Judaism circulating in early modern England," notions largely following the lines of gender difference. Where Jessica, Metzger argues, elects Christianity, capitalizing on her female ability to be bodily assimilated into her husband's family (according to Christian, patriarchal marital ideology), Shylock is both malignantly resistant to Christianity and unable as a marked, circumcised Jew to become Christian should he wish to do so.[31] Together, the characters provide both an example of absolute difference shoring up chauvinistic Christian self-image and a theologically gratifying example of conversion. To facilitate these opposed Jewish identities, the play pursues two representational strategies: Jessica is repeatedly depicted as "fair" and virtuous, a familiar type of heroine; Shylock is "villainous" and finally "alien." We are encouraged to further the opposition by reading the pair through the lens of period notions of gender and generational difference, and not through equally applicable period notions of family, religious, and racial similarity.

At some points, the play certainly endorses this opposition, fusing Jessica and her father into a complementary Jewish dyad that privileges her virtue using Shylock as a foil. Yet so long as Jessica relies on her father to be continually distinguished from him, in manners if not in blood, she is immersed in Jewish signification rather than liberated from it. Musing on this relation before he elopes, Lorenzo acquits Shylock of damnation on his daughter's account, with dubious effects for her:

> If e'er the Jew her father come to heaven,
> It will be for his gentle daughter's sake,
> And never dare misfortune cross her foot,
> Unless she do it under this excuse,
> That she is issue to a faithless Jew.   (2.4.33–37)

Lorenzo, unlike Jessica, emphasizes the import of her genealogy, her status as Jewish "issue." As if O. Henry were to recapitulate the logic of original sin, Lorenzo has the "gentle daughter" suffering for her pardoned father's sins in a strangely chiastic eschatology. Here is a Jewish dualism like the one Metzger believes operates throughout the play, yet the values associated with Jessica and Shylock seem to have migrated away from their respective sources, each tingeing the other with inverted consequences. These consequences are far more gratuitous and, of course, more dire, in Jessica's case. It appears that merely being distinguishable from her father may not be sufficient to redeem Jessica from the stigma of Jewishness or to ease her entry into Christian identity.

For Lorenzo's ambiguous praise of Jessica implies that, despite the functional opposition between Shylock and his daughter, her conversion is attended with intense and anxious rhetoric within her new Christian community. This rhetoric includes choice debate on such classic racialist tropes and topics as her color, her probable eschatological fate, and her effect on the Christian economy—all providing her with a persistent stigma as Jew. The volley of criticisms and "playful" name-calling that begin to adhere to her after her marriage and conversion seems to insist on her Jewishness, emphasizing it far more than earlier descriptions full of terms of feminine praise. Moreover, despite having agreed to become a converted Christian, Shylock does not occasion similarly anxious conversion debate at the end of the play, somewhat surprisingly for any working theory of the feminine gendering of racial and religious fluidity.[32] Unlike Jessica, Shylock has not married into Christianity, while his daughter is now in the delicate position of potentially becoming a mother of gentle and gentile Venetian offspring. While Shylock's conversion represents his final concession, his utter vanquishment, Jessica's is the expression of her independent (that is, gratified, not cowed) will. He is most Jewish before his enforced conversion; she, after her elective one.

Marriage seemingly renders Jessica vulnerable to a wellspring of anxiety taking the form of racial slurs and nonce racialization, inverting the imagery that connected her previously to feminine whiteness, virtue, and meekness. Before her marriage, she is "gentle" and "fair Jessica" (2.4.19, 2.4.28, 2.4.34, 2.4.39). Lorenzo, her lover, extols her beauty with puns on the fairness of her "hand"—both the fingers and their metonymized writing: "I know the hand, in faith 'tis a fair hand, / And whiter than the paper it writ on / Is the fair hand that writ" (2.4.12–14). In his miniature panegyric, any possible resonance of the darkness of the ink (traditional signifier of a dark or dark-eyed paramour) is displaced in favor of praise for the formal "fairness" of Jessica's handwriting and the ideal whiteness of its author's hand, lavishly imagined to be still whiter than the page itself. The analogy, lovely handwriting/pale hand, neatly captures the associations of beauty and whiteness animating the charged descriptor "fair," making Jessica seem a more than appropriate marital prospect.

Jessica's value in beauty is augmented by the wealth she brings to her marriage, and in this connection it will be useful to return to her elopement and theft from her father, and Gratiano's response, the approving award of "gentle" status. "Gentle," of course, conveys both a class status of high degree and a pleasing deportment (such as Jessica's virtue and beauty), assimilating the two in a strategic naturalization of class hierarchy. The semantic overlap of "gentle" and "gentile" further specifies the opposition between Jew and non-Jew, implying that religious difference participates in class difference and in national or ontological difference, such as that between different "peoples" (Latin *gentes*) or "kinds" (Latin *genera*). The only way to leave the identity of Jewishness fully behind would seem to be to become not only gentile but *gentle,* showing just how dependent Jessica's immediate transformation is on her filched dowry, that is, on the refiguration of Shylock's ducats and jewels from signifiers of Jewishness to guarantors of Christian gentility. Both forms of money are identified with Jessica through linguistic play: the aptly named "jewels" and the ducats she has fixed so closely about her person that she says she "gild[s] [her]self" with them. Draped in gold, Jessica heightens her desirability and dutiful provision for her husband but simultaneously comes dangerously close to embodying an iconographic Jewish acquisitiveness. Like Jessica herself, the wealth represents a drama of conversion, an attempt to detach a Jewish metonym from its Jewish origin and convert it to Christian identity and use.

The model of such marital conversion might be seen in Portia's example, which confers absolute disposal over all bridal holdings to Bassanio: "myself and what is mine to you and yours / Is now converted" (3.2.166–67). Portia's self-conscious use of the performative and temporally sensitive language of conversion echoes the transformative immediacy of Gratiano's "now . . . no Jew" that had awarded gentle status to Jessica.[33] Yet both moments of conversion are subject to retrospective qualification. At the very end of her offer, which seemingly would make Bassanio "lord" and "master" in her place, Portia shrewdly retains what she calls "vantage to exclaim" on her husband, should he violate her terms (3.2.167, 168, 174). When he gives her ring away, Portia's control over house, holdings, and husband is restored. Retrospective quibbles over Jessica's more literal conversion of self and wealth are less to her advantage, rather quicker to dissociate the taint of Jewishness from her wedding gift of ducats than from her person.

Insofar as Jessica converts to Christian wifehood, she loses hold over the chief passports to her gentle status, her fortune and chastity. Her money belongs to Lorenzo, to be conspicuously consumed in fashionable purchases, and once Jessica's fairness is partly compromised by the loss of her virginity, her conversion is more equivocal on the lips of her husband's friends. She is now referred to as "amorous Jessica" (2.8.9), and in Belmont, "Lorenzo and his infidel" (3.2.217). Launcelot, the servant and clown, reiterates Lorenzo's earlier eschatological predictions, consigning Jessica to hell as payment for "the sins of the father" (3.5.1). The promise of Jessica's manners falls short in consideration of her father's blood; accordingly, Launcelot offers only one mitigating possibility, one that renders her conversion superfluous: "you may partly hope that your father got you not, that you are not the Jew's daughter" (3.5.9–10).

Launcelot's solution, in which misogynist tropes are employed to further a wholesale *denial* of Jessica's relation to Shylock, is one Christian response to Jessica's earlier distinction between manners and blood, a distinction the Venetians do not appear ready to admit. Such a fantasy was of course immanent in Jessica's own prior wish that marriage would help her to "a father . . . lost." With a whimsical counterfactual, the sentence of Jessica's Jewish identification is rhetorically commuted by denying her parentage. The same strategy is occasionally engaged in by other characters, as when Salerio anxiously figures Jessica's conversion as more than skin deep in order to frustrate Shylock's claims on her "flesh and blood":

SHYLOCK: I say my daughter is my flesh and blood.

SALERIO: There is more difference between thy flesh and hers, than between jet and ivory, more between your bloods, than there is between red wine and Rhenish. (3.1.34–36)

Here the language of racial antithesis is bizarrely marshaled to drive a genetic wedge between father and daughter, one expressed in metaphors of commodification, as though the two were not actual "blood" relations, as though the father-daughter relationship depended solely on the will of the consumer. Because the gentle Venetians are reluctant to admit that manners may not supervene on blood, Salerio recasts Jessica's difference as physical and internal, imagining her body in the terms of a mercantile Petrarchism, her white flesh colored only

by the most refined blood, or her flesh and blood replaced by substances whose value is less ambiguous.[34] If for Launcelot no conversion is sufficiently complete to erase the stain of Jewish genealogy, for
Salerio the answer to the threat Shylock poses through Jessica is to try
to enlarge the boundaries of gent(i)le membership in order to show
that Jessica has been scarcely a Jew at all. [35]

Yet Launcelot imagines Jessica's conversion will make her enough
of a Christian subject to threaten economic strain: "if we grow all
to be pork-eaters, we shall not shortly have a rasher on the coals for
money" (3.5.22–23). That is, widespread Jewish conversion threatens
to raise the price of commodities reserved for Christians. Launcelot's
accusation is echoed in criticism that takes his point seriously, emphasizing Jessica's drain on Lorenzo's status and the larger threat she
may pose toward the Christian polity. Variously, commentators have
asserted that Jessica is effectively "nonproductive . . . economic dead
weight" and that "distinguished from Portia and Nerissa, whose
marriages work to secure the social standing of the men they love,
she is more saved than saving in her marriage to Lorenzo."[36] Such
reduplications of Launcelot's fretful critique of the economics of
conversion mark how unsuccessful Jessica's transformation truly is,
as servant and readers alike are quick to forget that both Lorenzo's
household and Launcelot's bacon are entirely sustained on Jessica's
contributions. Launcelot's gibe about supply and demand represents
a mystification of the true source of Lorenzo's income, just as, one
might observe, the bond plot itself generally serves to obscure the
fact that Bassanio's "gentle" posturings are enabled only by Shylock's
Jewish wealth.

Though their conclusions are different, Launcelot's qualms about
pork and Salerio's defense of Jessica's "ivory" flesh and robust blood
share a confidence in the fungibility of capital and commodity with a
larger ethics. For them, Christian and economic values are never incompatible. Jessica's stolen gold enters the world of Christian gentility smoothly, utterly stripped of its original connotations of Jewish
greed, while her flesh and blood continually vacillate between suspect Jewish and blameless gent(i)le embodiments. Nor is she the

only character in the play to undergo a trial by blood for spousal worthiness; the blood of Portia's suitors is similarly laid open to pointed scrutiny. The claims of *Merchant*'s gentility are sustained by a racial and class ideology as painstakingly detailed as that which stigmatizes the play's Jewish characters. As we will see, Portia's insistence that manners and blood overlap in gentility prepares the play's audience to find reasonable the claim that it is Antonio's Christian blood that insulates him from the threat posed by Shylock, an alien, excluded from the Venetian commonwealth both politically and corporeally.

Anatomy of Gentility

Portia's father's casket test aims at theorizing appropriate matches for his daughter—"who chooses his meaning," Nerissa explains, "chooses you, will no doubt never be chosen by any rightly, but one who you shall rightly love" (1.2.30–32).[37] Since Portia's fortune as well as her love is at stake, the conditions of her nuptials perfectly illustrate a Shakespearean trend according to which, however aleatory the path of love appears, the progress of money runs along surprisingly predictable channels, conservatively transmitting estates according to similarities of rank and (in this case) nation.[38] Portia's father fuses love and money in a test for spousal appropriateness that is explicitly a theory of value, superimposing the choice of wife onto a choice between gold, silver, and lead caskets.

As the dramatic focal point of the early scenes with Portia, the casket test codes Belmont as epistemically patriarchal and heterosexual.[39] Limited by the conditions her father's "will" imposes on her, Portia must submit her power of choice ("will") and sexual appetite (also "will") to his strictures or else, implicitly, lose her inheritance. She must also continually discuss and enact the casket test with all comers until a husband has been found. Amid the punning, Portia's father reaches out from the grave to direct events: "so is the will of a living daughter curb'd by the will of a dead father" (1.2.23–24). Portia's submission to an absent father's will can only

make a conspicuous contrast to Jessica's elopement—Jessica's assertion of agency through marital choice and theft preserves her own
dowry in the face of just such paternal prescriptions. Portia's obedience would seem to point to a Renaissance moral of female meekness, and yet the patriarchal imperative is complicated, as her father
remains dead and even unnamed, while, over the course of five acts,
Portia gradually assumes control of all the play's events.[40] However,
from the evidence of the casket test itself, there is no great reason to
believe that father's and daughter's objectives differ overmuch, since
the desires, or "wills," of both converge on Bassanio.

Ultimately, the constitutive elements of the casket "lott'ry" overwhelmingly endorse national and racial endogamy, while pretending
to an objective trial of the participants' spousal worthiness.[41] For instance, the distinctively international selection of participants seems
to advertise the contest's openness and cultural neutrality, even
while Portia's criticisms of her suitors center on their embodiment
of nationally stereotypic foibles. Similarly, the failure of national and
racial others to negotiate the casket test's moralistic metaphysical
apparatus successfully, with suitors left scratching their heads over
how to consistently value inside and outside, metal and virtue, sets
off the "untutored" test-readiness of the pointedly Venetian winner.
Many critics have noted irregularities in the test's administration,
such as hints Portia may provide Bassanio (the song rhyming with
"lead," her admonition that she "stand[s] for sacrifice").[42] But the
test's most invidious feature consists of its purported neutrality, designed to sustain a self-satisfied racial and national chauvinism and
to conserve Portia's inheritance in endogamy.

At first glance, the casket test participates in a Western tradition
suspicious of material goods and materiality, of surface appearance
as opposed to interior truth. As a philosophy, it is vaguely Christian
and Neoplatonic; more aptly, as the staple of fairy-tale diegesis that
Freud, among others, identified in the play, it embraces the under-
dog over his wealthier or more qualified brethren.[43] The renuncia-
tion of superficial value that governs the test has the perverse result
of Portia's worth being concealed in what Morocco contemptuously

calls "shows of dross" (2.7.20), the lead casket. Morocco declaims against the possibility of such misrepresentation, the lack of correspondence between inside and outside implied by the coupling of Portia and the lead casket. His argument is unobjectionable, a standard of Renaissance humanist and dramatic *sententiae:*

> Is't like that lead contains her?—'twere damnation
> To think so base a thought, it were too gross
> To rib her cerecloth in the obscure grave . . .
> O sinful thought! never so rich a gem
> Was set in worse than gold.   (2.7.49–55)

In Morocco's eyes, to propose a leaden Portia would be contrary to class decorum ("base"), positioning the prince himself as lacking proper delicacy ("gross") and even subject to a kind of secular "damnation" (a notable instance of the term, especially for a possibly non-Christian character).

Morocco's point is ironically amplified by the very scroll he finds inside his choice of the gold casket, which, far from undermining his metallic hierarchy, suggests nothing to value in gold's place. Instead, the scroll begins "all that glisters is not gold" (2.7.65), incoherently rebuking Morocco's choice by denying that the gold casket itself is, in fact, gold. The line hints at the ideology underpinning the casket test: while disavowing a visible greed, neither poem nor test goes so far as to renounce gold as a primary value. Though the casket is of course gold, the poem inside it acts as though Morocco has made an error in discernment or connoisseurship, not in desire.

The play thereby intensifies trends Shakespeare found in his source, a Christian allegory in the *Gesta Romanorum*. In the *Gesta* tale, a princess proves her worthiness to marry the emperor's son by choosing between gold, silver, and lead "vessells." The first two vessels are filled with worms, dirt, and "dead men's bones," which the tale's appended moral interprets as signifying the certitude of death and the torments of hell for sinners, while the lead container, full of precious stones, promises the joys of heaven. In the moral, the princess's correct choice proves her decorous love of poverty and her submission to "that [which] God hath disposed."[44] Yet the story can find no way fully to shun earthly values; it depends on the revelation of jewels to ratify the princess's decision (and to signal a love of poverty!) and dirt to signal material evanescence, expressing heavenly value solely through material signifiers and erotic and political allegory. Without Portia's wealth and beauty, she cannot occupy the role of even a figurative "golden fleece" (1.1.170), just as the princess's casket, lacking its cargo of precious stones, would not convey transcendent Christian bliss. In neither tale can lead be its own reward.

Correspondingly, none of Portia's suitors finds much to say in praise of the lead casket (which is to say in praise of undervaluing the goods, the bait and switch, or the lesser substance), *including Bassanio,* whose justification of his choice weighs in at under three lines: "thou meagre lead / Which rather threaten'st than dost promise aught, / Thy paleness moves me more than eloquence, / and here choose I" (3.2.104–7). Bassanio's is strangely faint praise, especially given that he has just berated the silver casket for being identically "pale" (3.2.103).[45] Yet the casket test prefers aligning Portia with lead, the possibility Morocco calls "gross" and "base," the better to forestall its opposite: poseurs, lead tricked out in gold's clothing.

The bulk of Bassanio's analysis of the caskets decries such tricks, "hiding the grossness with fair ornament" (3.2.80)—and sees them everywhere. As examples of disguised grossness, Bassanio cites social flaws that betoken a general cultural meretriciousness and a specific decline in the legal and gender order: immoral laws advanced by smooth-tongued lawyers, bearded men who nonetheless lack the courage of true masculinity, and in particular, false feminine beauty (3.2.73–101). Unsurprisingly, in Bassanio's speech the Renaissance opposition between grossness and fairness is racialized in gendered images of darkness, density, immorality, and ugliness. It is worth emphasizing that only the conjunction of femininity, falseness, and race spares Bassanio himself from being implicated, accoutred as he is in borrowed opulence. Bassanio's critique therefore zeroes in on feminine wiles: he deplores the process by which cosmetics (beauty "purchas'd by the weight") lead to "light" sexual morals. Ornament itself is "the beauteous scarf / Veiling an Indian beauty" (3.2.89; 3.2.98–99), with the latter term understood to be devastatingly ironic.[46] And Bassanio inveighs against "those crisped snaky golden locks" that are "often known / To be the dowry of a second head, / The skull that bred them in the sepulchre" (3.2.92–96).

Bassanio's portrait of an Indian beauty attempting to hide her "grossness" with the aid of ornaments such as scarves, makeup, and a blonde wig describes, on the one hand, an allegorically feminized version of a disingenuous suitor whom Portia's father's will was designed to keep from his daughter. As an "Indian," such a counterfeiter definitionally falls short of the true standards of Portia-like beauty, but like the boy actor whose props she is depicted as possessing, can jury-rig an external resemblance with the aid of art. Likewise evoking a drag sensibility, Bassanio's equation of artifice and a "snaky golden" wig recalls Jessica's attempt to possess the mantle of gentility, in particular the ducats with which she gilded herself from her own golden "casket" (2.6.33), and her subsequent bids to pass as Lorenzo's torch-bearing boy and Christian wife.[47]

Despite its seeming promotion of humility, the correct choice of lead only emphasizes the role of the profit-making motive in marriage. As readings stressing the play's mercantile values observe, the lead casket's inscription, "who chooseth me, must give and hazard all he hath" (2.7.16), embodies the philosophy of aggressive venture capitalism and justifies Bassanio's needling of Antonio for sufficient investment to compete in what is, after all, a highly lucrative prospect: "had I but the means . . . I have a mind presages me such thrift / That I should questionless be fortunate" (1.1.173–76).[48] No matter what abasement is required of the successful suitor (significantly less than of the failed suitors), he still receives Portia's house, servants, and considerable fortune, assets that have inspired her broad appeal to begin with. Portia herself is aware of her value and upon Bassanio's triumph experiences an elation that takes the form of an intense desire to be worth more, that is, lighter, lovelier, but especially weathier: "for you, / I would be . . . a thousand times more fair, ten thousand times more rich" (3.2.152–54). Indeed, she wishes that she might multiply her possession of all the accessories she already enjoys as a landed heiress, the markers of her status: "that . . . I might in virtues, beauties, livings, friends / Exceed account" (3.2.155–57).

Portia desires to embody a condensation of the values of gentility, effectively to "enclose infinite riches" in the "little room" of her "little body" (and its rather larger holdings).[49] That Portia's wish might thus be the equivalent of Barabas's self-descriptions in his opening monologue, or even to the desire that Bassanio finds so repellent—to put on (Jessica's?) wig of snaky golden ringlets—troubles the distinctions I have been arguing the play is at pains to set up. For if the desire to possess compressed wealth and virtues or to deploy them for the use of a worthy spouse similarly characterizes Jewish heroines, Jewish merchants, and Christian heiresses, then the "manners" that Jessica was hoping would distinguish her from her execrated father are never made fully distinct from those she wished to adopt, those of Belmont and Venice. Manners are insufficient. Instead, Portia judges human value according to different criteria.

The casket test's fusing of the values of fairness and wealth into the ingredients of gentility that are more than skin deep issues both in its trimming of unwanted suitors and its ultimate matchmaking. Here, the vocabulary of "gentleness" is once more deployed with abandon to strengthen classificatory differences between the characters. When Morocco is dispatched by his wrong choice, Portia views his departure as "a gentle riddance . . . let all of his complexion choose me so" (2.7.78–79). Portia's use of the valedictory "gentle" is at least as important as her use of the not-so-ambiguous "complexion" (which has occupied critical attention), for their conjunction implies the utter opposition between gentility and the continued presence of Morocco's skin color. However, as I have suggested, Morocco's own depicted values—manners—hardly diverge from Portia's. Addressing her as his "gentle queen" (2.1.12), Morocco defends his "complexion" but still concedes its potential to alienate Portia's affections: "I would not change this hue, / Except to steal your thoughts, my gentle queen" (2.1.11–12). Clearly aware of a potential bias, Morocco suggests a different contest in his defense: "Bring me the fairest creature northward born /. . . And let us make incision for your love, / To prove whose blood is reddest, his or mine" (2.1.4–7).

Eerily fusing the themes of Venice and Belmont, Morocco's proposed contest anticipates the trial's emphasis on cutting people open in a kind of human casket test. His eagerness to "make incision" is hardly a radical subversion of Portia's possible skin-color bias, which he anxiously tries to forestall. For Morocco simply proffers a different physical location where moral traits may be referenced by their colors. His proposal is no less racialist than the judgment he thinks to deflect. When Salerio distinguished Jessica's from Shylock's blood, Jessica's femininity was signaled by the paleness of her blood. Similarly, here, Morocco fantasizes a proof of masculinity in which the body would disclose its value through objective, physical properties: his own, most red blood.[50] Just as Salerio made his comparisons to deny metaphorically the evidence of Jessica's Jewish origins, Morocco reverts to metaphorical color contrasts when most uneasy about color prejudices he suspects of Belmont's lovely, yet captious, heiress.

Morocco's divination of Belmont's interest in matters of blood is confirmed by Bassanio's solution of the casket puzzle. Referring to the poem that awards Portia to him as "a gentle scroll" (3.2.139), Bassanio claims his prize—both Portia and all the elements of gentility she represents. As with Jessica, his change in status must be justified. Overwhelmed by Portia's bequest to him of house and property, Bassanio rhetorically gestures to verbal inadequacy and hypes his redeeming quality in language not unlike Morocco's: "Madam, you have bereft me of all words, / Only my blood speaks to you in my veins" (3.2.175–76). The sexual charge conveyed in Bassanio's eloquent blood relies on the worthiness of that blood for it to substitute inoffensively for the flowery gratitude that might be more appropriate to display here. The logic recalls Portia's earlier play on "will," in which her sexual desires were shown to be at the service of her father's prescribed priorities for her. When Antonio's dire situation is almost immediately revealed, Bassanio quickly clarifies the precise nature of his blood: "Gentle Lady / . . . I freely told you all the wealth I had / Ran in my veins,—I was a gentleman" (3.2.251–54). Bassanio's repetition of "gentle" surely aims to cushion the blow of his own "counterfeit" displays of "mannerly" wealth; according to him, that blood is its own wealth. Antonio's similarly impoverished, gentlemanly blood is also on display in the scene, as Bassanio claims to see it in the letter, whose "every word" is "a gaping wound / Issuing life-blood" (3.2.263–64). It is this blood, and its resemblance to Bassanio's, that enlists Portia's direct aid in Antonio's trial, while the blood's ideological value ensures the trial's outcome.

The solution the Venetians find to the problem posed by Shylock's bond is, of course, to distinguish between Antonio and Shylock on the bases of citizenship and blood. Their logic has been prefigured by the speeches before the caskets: both Bassanio and Morocco, as we have seen, provide rhetorical precedents for inflexibly materialist human categorizing. The furthest reach of the law as interpreted by Portia (dressed as Balthazar) prevents Shylock, as "an alien," from "direct, or indirect attempts [on] . . . the life of any citizen," on penalty of death and loss of property (4.1.345–47). Thus safeguarded as a Venetian citizen, Antonio is additionally protected as the possessor of "Christian blood," of which one drop spilled by Shylock renders the latter's property "confiscate unto the state" (4.1.306–8).

The conceptual overlap of Christian and citizen, that is, gentile and gentle, is made explicit when each term is contrasted with the term it opposes and excludes, the Jew.[51] Definitionally "strangers," partly by virtue of belonging to their own "nation," Jews cannot be citizens, irrespective of their economic status or birthplace. (The irrelevance of their birthplace to their legal status as permanent noncitizens ensures that such biographical data is almost never provided in Renaissance drama.) Thus, the designation "alien" or "stranger" is often of strategic value to non-Jews.[52] In Venice, it governs Shylock's vulnerability to the juridical apparatus of the state and colors Venetian interpretations of his affective stance, for example, in the Duke's words, of his "strange apparent cruelty" (4.1.20), a phrase that attempts to characterize Shylock's vindictive relish as non-Venetian.

Where Shylock defends his actions toward Antonio as paralleling Venetian treatment of their own "purchased slave[s]" (4.1.90), the Venetians implicitly contrast themselves with the "strange nature" (4.1.172) of Shylock's bond, which they construe as corresponding to his alien Jewishness. That a Venetian law exists to defend citizens from the predations of aliens reveals the suspicions inherent in the framework in which alien and Venetian difference is asserted, against Shylock's parallel. In his plea that Shylock have mercy on Antonio, the Venetian Duke never abandons the assertion of Jewish-Venetian difference. His request emphasizes instead the degree to which the Venetians appropriate the discourse of forgiveness and mercy, as both subjects and objects, while excluding those outside of mercy as religious and national aliens:

> But touch'd with human gentleness and love,
> Forgive a moiety of the principal,
> Glancing an eye of pity on his losses . . .
> Enow to . . . pluck commiseration of his state
> From brassy bosoms and rough hearts of flint,
> From stubborn Turks, and Tartars never train'd
> To offices of tender courtesy:
> We all expect a gentle answer Jew!   (4.1.25–34)

Attempting both to cajole and isolate Shylock, the Duke extends the quality of "human gentleness" to Turks and Tartars, whose mineral organs, brassy and flinty, nonetheless retain a sense of their own alien, not-so-human makeup. But having seen the definition of "gentle" that prevails in Venice and Belmont, we can read this "gentleness" along with the "gentle answer" the Duke solicits as conforming to an ideology precisely characterized by its refusal to include Jews within its privileged sphere.

The "gentle answer" expected by the Duke's speech, then, attempts to interpellate Shylock into gent(i)le subjectivity, whose gentleness and pity "forgive a moiety" of debts owed by gentles to Jews. Such interpellation also occurs as a by-product of Portia and Antonio's working out of the trial's verdict, which ultimately requires Shylock's conversion to Christianity and grants a "moiety" of his estate to Lorenzo and Jessica after Shylock's death. Detailing this dispensation, Portia tutors Shylock in the gentle answer expected to the trial's resolution: "art thou contented Jew? what dost thou say?" (4.1.389). Shylock: "I am content" (4.1.390). In allowing the context of Shylock's powerlessness, rather than explicit force, to elicit this response, Portia pushes Shylock to simulate the desired gentleness. That it *is* simulation is also desired, since Shylock's very inability to say what he might wish demonstrates that gentle and juridical meanings are now perfectly aligned. Portia uses this alignment to refigure Shylock: he is made to appear willing in submitting to his loss of property and forced conversion and to assert that any hunger for revenge has been not frustrated but sated.

Later hearing of Shylock's "bequest" from Portia—who doesn't mention Shylock's conversion to Lorenzo or Jessica—Lorenzo invokes a hunger of his own. He describes Portia's judicial activism with Shylock's fortune as yielding providential subsistence: "you drop manna in the way / Of starved people" (5.1.294–95). That part of Shylock's possessions that served as Jessica's portion has apparently only sharpened Lorenzo's appetite. Prompted by the offering of further Jewish belongings, Lorenzo represents himself as "starved," an avariciousness posing—or understood—as physical need. Here, the signature appropriation in this play is performed once again and rhetorically extended by an even older, parallel appropriation, in which a biblical trope is converted from its original Jewish function to Christian use. Lorenzo evidently experiences no irony in presenting himself as a famished Jew in the desert in order to figure the complete reversion of Shylock's estate to Christian control.

The Merchant of Venice presents powerful linked fantasies of exogamous alliance and familial estrangement. But the possibility of a full transfer of identity is progressively abandoned as Shakespeare endorses a troubled endogamy, one always implied by the play's vocabulary of human classification, which carries substantial ontological and moral weight. Still, while Jessica's and Shylock's hopes are differently frustrated, Jewishness is not fully discarded as cultural waste. The material components of Jewish identity (those Marlowe's Barabas would recognize) are readily put to use by the Venetians, even to enable their truest self-representations—Bassanio as comely wooer; Lorenzo as spendthrift. *Merchant*'s ambitions to absorb desirable Jewish qualities, while disavowing Jewish manners and blood, are thereby revealed in the profit accrued to the gentles of Belmont and Venice, dropped like manna, that selective, biblical mercy, "as the gentle rain from Heaven" (4.1.181).

THREE

The English Italian

✿

Inglese italianato è un diavolo incarnato.

—Roger Ascham, *The Scholemaster*
(The Italianated Englishman is a devil incarnate.)

Reading Italian

When she disguises herself as a young doctor of the law during the trial scene of *The Merchant of Venice*, Portia takes the name "Balthazar" (4.1.153), the name of the youngest Magus to visit the Christ child, a Magus conventionally represented as African. It is also the name of her trusted servant (3.4.45), who, because of his name, is possibly African as well.[1] Portia's selection of this particular name can help specify some of the associations her cross-dressing might possess for a sixteenth-century English audience. In particular, "Balthazar" supports an interpretation in which cross-dressing is seen as generally analogous to racial darkening, and gender difference as analogous to racial difference.[2] In this chapter, I will pursue the implications of a further determinant of Portia's identity—Italianness—for her figuration here, for the figuration of countless other characters in English Renaissance drama, portrayed, like Portia, by English actors, and, indeed, for the self-figuration of several generations of English poets. As the range of this list suggests, Italian identity possessed a special significance for the early modern English. An investigation of the period meanings of Italianness will in turn shed light on the racial component of nationality during this period.

In what ways might Portia's Italian identity also enable her cross-racial figuration? Elsewhere, Portia is described according to the classical terms of a Petrarchan *blazon* (3.2.115–29) and lauded for her golden-haired beauty (which, partly thinking of her fortune, her suitor Bassanio calls a "golden fleece" [1.1.170]). "Fair" Portia's ability to be figured both as a Petrarchan beloved (1.1.162) and, however faintly, as an iconographic African king indicates, I would argue, the full, intriguing range of associations Italy possessed for the early modern English: simultaneously a site of radical, racialized, and/or immoral otherness, a center of international trade and wealth, and the origin of intellectual and courtly high culture that exerted a definitive influence on the English.[3] As an icon popularized in Italian Renaissance painting, indebted to scenic norms encouraging *varietà* (norms corresponding to Italian experiences of international diversity), the figure of Balthazar himself combines elements of all three components of Italian signification.[4] The Italian setting of the play thus facilitates the possibility of Portia's brief instantiation of this icon, even as her transformation complicates the meanings of her own Italian identity.

Racial and national overlap such as that between Portia and Balthazar is especially prevalent in English Renaissance drama when the setting is foreign. Indeed, foreign settings, somewhat symptomatically, are fertile sites for the depiction of racial and national difference. It is no accident that the plays I have discussed thus far, plays interested in racial, ethnic, and religious diversity and strife, are set in Mediterranean, mostly Italian venues. But Italian settings do not merely serve as places where difference can exist, conveniently distanced from England: thematized Italian diversity is itself located within London and enacted on behalf of English playgoers. The popular, public context of their enactment in London means that English Italianate dramas effectively testified to and promoted experiences of diversity and alterity within the imagination of the English subject.

Such experiences are the more remarkable in that they occurred with surprising frequency; as is well known, English playwrights routinely set comedies and especially tragedies in Italy, France, and other Mediterranean countries.[5] The strangeness of using foreign, Catholic settings as routine, even default, locations for English fictions is difficult, I think, for us to fully appreciate, though a consideration of the relentlessly nationally domestic settings of our own popular entertainments, on television and in film, can perhaps begin to evoke its estranging potential (imagine thinking nothing of *CSI*, *Friends, Sleepless in Seattle,* or *Seven* set in Florence or Rome and featuring Italian characters played by American actors). Moreover, the English convention was a native one: it is worth pointing out that other European dramatic canons lack corresponding foreign settings—Italian drama is set in Italy. To be sure, London's own urban scene generated ample occasion for (and helped to motivate) dramatic representations of international encounters.[6] Yet Mediterranean settings evidently provided playwrights with fantasies of even more densely diverse interactions, thereby promoting labile transnational and transracial identifications. English beliefs about the nature of Italian identity supported these fantasies, and we will explore these beliefs in detail, after a brief consideration of the general meaning of nationality in early modern England.

By the beginning of the seventeenth century, the word "nation" implied more than groups mythically united by geographic and tribal accidents of birth *(natio).*[7] Building on Benedict Anderson's seminal work, recent models of the formation of early modern English nationalism have depicted a national community that wills itself into being in an individual and collective enterprise, imagining itself as having common structures of sovereignty and subjecthood, and common history, culture, law, language, and bounded geography.[8] In addition, imagined national coherence drew on older beliefs about common national temperament, spirit, and morality, for instance, thought to be derived from common ancestry, history, and location of birth. Belief in these components of national specificity was particularly instrumental in advancing nation building through imaginative contrasts with the temperament, culture, politics, or history of other nations. For instance, Jean Howard writes that early modern English nationalism "shares with modern nationalism a supposed fraternity of subjects within an imagined community defined in part by a bounded geographical essence and in part by cultural and racial *differences* from other such imagined communities."[9]

In Howard's account, national difference is partially constituted by, and shades into, cultural and racial difference.[10] The slippage is not surprising, since some of the elements that produce a specific national identity, such as assertions of genealogical or historical continuity, of a common spirit, or even of a climatically influenced character, are instrumental in generating racial meanings as well.[11] Early modern English vocabularies of national and racial difference share terminology, trading on imagery of moral and physical blackness or alien subjectivity, emphasizing genealogical relationships, and exhibiting a heightened concern with questions of blood and its purity.

A central role has been claimed for literature in solidifying and circulating such tropes.[12] The development of a national vernacular simultaneously serves the bureaucratic interests of the state and privileges emerging nationalist literary expression. From Anderson himself to Claire McEachern and Richard Helgerson, the study of national identity has entailed careful study of literature. For all these writers, analysis of literary texts highlights the unique efficacy with which such texts solicit a community's collective and corporate identification. But if a nation's imagined boundaries are definite, the contributions and functions of its privileged language—I'll call it English—are not likewise delimited or exhaustively scripted. The multiple voicings and uses of English point to equally multiple visions of nation and selfhood. Helgerson's masterful work on a variety of English "forms of nationhood" emphasizes this multiplicity. Helgerson shows that even within the distinctive fields of law or chivalric epic, populist historiography or religious apologetics, authors drafting new national idioms were themselves continually engaging, displacing, and revising older and contemporary models and "openly or latently competing form[s]."[13] Similarly, referring to the impact of this ferment of consensus and division, McEachern writes: "England, English, and Englishness are spoken in many ways in this moment [the beginning of the seventeenth century], by many persons and in many places."[14]

Helgerson's and McEachern's work, like most considerations of the early modern literary texts that helped to articulate English national identity, focuses on the figuration of English problematics and localities. In contrast, I am concerned with the significance of English figurations of other nationalities, such as Italian, and with the impact of English writers, actors, and theater audiences imagining that they belong to other national communities. It is striking that despite the influence of Anderson's model of imagined communities, the question of what happens when an audience routinely imagines itself as belonging to other national communities has gone virtually unasked. Yet communal imaginings do not limit themselves to domestically familiar ground. The importance of imagining and fiction to Anderson's and subsequent arguments about nationalism might suggest that we must account for imaginative hybridity, as well as imaginative limits, for the productive overlap between cross-identification and self-constitution.[15] If, in accordance with Anderson's dicta, the English imagine their geographic borders as finite, the cultural and psychological borders of their imagining community are decidedly more porous. In part, therefore, my argument assesses the role of imaginative contrasts with Italy in shoring up English identity, but more importantly, I wish to argue for an Italianate identification as itself fundamentally English. For McEachern's sentence still seems strangely true when paraphrased as follows: "Italy, Italian, and Italianness are spoken in many ways in this English moment, by many English persons and in many English places."

One way of glossing my paraphrase is to refer to commonplaces of literary history that assert the signal influence of Italian literary form on the English, as when Jonathan Bate writes, "The English Renaissance began when Sir Thomas Wyatt and the Earl of Surrey discovered, translated and imitated the poetry of Petrarch."[16] We are used to accounts of the traffic of poetic form across national borders, but I wish to make this familiar narrative strange by insisting on the peculiarity of its national trajectory, in which a specific kind of Italianness serves as originary ground for a specific kind of Englishness. Just what is "English" about the Renaissance Bate references? Does an English Renaissance begin to appear within the disjunctions between the literary intentionalities he lists—naive "discovery," knowledgeable "translation," and corrupting or improvisatory "imitation"—or is Italianate poetic subjectivity simply being increasingly internalized?[17] How does the English Italian of Petrarchan-derived forms relate to the Italian in other English genres?

Early modern English figurations of the Italian draw on a tradition of English veneration for Italy, imagined as a culture that exports humanism, Petrarchism, courtiership, and literary sophistication, but alongside veneration, they express English fascination and contempt. For English dramatists in particular, Italian subjectivity was depicted in as charged a discourse of otherness as the English xenophobic imaginary had to offer. Italy represented a nation among whose most famous identity-effects were popery, atheism, sodomy, murder and poison, deceit, "practice," erotic obsession and sexual promiscuity, and a preternatural propensity for revenge, any and all of which were available for the playwrights' use in plot devices that both shocked and titillated.[18] The drama's Italy thus confirms the most disapproving Protestant suspicions of Catholicism and Machiavellianism, though critics have taught us to read it also for covert responses to the native, Jacobean regime and culture.[19] Imagined as possessing separate spheres of literary and moral influence, Italy is often thought to provoke the English according to predictable rules and disjunctively, for better *or* for worse, inviting either admiration for literary virtue or abhorrence for social transgression. Indeed, criticism seeking to weigh the effect of Italian representations on English writers and readers often adduces such binarisms as models of English reader response, as though English subjects would interpret depictions of Italian virtue and vice as discrete entities. Such readings downplay the breadth of Italian models for English high and popular culture and the interaction of high and low. In fact, Italian dramatic settings and characters ventriloquize a full spectrum of English interpersonal thematics, not merely iniquitous ones, while Italian poetic form nurtures desires repeatedly characterized as threatening to self, beloved, and community, not merely elevated passions.[20]

In the past, then, English Petrarchan poetics and English Italianate drama have not been seen as having much to say about one another. English flirting with Petrarchan consciousness may be a pleasurable, if dangerous, adoption of foreign subjectivity—one which is acceptable because it signals the knowledgeable refinement of the poet's humanist Englishness. But in drama, the compulsive English interest in an Italian thematics threatens to convert international humanist cosmopolitanism and refined Petrarchan longing into morbid and sensationalist, even criminal, degeneracy. There are elements in common here, nonetheless: the use of Petrarchan stylistic and thematic norms in structuring expressions of desire; the loss of self-possession occasioned by that desire; and the related possibility of transnational identification, staged both in disguise plots and in the fact of English actors personating Italians, are featured in both English Petrarchism and Jacobean drama. Both genres stage an alienated self as a desirable literary achievement, a peculiar property of the English Italian. I will trace these associations in John Milton's Italian sonnets as well as John Webster's Italianate drama, texts that figure and reflect on Italian influences on the English in especially explicit and innovative ways. In so doing, I intend these texts to stand in for the larger sweep of English Petrarchan-derived poetry and drama that treats Italy as its cognitive and topical center.

Milton's Strange Tongue

Perhaps no example of English Petrarchism more clearly dramatizes the estranging effects of Italianate poetics on English subjectivities than Milton's Italian sonnets. The sonnets first present the quintessentially English view that a literary discourse of erotic intensity is a properly foreign impulse—even if one wholly employed in English contexts and for English uses, not excluding humanist authorial self-promotion. The poems then both ratify and ironize that view by literalizing the poet's estrangement in their Italian language, versification, and content and in their italic typeface.[21] In repeatedly and emphatically marking the self as so estranged and translated (that is, not originally Italian), they reveal the underlying Englishness of the whole exercise and of the author himself. The presentation of the sonnets in Milton's debut publication of verse also names its Italianate enterprise as English.

For Milton's 1645 volume of poetry is titled *Poems of Mr. John Milton, both English and Latin, Composed at Several Times* and is divided into two sections, containing, respectively, English and Latin poems. Interestingly, the "English" section is the locus of the six poems in Italian, probably written around 1628, in which the poet represents himself to be deeply in love and hence, according to an overdetermined yet nonetheless original and Miltonic logic, finds himself inexplicably speaking Italian. Publication in Italian is itself highly unusual; Milton's labeling the Italian poems "English" produces an outrageous decorum. That is, Milton's Italian literalizes an equation between love and Italianness suggested nearly a hundred years earlier by Wyatt and Surrey. Wyatt and Surrey's popular English translations or approximations of Petrarch's sonnet and canzone forms made English expressions of desire seem inevitably rooted in an Italian poetics. Indeed, Wyatt and Surrey specified the experience of desire further, decisively linking erotic (and/or political) sophistication, anguish, manipulation, submission, devotion, regret, and occasional, fleeting satisfaction, with the thematics and forms of a stranger poet, conventional, Italianate associations with desire still familiar to us today.

Milton's poems up the ante, drawing attention to the oddness of such associations by claiming that those in love must actually *speak* Italian, and his sonnets are well aware that such a stance is open to accusations of scandal and obscurantism. The poems repeatedly discuss their linguistic transformation—indeed, a significant portion of their content is given over to these metalinguistic observations. For instance, the poet reflects on his estranged cognitive geography— *"E'l bel Tamigi cangio col bel Arno* [I exchange the fair Thames for the fair Arno]" (Sonnet 3.10)—the rivers metonymically signaling in geographic terms his new affective nationalism.[22] Milton also depicts a dismayed chorus of what he calls *"ridonsi donne e giovani amorosi* [laughing ladies and amorous young men]" who surround the poet and demand, *"Perchè scrivi, / Perchè tu scrivi in lingua ignota e strana / Verseggiando d'amor, e come t'osi?* [Why, why do you write love poetry in an unknown and strange tongue, and how do you dare to do it?]" ("Canzone," 1–4).

Oddly, the language the poet is speaking is always referred to in these terms as a "new" or "strange" *("strana")* tongue; it is never named as Italian. The repeated observations of the language's "strangeness" mark its ongoing foreignness to the poet in a conceit that heightens the supposed untutored quality of this experience of self-translation, as though the transition has happened unexpectedly to the poet. Such a claim of course mystifies Milton's own history of language study, his calculated deployment and display of humanist learning. At the same time, the language's "strangeness" underlines the poet's claims that love itself is strange, is foreign to the English, makes the English strange.

In his second Italian sonnet, the narrator describes the experience of his coming to speak this foreign tongue with an analogy:

Qual in colle aspro, al'imbrunir di sera,
L'avezza giovinetta pastorella
Va bagnando l'erbetta strana e bella,
Che mal si spande a disusata spera . . .
Così Amor meco insù la lingua snella
Desa il fior nuovo di strania favella   (Sonnet 3.1–7)

As on a rugged hill at dusk,
A young skillful shepherdess
Waters a strange and lovely herb,

Which scarcely spreads its leaves in the unfamiliar place . . .
So Love in me wakens on my lithe tongue
The new flower of a strange speech

Speaking the new language is like the growth of a foreign plant, but a plant that must be knowledgeably tended or die in its basically unsuitable environment. The poem identifies, in part, with the Italianate plant/tongue, distancing itself from Englishness, since Milton's lithe, English tongue *("lingua")* corresponds to the "unfamiliar" *("disusata")* site of the displaced plant's tending. Describing his Italianate love experience in this way, Milton equivocates between natural and unnatural vocabularies, implying, respectively, an out-of-control, unmediated experience (the plant is strange) and a careful humanist performance (the plant is skillfully, that is, knowingly, watered). Between the two options lies an authorial *sprezzatura,* studied carelessness, which also puts Milton in an agreeable Italianate position. Though here the gardener is said to be Love, planting an unfamiliar speech on the narrator's tongue, Milton too occupies the roles of Love and the skillful shepherdess, dictating which language will be planted, tended, and spoken.

If the poet has been transformed, he is responding to some degree mimetically not only to the literary decorum associating Italianness with love poetry but also, he tells us, to his beloved, who defies English conventions of beauty:

Nè treccie d'oro, nè guancia vermiglia
M'abbaglian sì, ma sotto nuova idea
Pellegrina bellezza che'l cuor bea . . .   (Sonnet 4.5–7)

Neither golden locks, nor ruddy cheeks
Dazzle me so, but modeled on a new and strange form,
A foreign, rare beauty which delights my heart . . .

The newness *(nuova idea)* of Milton's beloved includes her darkness—her lack of golden hair, and her eyes *"d'amabil nero* [of a lovely blackness]" (Sonnet 4.9)—and her darkness is referred to the almost Platonic "*Idea* (form)" of her foreignness. Darkness here is delightful. The beloved encourages the poet to echo her foreignness verbally, telling him, "*Questa è lingua di cui si vanta Amore* [This is the language of which Love is proud]" ("Canzone," 15). In the first Italian sonnet, her name is riddlingly said to be "*il cui bel noma onora / L'erbosa val di Reno, e il nobil varco* [(she) whose fair name honors the grassy Reno valley and its noble ford]" (Sonnet 2.1–2). Critics have thereby identified her with the region of Italy called Emilia.[23] While the name would in theory particularize or historicize the beloved, it instead abstracts her, partly because this is the only instance when the poet even indirectly names his *donna*—like the word "Italian," the word "Emilia" becomes one of the sonnets' conspicuous absences. Milton does not say that she is actually Italian—instead, her identification with a region of Italy may represent that she, like the narrator, has been made foreign by love.

In any case, the suppressed "Emilia" is a name Milton has chosen. As with iconographies that identify a region or nation with an allegorically female personification of the land, Milton's portrayal of his sonnet sequence's beloved as a person named only with reference to a foreign territory performs nationalizing (hence generalizing) work, assimilating people to land and, in this case, language.[24] What I want to point to here is Milton's project of writing himself into this Italianate chorography or place-writing, through which it seems that an affective identification with the territory Emilia is as significant for the poet as his erotic fixation on the person he calls "Emilia." That is, it is not simply that the poet is in love, hence speaking Italian; he is also depicted as speaking cultural and topographical Italian.

Milton provides a striking literalization of the alterity that is a perennial feature of English Petrarchism. Yet so long as it is named the "*lingua strana*" or "strange tongue," alterity continues to imply an English identification, as English remains the normative, familiar language. On the one hand, the poetic speaker represents himself as transformed by passion; on the other, he constantly signals his resistance to complete or earnest surrender. The conflict may be seen to motivate the larger sequence. The constant discussion of the language being spoken—which is, through the omission of the word "Italian," also a constant refusal to discuss the language being spoken—is itself one sign of this resistance.

This is apparent in the aforementioned "exchange" the speaker claims to have made, Thames for Arno: the line announces not only a national reaffiliation but also a linguistic alteration, one staged in the translation of English "Thames" into Italianate "Tamigi." Yet knowledge that English is being translated into Italian is the condition of possibility for the reader's comprehension of the sonnet— placed, the reader will recall, in a collection of Milton's "English" poems. The sentiment evoked by the claim of exchange, then, may be recognized instead as equivocation, linguistic nostalgia. By discussing the newness of the new language, the speaker reveals a prior identity in the guise of discarding it and defers any authentic participation in a newly strange interiority by describing it rather than fully participating in it.

This may be because the exercise, however pleasurable, simultaneously flirts with high literariness and the dubious morality of submission to desire. In the following sonnet, an announcement of the Italian love project addressed to Milton's childhood friend Charles Diodati, the troubled moments do not take the form of revelations of incomplete metamorphosis but rather sabotage the poet's professed devotion in self-reference and in typically Miltonic polysemy. The poem begins, *"Diodati, e te'l dirò con maraviglia, / Quel ritroso io ch'amor spreggiar soléa* [Diodati, and I say it to you with amazement, that unwilling I who used to disdain love]" (Sonnet 4.1–2). Until this point, the speaker has remained unnamed, just as "Emilia" herself is never directly named. The poems have conveyed their subjective effects through an unidentified—indeed, a generic— first-person narrator. By invoking Milton's actual friend, the fourth sonnet maximizes the reality effect of the poem and its myth of affective immediacy, the illusion that speaker and author are collapsed and that the person in love really is the author, John Milton. Just

as the italic typeface in which the poems were printed marks their
adoption, their naturalization of foreignness through the graphic
conventions of English printers, the identification of Diodati calls
attention to the poems' author and to his careful placement of them
in support of the construction of his own authorship.

At the same time, Milton performs etymological sleight-of-hand,
diluting any immediacy with intricate puns that suggest the author's
resistance to the supposedly overwhelming Italianate force of desire.
"Ritroso" ("unwilling"), most obviously expressing the lover's reluctance in love, also implies backward, retrograde, even wayward motion: the lover's fall into carnal desire and subjectivity-made-foreign.
Describing the beloved to Diodati as a *"pellegrina bellezza"*—"foreign,
rare beauty" (4.7)—flavors the enticing estrangement of the foreign
with the "waywardness" implied etymologically by the lover's national errancy (compare Latin *peregrinus*). Similarly, Milton earlier
capitalizes on the hidden, ominous (Italian and English) *alteration*
in Italian *altera,* with which he evokes the beloved's admirable pride:
"Mentre io di te, vezzosamente altera, / Canto [As I sing of you, gra-
ciously proud]" (Sonnet 3.8–9).

These multiplicities produce a disjunction between author and
speaker: the reader may interpret the Italian as surface, the poem as
palimpsest, revealing Milton's wholesale critique of the emotions,
national fluidity, and Italian temptations he conjures. In reactivat-
ing familiar Anglophone xenophobic resonances that equate the
foreign with the errant within the Italian words themselves, Milton
reclaims the English persona who was so happily celebrating self-
translation into an affective and national stranger. This disjunction gives the lie to the poetic conceit, the fable of affective and
linguistic immediacy in what purports to be an autobiographical
poem. The double consciousness of English and Italian traditions,
which Milton briefly occupies simultaneously, recasts the emotional
content heretofore associated with Italian—previously figured as
a strange, attractive language, charged with desire spontaneously
converted and deployed.

Most of all, the fourth sonnet's choice of address to Milton's close friend, Diodati, immediately removes it from the state of erotic absorption on which it purports to remark. As the sonnet begins with the proper name, "Diodati," the poem could, in theory, be written in either language (it is still printed in italic). What happens when a proper name is translated? Writing letters to each other in Latin and Greek, Diodati and Milton had transliterated and transposed their names—"Diodati" became the Greek "Theodotos" and the Greco-Latin (vocative) "Theodote."[25] The names "mean" the same thing, "god-given," but the languages invoke different notions of names, gods, and gifts, while the polyglot, retrospective context in which the names are inscribed also alters the meanings with which they are read.[26]

In these humanist hands, as names are altered, alterities pile up. In the fourth sonnet, Milton stages the possibility that Diodati, written into Italian, has been made Italian. Indeed, though born and raised in England, as the son of an Italian father and English mother, Diodati himself serves as an especially apt figure for the hybrid Anglo-Italian subjectivity the sonnets explore and dramatize.[27] Thematically, Diodati plays the familiar courtly-love role of friend and confessor, and also that of addressee and object of the sonnets' energies: the principal affect communicated in the fourth sonnet is not Milton's desire but his Diodati-directed *"maraviglia"* ("amazement") at his self-translation. In this sonnet, the entire love experiment may be legible as a project in which Milton positions Diodati as humanist transfer point for Milton's own affections (Diodati knows about love and the grand tour; he can, naturally, read Italian). In this reading, the foreign beauty, not Diodati, becomes the enabling fiction for the expression of Milton's (now recognizably English humanist) homosocial and homoerotic desires. The radical alterity here, if we had to place it in a taxonomy, is Italianness covering up for an Anglicized Latinate and Greek alterity, echoing the two youths' letters, in which they express properly Greek longing for a brilliant young companion to converse with.

Using the building blocks of humanist linguistic play and tropes of Petrarchan desire, Milton's Italian sonnets imagine a radical transformation of the self into something unfamiliar, foreign, full of alienation and longing. Desire in these sonnets is revealed to be as compelling as estranging. Pointedly, a self inhabited by such estranging desires is thought in particular to find its nationality—its Englishness—eroded, implying that given nationalities have given affective orientations (and vice versa). Correspondingly, the new self is imagined to gravitate toward a recognizably Italian identification. Yet from another perspective, the vacillation between English and Italian norms of selfhood that Milton depicts is itself a familiar English gambit, and not only in coterie publication of Italianate lyrics. Such transformations had been in vogue upon the Jacobean stage for more than two decades before Milton's sonnets were written, depicted in plays that also liked to imagine their subjects and settings were Italian.

Painted Devils

If Milton's sonnets reveal one possibility for English feelings about Italianness, dramatizing the fine line between Englishness and otherness and between the experiences of otherness and of desire, Italianate drama expands on and complicates the relevant senses of otherness. For as in *The Merchant of Venice* or *Othello*, representations of Italians in Italianate drama are nearly always bound up with representations of other groups, such as Jews, Moors, and Turks. The presence within the Italian context of characters whom the English would certainly have seen as racialized, alongside Italian characters, points up the racial content of national difference for the English.

In addition, where the Petrarchan lyric lavishes praise on the beloved (though this may be sometimes tempered by moments of ambiguity or self-aggrandizement), the women of Italianate drama elicit considerably more ambivalent representations. This is partly because of the radical difference in female sexuality between the two genres: the Petrarchan beloved withholds sexual favor, while female characters in Italianate drama indulge in both licit and illicit sexuality and are chastised (in either case) accordingly.[28] In Jacobean

Italianate drama, female sexual license is coded within the monochromatic antitheses of light and dark that we have seen attend and signal processes of racialization. These antitheses exaggerate and further stress the physical darkness of even Petrarchan Italian beauty and construct the English Italian as a site for racially complex depictions and identifications.

Plays cultivate the portrayal of a convincing and specific Italianness, for instance, in the accumulation of detailed expository references to Italian things and places, while exploiting awareness of the English audience and metatheatrical conditions of playing—John Webster's plays especially so.[29] Generally, the Italian settings of Jacobean tragedy and tragicomedy allow the English to depict disturbing tendencies toward immorality, religious errancy, and sexual license as the native province of national others. Still, as with the ambiguously foreign forms of Petrarchan poetry, adopted, naturalized, and celebrated by English poets, the presence of such depictions on English stages, in the persons of English actors, allows for substantial English identification with and pleasure in these representations. This persists even when stereotypes of Italian moral darkness combine with notions of Italian physical darkness and Italy's diverse populations to read national difference as constitutively racialized.

Webster's *The White Devil* presents just such a dense combination of dis- and cross-identification, English and Italian, nation and race. The racialization of English-Italian doubleness is staged first of all in the play's title, an oxymoron to the English, who by visual convention depicted devils as dark-skinned. Though "the white devil" names an Italian character or characteristic, the English pun specifies the nationality of the subject position from which the oxymoron can be read.[30] The white devil is ostensibly the play's antiheroine, Vittoria Corombona, endowed with antithetical whiteness (her beauty) and blackness (her indulged sexuality and the trail of dead men and women she leaves in her wake). This use of an ambiguous female character who may operate alongside immoral male counterparts while nonetheless becoming the focal point of the play's moral qualms is generically typical. Vittoria occupies the same function in relation to the play's title as Barabas in *The Jew of Malta:* both one example among many and *the* type of "White Devil." Vittoria thus emblematizes a misogynist view of corruption and hypocrisy that was at once stereotypically Italian and proverbially English: "the white devil is worse than the black."

The White Devil graphically enacts an ample number of similar English stereotypes of Italianness—of which adultery, consummated onstage, is hardly the most dramaturgically outrageous. The play also features the ascension of a cardinal to the papacy, acts of sorcery, betrayal, murder, and arcane poisoning—in this case a painting poisoned so that a faithful wife dies upon kissing the lips of her painted husband in a ritual that, for all its marital devotion, is redolent of Catholic image worship. These plot elements certainly present and further a view of Italy as steeped in religious, sexual, and criminal license, that is, as a world in which Catholicism, atheism, and "nigromancy" (2.2.8) seamlessly blend through their manifestation in homologous sexual and violent crimes.[31] Nonetheless, an audience's likely pleasure in dramatic spectacle (such as would be involved in staging the election of a new pope), in the characters' powerful rhetoric, or in the actors' charisma complicates any reading that would imagine the English to be simply revolted by the portrayal of Italianate excess.[32] The pleasure of shock value identified with Italy was what made this a genre, rather than an exception.

Alongside acts of passion and crime, *The White Devil* also thematizes racial and national multiplicity and concomitant fluidity. In the play, the Florentine and Roman scenes are populated with national others, many of whom are not what they seem: Moorish servants; a troupe of vengeful Florentines disguised as Hungarians-turned-Knights-of-St. John-turned-Capuchins; the Florentine Duke Francisco, likewise disguised as a Moorish general; and even a set of ambassadors from Spain, Savoy, France, and England, who showily pass across the stage in dumb show and later participate as judges in the trial of Vittoria for murder and adultery. As I have suggested, the range of these characters and the fluidity of their disguises suggest the degree to which English playwrights and their audiences associated Italy with an especially heterogeneous national and racial scene. At the same time, as conventional characters, they necessarily locate such heterogeneity within the English dramatic tradition, for the characters recall the specific diversity of other casts in English Mediterranean plays.

In this case, the Florentines pose as retired Knights of St. John, that is, crusaders against the Turks, knighted in Malta. One of them is even called "Farnese" in the stage directions. The group thus self-consciously evokes the dramatis personae of *The Jew of Malta*. Their leader, Francisco, posing in Rome as "Mulinassar," a Moorish general for hire against the Turks, is described as a latter-day Othello: "He hath by report, serv'd the Venetian / In Candy these twice seven years . . . I never saw one in a stern bold look / Wear more command, nor in a lofty phrase / Express more knowing" (5.1.9–10, 34–36). The echoes of Marlowe and Shakespeare constitute a characteristic metatheatrical joke for Webster but also emphasize the meaningfulness and longevity of these culturally and racially diverse character configurations on the stage: cynical, opportunistic Maltese; hypercompetent Moorish rhetor-warriors; unidentified, menacing Turks. The English imaginary reverts to these characters, a sort of English *commedia* stable; the setting is a distinctively English Mediterranean.

However, national heterogeneity and transnational disguises do not evoke an entirely benevolent Italianate multiculturalism. Though their diversity undoubtedly points to the centrality of Italy to international trade and rounds out the dramatic spectacle of courtly wealth, importance, and variety, many of the international personae who populate the play are also represented with varying degrees of contempt. Meanwhile, contempt itself is expressed through tropes of cross-racial figuration. Thus, as diplomats, judges, and witnesses to the play's murderous denouement, the ambassadors possess cultural and epistemic authority, but as representatives of other cultures, they also provoke epigrammatic bouts of mockery for their nationally determined humors and foibles, reminiscent of the treatment of Portia's suitors in *The Merchant of Venice* (3.1.65–78). More heightened scorn invariably affixes to Vittoria's Moorish servant Zanche, who is the butt of general, racist loathing that emerges in epithets such as "black," "Irish," and "gipsy" (for example, in 5.1.86; 5.1.161; 5.3.233–41; 5.6.227).[33] Similarly, when Vittoria herself is repudiated by a lover, descriptions of her beauty are replaced with the accusation that she possesses the bestial insincerity of "dissembling . . . howling . . . Irish" (4.2.95–97).[34]

Nor are the Irish the only group used by the play's characters, who prove well aware of the uses of international scapegoating. For instance, Francisco's band of avengers employs their disguises to avail themselves of a cynical and racially exploitative realgeopolitik: both the "Hungarians" and "Mulinassar" use the threat of the Turks as a convenient, fictive pretext for their presence in Rome.[35] Yet even the Turks do not function simply as a unifying, all-purpose enemy. Like *Othello, The White Devil* does not actually depict Turks or representatives of the Ottoman Empire. When Francisco, disguised as Mulinassar, offers to lead an offensive against Florence (Francisco's own city) on behalf of Rome (his own enemy), he therefore reveals threatening possibilities never openly voiced in *Othello*—the Moor turning against the Italians; the Italian cities warring against each other; the "general enemy Ottoman" (*Othello*, 1.3.50) failing in its traditional capacity to unify occasionally antagonistic Christian polities against a more clearly "common" foe.[36] The fluidity of racial identity associated with Italy threatens to leave an erosion of individual values and loyalties in its wake.

But the disturbingly fluid and amoral effects on identity depicted here do not only reflect an English indictment of foreign failings. The involuted disguise plots and cross-racial labeling possess direct significance for the notion of Englishness as well. Typically, Webster does not let the audience forget that disguises such as Francisco's Moorish persona represent no more artifice than the "Italian" disguises of Webster's English actors, metatheatrically directing the audience's attention to the conditions of playing. The imposture of foreignness, put on and off at the characters' will, pointedly includes the performance of Englishness in the figure of the English Ambassador. This character offers a rare opportunity for the audience to view its own nationality as an other in the Italian context, inverting the situation of the play itself, in which Italian alterity is the compelling spectacle on the English stage.[37] Interestingly, Webster depicts the English Ambassador as consistently sympathizing with Vittoria. "The Cardinal's too bitter" (3.2.107), he mumbles in aside during her trial, and he observes out loud that "she hath a brave spirit" (3.2.140). Thus, while drawing attention to the foreignness of Englishness in the person of the "foreign" English Ambassador, Webster aligns English sensibilities with Italianate white devilishness.

Italian and English are further aligned through Vittoria in their overlap in an identical vernacular. Like Milton, Webster calls attention to linguistic difference in a gesture that unsettles the stability of national difference. When the lawyer accusing her begins his prosecution in Latin, Vittoria objects: "By your favour, / I will not have my accusation clouded / In a strange tongue: all this assembly / Shall hear what you can charge me with" (3.2.17–20). Vittoria's objection is explicitly mounted on behalf of the audience; indeed, the prosecuting Duke Francisco responds to her objection incredulously: "why you understand Latin" (3.2.14). Vittoria admits her understanding (positioning herself as a product of humanist education whose English and Italian manifestations would have had much in common)—and in fact quotes the language sententiously later in the trial to downplay the significance of having been the object of adulterous, seductive attentions: *"casta est quam nemo rogavit"* ("she is chaste whom no one has asked," 3.2.200).

Though accused by a duke and judged by a panel of ambassadors, Vittoria evidently cannot claim that the trial's Latin excludes her—as it might her audience—from understanding the content of the proceeding in which she is judged and by implication from comprehending the power structures that are being aligned against her. Instead, Vittoria's protest of the "strange tongue" seeks to enlist popular sympathies, since she notes that "amongst this auditory / Which come to hear my cause, the half or more / May be ignorant in't" (3.2.15–17). The trial's "auditory" refers to the play's own audience; Vittoria casts the audience members as players in the drama, specifically, as prurient Italian trial goers. Since the "strange tongue" she objects to is Latin, she implies that the Italian she is already speaking is familiar. That is, unlike Milton (though she uses the same phrase to describe it), Vittoria's "strange tongue" *naturalizes* a foreign vernacular. Of course, the Italian, in this play, is spoken in English, and the play's English-speaking audience, cast as Italians, is by implication leaving the theater speaking a kind of Italian too. The English comprehend the language of Italian policy and misdeed fluently enough.

Yet while sympathy with Vittoria is occasionally, subtly written into a linguistically and politically English identification, the play is also liberally critical of her—criticism hardly mitigated by the fact that her Italianate alterity proves capable of assimilating itself to the English language. As I have argued, Vittoria is emblematically figured as a "white devil" whose dark interior is concealed by seductive and false exterior attractions. Applied to Vittoria, the trope hints at English suspicions of an anti-Petrarchan reality inhabiting the heart of "Italian" beauty itself. In fact, Vittoria's brother Flamineo, seeking to disarm her husband's jealousy, critiques the application of Petrarchan forms to his sister, on the basis of her violation of Petrarchan aesthetic norms: "what an ignorant ass or flattering knave might he be counted, that should write sonnets to her eyes, or call her brow the snow of Ida, or ivory of Corinth, or compare her hair to the blackbird's bill, when 'tis liker the blackbird's feather" (1.2.115–19).[38] However, Flamineo's reassuring words are disingenuous—he himself is arranging a tryst between his sister and Duke Brachiano. Flamineo relies on Vittoria's husband's (amply) foolish inability to recognize the allure of the very darkness of her dark beauty, whose elements are signs of her duplicity and "blackness."

Not only dark-eyed and dark-haired, Vittoria is possessed of what one character describes as "black lust" (3.1.7) and what Francisco speculates may be "a soul so black" (3.2.183) that she might be personally responsible for several of the play's deaths. Vittoria's beauty, darkness, and illicit sexuality ("lust") tend to coalesce; unlike Jessica's or Desdemona's, her beauty is tainted from the beginning by her adulterous sexuality, and adultery seems to be the sole sphere in which she is sexual. The desires of her husband Camillo are suf-ficiently confused that he is fooled into sleeping apart from her to "cross her humor" (1.2.166). In her first scene, Vittoria gulls Camillo, engages in extraordinarily elaborated sex-play with Brachiano, sug-gests that Brachiano murder her husband and Brachiano's wife, and is cursed by her own mother. Later, even indictments of her are routed compulsively through discussions of her beauty—its dark-ness and simultaneous deceptive "fairness" (1.2.6). The paradox of this beauty's nature proves to be of obsessive interest for the play's characters. Speaking out of a jealous disenchantment, Brachiano echoes the play's title and blames Vittoria's beauty for his criminal involvement with her:

> Your beauty! O, ten thousand curses on't.
> How long have I beheld the devil in crystal?
> Thou hast led me, like an heathen sacrifice,
> With music, and with fatal yokes of flowers.   (4.2.87–90)

Brachiano is unable to separate blame from the elegiac irony with which Vittoria's beauty is linked to a "devilish" darkness. Vittoria's beauty leads directly to fatal acts of murder, adultery, and (in this case) jealousy, but as Brachiano tells it, the cost of its thrall is immea-surably increased less by resultant immorality than by the doubleness of her beauty itself. Brachiano laments the appeal of this doubleness, laments the darkness he now claims to see reflected within Vittoria's "crystalline" surface; he casts himself, not the people he has mur-dered and poisoned, as the true victim of what he terms a "heathen sacrifice." The heathen sin is the Italian sin: not just human sacrifice but a fatal and seemingly unethical deployment of aesthetic cues, a "savage" and malign misappropriation of Eurocentric decorative (here musical and floral) norms.[39]

In the wake of a jealous reorganization of his affections, Brachiano's outrage reclassifies Vittoria's beauty as a sinister pairing of the dis-ingenuous and culturally alien. Collating beauty, artificiality, and the cultural import, Brachiano echoes Milton's depiction of the erosion of agency in response to a compelling foreign aesthetic. Not co-incidentally, it is here that he compares Vittoria to the Irish: "what? dost weep? / Procure but ten of thy dissembling trade, / Ye'd furnish all the Irish funerals / With howling, past wild Irish" (4.2.94–97). The Irish accusation surely reinvokes the play's English context, attempting to recast Vittoria's Italian allure as a far less appealing, bestial ("howling, past wild") show. In the reference to an Irish "dissembling trade" in grief, as in the prior analogy involving deceitful "heathen" paraphernalia, flowers and music, Brachiano presents a view of Vittoria's beauty and emotion as artificial, prosthetic, and immoral.

The accusation verges on a critique of Petrarchism itself, that most exalted and influential Italian import. Brachiano's connection between deceit, immorality, and ambiguous beauty is found throughout the play. After the dismissal of the Latin-speaking attorney, for instance, Cardinal Monticelso initiates prosecution by warning Vittoria of his own forthcoming, more direct accusations. According to Monticelso, the language of his charges does not demonstrate the falseness of her actions so much as the falseness of her appearance:

> I shall be plainer with you, and paint out
> Your follies in more natural red and white
> Than that upon your cheek.   (3.2.51–53)

Ostensibly, Monticelso means that by eschewing the "colors" of rhetoric, his plain descriptions of Vittoria's adultery and participation in her husband's murder will in their simplicity belie her own pretense of cosmetic honesty, though it is equally possible to construe his words to mean that his (possibly florid) "painting" of the facts will correspond more closely and appropriately to the truth than her cosmetic painting, or that he simply intends to paint *over* her falseness in a new, "truer" layer of paint. In any case, Monticelso suggests that Vittoria's deceitful simulation of innocence exactly corresponds to her artifice in beauty.

Both innocence and beauty require Vittoria's display of "red and white," through the ruddy lip, rosy cheek, and pale skin of English and Italian idealized femininity and through the blushing and blanching that would be Vittoria's necessary and most appropriate response to false and shocking indictments of her virtue. The phrase signals a Petrarchan aesthetics, yet while depictions of affective and cosmetic fluidity are ultimately derived from Petrarch himself, their closer, more abundant sources are found in English Petrarchism.[40] Her "red and white" thus once more marks Vittoria as Italian in an English idiom. The catalog of complexional and emotional shading associated with the phrase indicates that English standards of female beauty are demanding ones, requiring frequent and fluid demonstrations of shame and shock, blood marking feminine (im)modesty. These requirements also highlight the disturbing implications of English norms. Blushing and blanching are something of a problem, for sudden blushing indicates that seeming fair skin may always transform into (or already conceals) darkness, and sudden paleness implies that skin was never as light as it might have been.[41] In general, the commixture of feminine red and white itself, as Jonathan Crewe has suggested, represents a suspect and internal multiplicity: "the red and white, respectively signifying the desire of her blood and her chaste spiritual purity, remain at odds." For Crewe, such conflict strongly anticipates a discourse of miscegenation.[42] If so, a miscegenistic potential inheres in idealized femininity itself, inciting Petrarchan desires with the selfsame signs of its conflicted doubleness.[43]

Monticelso, of course, calls the authenticity of Vittoria's "red and white" into question to begin with. In his challenge, as in his other extended descriptions of her in the trial as a "whore" (3.2.78–106) that figure her as a "counterfeited coin" (3.2.99) or "counterfeit jewels" (3.2.141), he implies that the dissimulation of Vittoria's beauty is identical with her moral deceit, just as the worthlessness of counterfeit valuables derives from their artificiality. He also figures her as not only false representation but also a representation of something false: "If the devil / Did ever take good shape behold his picture" (3.2.216–17). Vittoria's equation with a white devil underlies Monticelso's initial heightened concern with her physical color—as though signal proof of her criminality lies in her hypocrisy in over-application of cosmetics.

Though she denies her guilt, Vittoria's defense does not fundamentally rework the terms Monticelso has set up. Her further reproofs of Monticelso and her other accusers simply cast them as the "white devils" and herself as just the complementary, fair and glassy yet unbreakable surface that Brachiano decries as essentially deceptive when he calls her a "devil in crystal." To Vittoria, Monticelso's accusations are "painted devils," but not least because they seem to dim or falsify her true brilliance and impervious hardness, fairness asserted with a threat that should her enemies

> . . . strike against this mine of diamonds,
> [They] shall prove but glassen hammers, they shall break,—
> These are but feigned shadows of my evils.
> Terrify babes, my lord, with painted devils.   (3.2.144–47)

Having converted the terms with which she is accused into accusations, Vittoria's deflection nonetheless contains a rather ambiguous boast of her own virtue—either uncorruptible or far beyond their "shadowy" imagination in villainy. Defending herself, Vittoria does not deny the fact of corruption in the sphere of her fairness or her actions, relying on the copresence and complementarity of light and dark to affirm her inviolable, metaphorical luster the more for its interaction with darkness: "through darkness diamonds spread their richest light" (3.2.294). Refusing to untangle ethics and aesthetics, light and dark, the aphorism functions as a kind of slogan for Jacobean Italianate drama.

The accusations traded between Vittoria and the Florentine faction during the trial are central to the play's theory of Italian character and plot; nearly all of *The White Devil*'s actions—both offending and avenging—unfold through tropes and processes of disguise and deceit figured as both internalized and externalized, but only partial, darkening. In comparison to such figurations, the character Zanche would seem to stand apart as figured in unequivocal blackness, exempt from the ambiguously positive connotations of white devilry. A rare female Moorish character, she is the object of casual scorn or violent loathing from virtually all the characters (Vittoria excepted), which is often shocking in the specificity of its racism, as when the brother of Zanche's lover Flamineo abruptly kicks her for allegedly bragging that Flamineo will marry her, averring that "I had rather she were pitch'd upon a stake / In some new-seeded garden, to affright / Her fellow crows thence" (5.1.194–96).[44] It is significant that whereas the Moorish general Mulinassar (Francisco in disguise) is admired, Zanche is routinely insulted and mocked; the difference in their treatment is a function not only of her gender and her role as Vittoria's sexual accomplice but also of her class status as servant.

Indeed, as Ann Rosalind Jones has noted, Zanche is placed "at the absolute bottom of interlocking cultural, racial, gender, and class hierarchies." Jones is one of the few critics to register the effect of Zanche's class status on her figuration; being a servant renders her sexual desires for Flamineo and, later, the disguised Francisco presumptuous and makes her vulnerable to the insults and ready blows of the other characters.[45] Both Zanche's desires and the violence directed at her are then racialized, demonstrating the importance of class structures to the development of institutionalized racism and in no small measure prefiguring the evolution of the large-scale, class-based system of slavery.

Important for the intersecting discourses of race and Italianness presented in the play, Zanche is also presented as being unable either to blush or to blanch. Approaching Mulinassar, she declares that "I ne'er lov'd my complexion till now, / Cause I may boldly say without a blush, / I love you" (5.1.213–15). About to be stabbed to death, she likewise shares the doomed bravado of co-conspirators Vittoria and Flamineo: "I am proud / Death cannot alter my complexion, / For I shall ne'er look pale" (5.6.229–31).[46] In both instances, Zanche's satisfaction with the stability of her complexion contrasts with Vittoria's red and white fluctuations, which simultaneously and indiscriminately broadcast (and, to some, dissimulate) her beauty, desire, shame, and fear.

Zanche's invocation of her self-similar blackness removes her from the red and white affective economy that grounds much of the racial representation of the other characters, seeming to place her in a racial category separate from the Italians, though both groups are described with the discourses of blackness. Yet elsewhere, Zanche is figurally as well as thematically linked with the Italians. Both she and Vittoria are associated with the Irish; in their capacity as femmes fatales, both are compared by male characters to wolves (4.2.92; 5.1.155). In addition, as we have seen, the Italians are consistently depicted in proximity to Moorish characters and as impersonating them. Francisco's disguise as a Moor in particular suggests the dramaturgic proximity of and overlap between the two groups (the Italian, taking on the Moorish disguise, reveals himself as a white devil). Zanche's subsequent, misguided infatuation with him draws attention to their difference (through dramatic irony), yet the physical resemblance—and, given their portrayal by two English men in blackface, the utter metatheatrical equivalence—of the two characters on stage would argue for their likeness.

The task of personating both femininity and dark skin, as Dympna Callaghan reminds us, was itself achieved through the prosthetic layering of "surfaces of difference": whiteface, rouge, and blackface.[47] From the point of view of the technologies of theatrical representation—the antithetical, yet analogous, application of makeup—the embodiment of "fair" femininity strongly resembles that of "dark" nations, races, and ethnicities. Indeed, the representation of "black" beauties might well have taken a mediate position—as when the Veronese Julia, disguised as a man in *The Two Gentlemen of Verona,* describes the alteration of her own appearance to unknowing Silvia: "since she did neglect her looking-glass, / And threw her sun-expelling mask away, /. . . now she is become as black as I."[48] Presumably, the actor would now lack whiteface, bear some cosmetic simulations of tanning (or simply the actor's own skin)—

since darkening of the skin would compose part of her disguise of masculinity—and possibly maintain a certain amount of rouge to indicate to the audience her "underlying" femininity and her assumed role of boy.

Julia is an unqualified heroine, her disguise put on to serve her constancy: the rigors of *Two Gentlemen* are not primarily the cultural anxieties provoked by the attractions and threats of female dissimulation or immorality. By contrast, in Webster's drama, English metaphoric exchanges between moral and cosmetic darkness are continually explored, exploited, and urgently linked to questions of moral and cosmetic imposture. Webster's characteristic fascination with dramaturgic paradox emphasizes the material and metatheatrical components of these connected representations: the embodiment of artificially "self-similar" blackness; the prosthetic portrayal of feminine fairness; and the (related) accusation of complementary, hidden feminine darkness. Racialized blackness and the moral darkness of revenge plots are mutually enabled by and projected onto the play's Italian fiction.

The same array of raced and gendered parallels and crossings is still more compactly figured in the closing tableau of Webster's *The Devil's Law-Case,* to which I turn in conclusion. The action of the play, which relentlessly thematizes doubling, is poised to resolve at the entrance of two female characters: Angiolella, a nun impregnated by the merchant Romelio; and Jolenta, Romelio's sister, who has spread a rumor that she herself is pregnant, naming three different fathers (including her brother). Led by a doctor disguised (for no discernible reason) in a Jewish costume, the women enter dressed as nuns, pregnant Angiolella all in white and Jolenta in black (5.6.29). As the doctor introduces them—"this is a white nun / Of the order of Saint Clare; and this a black one" (5.6.31–32)—he lifts Jolenta's veil to reveal she is in blackface, *"her face color'd like a Moor,"* as the stage directions have it, beneath her black habit. In response to the combination of dark habit and dark skin, another character underscores the dramaturgic *rime riche:* "she's a black one indeed" (5.6.33).

The "joke" turns out to have been arranged at Angiolella's expense:

Jolenta, whose rumored, possibly incestuous pregnancy has understandably vitiated her reputation for virtue, indulges in a heavy-handed irony by dressing the pregnant Angiolella in a garment whose color and function symbolize virginity. Without the spectacular travesty of a pregnant, white-garbed nun as contrast, Jolenta's darkened skin would simply figure forth her own supposed promiscuity, and her nun's habit would exaggerate her crime, as it does Angiolella's. But with Angiolella as a foil, Jolenta's display instead creates a cognitive dissonance, neither redefining nor wholly inhabiting the traditional connotations of whiteness and blackness. The questions raised by Jolenta's use of color are the same as those raised by and about Vittoria and Zanche in *The White Devil*. Is blackness an aesthetic and moral liability, a sign of dissimulation, or does it imply a fundamentally virtuous, straightforward self-similarity?

On the one hand, Jolenta resists some elements of the conventional connotations of fair and dark by equating enveloping darkness with a salutary black-and-white mixture in her subsequent masque-like speech: "the down upon the raven's feather / Is as gentle and as sleek / As the mole on Venus' cheek" (5.6.35–37). This contrast recalls Vittoria's defense of the admixture of darkness used to set off fairness: "through darkness diamonds spread their richest light." Yet in order to consolidate her reputation, Jolenta retains some traditional symbolism of whiteness and blackness as she points to the "white" consistency of internal virtue, which, she hopes, dispels the implications of her outward appearance of "darkness":

Which of us now judge you whiter,
Her whose credit proves the lighter,
Or this black and ebon hue,
That, unstain'd, keeps fresh and true?
For I proclaim't without control
There's no true beauty but i'th'soul.   (5.6.44–49)

Of course, without Jolenta's darkened skin to suggest an oppositional logic between the two colors and women (a logic strengthened by the couplets in which she speaks), she would resemble Angiolella too much for their appearances alone to allay the public doubts about Jolenta's own sexual innocence. In impugning Angiolella's "whiteness," Jolenta does not undermine the negative connotations of blackness, though she hopes in this instance showily to circumvent them.

However, Jolenta's hopeful lines about "true beauty" aside, her use of blackness does succeed in substantially compromising the virtue, beauty, and purity supposedly signified by feminine whiteness, as disdainfully revealed in Angiolella's demonstrably "light" credit and white habit. Jolenta's own resort to disguise (not to mention her false disclosures of incest) succeeds as a diversion, but her display and poem fall uneasily between a bold Platonic refiguration of color (blackness as constancy) and satiric self-incrimination (blackness as wantonness). Her use of the nun's habit further underscores her ambiguous moral rehabilitation, for though Jolenta is not visibly pregnant, she in no way means to pursue a life of chastity. The uncertain destabilization of whiteness she desires is therefore eased along by the Catholic regalia that were, according to the officially sanctioned English logic, already symbols of hypocritical virtue. The nuns' habits and the gratuitous Jew's costume reveal the suspiciousness of Italy's religious diversity. Jolenta's gambit is in part achievable because Italian whiteness is never, in England, fully white. In this context, we may more easily access the palpable ridiculousness of her suitor Ercole's response to the ending of her speech, truly remarkable in light of her costume: "O, tis the fair Jolenta!" (5.6.50). With such jokes, Webster employs his characters both here and in *The White Devil* to acknowledge and endorse the possibilities afforded by the aesthetic of dissimulation and mixture presented both thematically and metatheatrically in Italianate drama.

In the English Italian, race fluctuates as it is used to figure shifting national and gender identities. The drama's many crossings between "English," "Italian," and "Moorish" and between schemata of morality and gender fracture any proposed contrast between "Europeans" and "others," offering instead a dense map in which identificatory structures are internally hybridized and where different nationalisms are put to work on English problems. The associations of Italy with racial diversity, literary sophistication, alluring sensationalism, and a simultaneous awareness and fluidity of self make Italy an especially fruitful and momentous site where the English can project, claim, and experiment with formulations of their own national identity. In this way dramatic and poetic texts, with their frequent gestures toward metatheatricality, do not fail to remind their imagining community of who produces them. Nor does Webster, Milton, or their lyric forebears forget whose desires they figure in the persons of Italians.

FOUR

Race, Science, and Aversion

꒛꒜

I find a contrariety in nature
Betwixt that face and me.

—Middleton and Rowley, *The Changeling*

A Certain Loathing

In this chapter I return to some of the concerns about the periodization of race and racism with which I began. In my Introduction,
I argued that an overzealous identification of race with the epistemological protocols and classificatory expressive styles of post-
Renaissance science tends to occlude both Renaissance and modern
racialist meanings and operations. Instead, reading for the multiple,
often illogical or contradictory discourses and logics that sustain
beliefs in group differences, and for the shifts in individual racial
identity that permeate Renaissance texts, we find racial meanings to
be pivotal within the period's understandings of gender, nation, religion, sexuality, and class and frequently underlying and intensifying
the pleasurable tensions depicted in comedy and tragedy.

But what role do Renaissance theories of epistemology and science play in this account? The plays under consideration are all written long before the sea change in science production that would
occur in the eighteenth century and even significantly before the
changes in scientific epistemology in the 1650s and 1660s associated
with the New Philosophy—the revolution in scientific methodology
that attempted to replace inferences based on pure reason with experimental empiricism as means and assurance of accessing scientific

truths. For historians of race and racism, the discrepancy between methodologies before and after this revolution has often proved decisive in limiting truly racist expression to the later period, when racial "facts" began to be classified, arranged in hierarchical orderings, and referred to biological causes.

Nonetheless, revisionist accounts of this periodization are emerging. For instance, at one time, David Theo Goldberg, a philosopher extremely sensitive to the logics and nuances of racist discourses, wrote that "the ethnocentrisms of socioepistemic conjunctures prior to the seventeenth century, although forerunners of racism, were not themselves forms of racist expression . . . they make no legitimating appeal to any concept having its originary place in scientific discourse the way race has."[1] However, in more recent work, Goldberg describes in detail changing paradigms of racial signification, arguing "that 'race' is a fluid, transforming, historically specific concept," which allows him to conclude that "the primary senses of 'race' and the conflation of natural with the social kinds they promoted were already well rooted nearly two hundred years prior to the Enlightenment!"[2]

Goldberg's sense of surprise at his conceptual revision is eloquently conveyed by that exclamation point, and he notes that the contrary view is "widespread."[3] It remains so. Partly in response to the contrary view, throughout this book I have presented evidence for the presence and features of early manifestations of the conflation of natural and social kinds in metaphors of blood, color, lineage, and racial transformation. Interestingly, the quotations that Goldberg uses to adduce the earlier presence of "race" are dated 1580–1605 (while "well rooted" hedges even that origin), overlapping the dates of the plays under discussion.[4] The early modern period thus appears to be a critical time in which the modern forms of race and racism emerged and began to calcify. For the English, the popular drama of this time, which favored plots of interracial desire, racial disguise, and racial fluidity, was instrumental in transmitting some of the central, enduring tropes that would characterize race in modernity.

Of course, appealing to science as the origin of racist discourse is not the same as science upholding racism. I have argued in this book that other interests and beliefs, including philosophical, aesthetic, religious, political, and economic ones, in fact motivated and justified racism and dictated the questions and results that the new science would generate. Yet an appeal to science—in particular to the impersonal facts or natural order that science might be thought to disclose—is enticing as a way of validating more personal, subjective intuitions about or reactions to difference. One such reaction, aversion, and the differential treatment that it may prompt are often in particular need of external justification. And this desire, too, for an objective epistemology that would bear out individual viewpoints is anticipated in drama several decades before New Philosophical reforms.[5]

In preceding chapters, I have repeatedly described how ambivalent expressions of desire precipitate racialist expression. Now, in readings of Middleton and Rowley's *The Changeling* and (once again) *The Merchant of Venice,* we will consider desire alongside racializing and materialist expressions of aversion. These plays put forth a view of aversion as the unavoidable and arbitrary effect of the vagaries of individual humoral physiology and, in *The Changeling,* as bodies disclosing hidden truths. However, as we will see, those aversions labeled "arbitrary" in fact emerge within narratives that richly detail the social causes of racially inflected tension. Such narratives motivate the humoral account: they are suppressed or dismissed in favor of a (diversionary) materialist explanation. Thus, we are presented with early examples both of an attempted naturalization/biologizing of the origins of racial antagonism and of the mystification of the social motivations in fact underlying that attempt. Like the charts of comparative physical and intellectual measurements that would come to document supposed differences and justify racist exclusions and abuses, humoral theory is used in these plays to present materialist, physiological "facts" in order to preempt histories of social prejudice and conflict. This application of the theory of humors anticipates the use of science as both prescriptive and descriptive agent of racial difference. However, though similar arguments would attempt to naturalize racial antipathies in later centuries, the humoral discourses that structure the understandings of aversion we will see here provide a historically specific (and hence contingent) form for aversion to take.

In the doctrine of humors, we have seen that the interrelation of physiology and psychology facilitated the racialization of individuals or groups, as when Desdemona ironically absolves Othello of a tendency to jealousy, assuming that the hot climate of his formative years "drew all such humours from him" (3.4.31). Humoral theory also implied a metaphysics, one that was profoundly materialist, according to which understandings of the self, and changes in health and also in mental states (such as jealousy), were alike referred to personal configurations of humoral flow and their interactions with nature.[6] Surviving today in a collection of vestigial metaphors ("catching a cold") and intuitive self-understandings ("this sadness inside me"), a rich and complicated vocabulary arose to describe the experiences, often dynamic ones, of interiority in accord with humoral theory.[7] Humors emphasized the multiple fluid interactions, influenced by climate, diet, exercise, and other forms of self-care, that forged individual temperaments, or "complexions." The intricacy and flexibility of this vocabulary allow modern readers to find Renaissance humoral evocations of the self sporadically satisfying and communicative and even, in a word that will presently take on a slightly ominous tone, "natural."[8]

Though they were always, quite literally, in flux, humors nonetheless had the potential to lend inflexibility to theories of individual personality and physiology, such as guides Desdemona's presumption about Othello, and provides the premise, for example, for the fantastic and intractable characters that populate Jonson's comedies of humors.[9] The combination of materialism and inflexibility meant that humoral theory, appealing to the natures of differentiated bodies and substances, could support the sedimentation of various invidious social distinctions. Indeed, Gail Kern Paster notes, "the materials of early modern humoral theory encode a complexly articulated hierarchy of physiological differences paralleling and reproducing structures of social differences."¹⁰ Paster directs her argument toward humoral enforcement of the social differences of gender and class, but her claim applies equally well to the reproduction of racial differences. Many of the humoral tropes she observes to maintain gender hierarchies—distinctions among disordered as opposed to disciplined bodies, impure as opposed to pure blood, gross as opposed to refined matter—we have seen simultaneously structure and intensify racial hierarchies.

As we will see in detail, humoral theory had the further potential to naturalize antagonisms between or inclinations toward differentiated individuals or groups, by connecting the perception of psychical and physical differences to systems of affect, especially attraction and repulsion.¹¹ In *The Changeling*, such a physiological account of attraction and repulsion advances a racialist tragedy of moral and bodily degeneration, a tragedy whose social and interpersonal origins are simultaneously obscured. Shylock's account of his repulsion for Antonio during the trial scene in *The Merchant of Venice* likewise uses humoral theory to suppress the social and interpersonal causes of *Merchant*'s tensions. Shylock's gambit is striking in a play that does not elsewhere rely on humoral vocabulary to generate its racial content; its presence, out of place in its own play, underscores the emerging appeal of using the persuasive discourse of materialist objectivity to validate gratifying emotions.

The origins of the tragedy in *The Changeling* are diffuse, for the play's racial content is intensified by associative links the play makes among its chaotic constellation of plot elements. These include first of all its setting in Spanish Alicante, on the Mediterranean coast directly north of Algiers. Though Africa is not mentioned in the play, the detailed attention given to the "strengths" of Vermandero's castle (1.1.164; 2.2.158; 3.1.4; 3.2.7–9) suggests the city's defensive stance against a potential North African threat.¹² At the same time, depictions of the castle's defensive apparatus maximize the pathos of more potent dangers, implicitly surpassing the African threat, including an internal breakdown of norms of female chastity, filial and marital responsibility, hospitality, class stability, servant loyalty, and a general ethical integrity.[13] As with the Jacobean Italianate drama discussed in chapter 3, *The Changeling*'s setting in a Mediterranean Catholic country—one especially hated and feared by the English—makes the play suggestive as a site of otherness, coarticulated in tropes of immorality and physical difference.[14] In this case, the affair of its morally "black" heroine (5.3.193) with a disfigured servant, their murderous plots, and her resultant refiguration as "all deform'd" (5.2.77), by insisting that manifestations of immorality are visually abhorrent, racialize class and gender transgression.

Michael Neill writes that *The Changeling* is "a play that could scarcely have been written without *Othello*," yet he reads *The Changeling* as engaging tensions around degree (that is, social rank) rather than race. The play "shifts attention from the racial anxieties at the center of the earlier tragedy to the bitterness about rank and status evident at its margin" and replaces the jealous husband with "a bland and colorless figure."[15] Nonetheless, the profusion of derogatory visual imagery—rounded out with images of sickness, darkness, immorality, and impurity—that attaches to the play's villain, De Flores, suggests that questions of status, rank, and their stability, in this play, are closely linked to questions of race.

The play's insistent links between De Flores's status and quality of blood, on the one hand, and his external appearance and desirability, on the other, present racial content in ways we have seen before. What is most significant for the concerns of this chapter is the mechanism by which these connections are established and justified: through an appeal to nature. In *The Changeling*, distinction between classes and antipathy between characters are given maximum moral and suasive force by an account of social interactions that emphasizes the rules governing natural kinds. These rules are invoked to discipline De Flores's sexual desires and, importantly, to explain the repulsive effects he has on others.

As De Flores tells it, he "tumbled into th'world a gentleman" (2.1.49) but has suffered a reversal of fortune and is a servant. Yet

either his "gentle" origins have been obscured or his original distance from aristocratic Beatrice is sufficient that she rebuffs his advances with an appeal to the differences inherent in their "blood":
"Think but upon the distance that creation / Set 'twixt thy blood
and mine, and keep thee there" (3.4.130–31). This "distance" in
rank, later bridged by their illicit sexual liaison, is at first rhetorically augmented by repeated references to De Flores's ugliness and/
or deformity (a distinction between the two is not maintained),
contrasted with Beatrice's beauty. His ugliness repels many of the
other characters and figures forth his villainy in tropes that at times
become extreme. Yet as though an aversion to ugliness cannot be
easily explained, these characters repeatedly dwell on the reasons for
their alienation from De Flores, often citing the agency of creation
and the laws of nature (as Beatrice does above). The play's focus on
De Flores's appearance therefore becomes notable not just for the
responses of aversion De Flores occasions in the play's other characters but for the routine validation of those responses by discourses
of nature.

For instance, when Tomazo de Piracquo seeks the murderer of his
brother Alonzo, he encounters De Flores, who is, in fact, that murderer. Unaware of De Flores's crime, Tomazo nonetheless describes
De Flores as an object of revulsion and, indeed, contagion:

I find a contrariety in nature
Betwixt that face and me: . . . he's so foul,
. . . so most deadly venomous,
He would go near to poison any weapon
That should draw blood on him . . .
He walks a'purpose by, sure, to choke me up,
To infect my blood. (5.2.13–25)

In the characteristic logic of this play, the strange passivity with which
this virulent speech begins—Tomazo, almost reflectively noticing that
"I find a contrariety"—bespeaks his unknowing "instinct" that De
Flores is his brother's killer. "Instinct" is a word De Flores supplies

(5.2.40), with which he explains Tomazo's sudden but seemingly untutored hatred for him. That is, the two agree on the mechanics at work in this upsurge of aversion: instinct is revealed in "natural" antipathy, a "contrariety in nature." Yet given Tomazo's focus on De Flores's foulness and "face," the aptness of this instinct depends on metatheatrical conflation of De Flores's hidden evil and manifest, off-putting disfigurement. Here and throughout, the play's connections between De Flores's inferior, infected blood, "foul" appearance, villainy, and lasciviousness lead, unsurprisingly, to his racialization. Perhaps more disturbingly, the play uses these connections to endorse the "instinctive" antipathy felt by the other characters, although that instinct is repeatedly emphasized as predicated merely on appearance, not on De Flores's villainy. Though De Flores's appearance is unique (he is not a member of a visually identifiable group), I would suggest that the play's narrative sanction of its characters' visual aversions is suggestive for any analysis of the workings of racial antipathies.

Indeed, for modern audiences, the subjective alienation created by De Flores's class position, disfigurement, and repugnance to Beatrice and others has frequently been conveyed through racialized casting and makeup. For instance, Neill cites "Richard Eyre's 1988 production for the National Theatre . . . which cast a black actor (George Harris) in the role of De Flores, and set him against a blonde Beatrice (Miranda Richardson)."[16] In Christine Morris's production of the play at Duke University, De Flores was ambiguously racialized, when his ugliness/disfigurement was represented by a large, slightly raised, dark spot that covered most of the right side of the actor's forehead and cheek.[17] The importance of race in modern culture makes such choices especially resonant and topical ones, yet they are not for that reason utterly ahistorical; instead, they mark a consonance between Renaissance and modern racial logics, as similar connections are made between alienation and appearance in *The Changeling* itself. However, modern audiences are less likely to find quite as "contemporary" some of the play's other discursive connections to race: its interest in tropes of infection (in line with the play's humoral matrix, infection spread through blood and purged by bloodletting); its intense concern with the bodily and aesthetic implications for Beatrice of her adulterous relationship with De Flores; and its further, centripetal associations between the beastlike, "howling, braying, barking" madmen (3.3.197) of Alibius's madhouse and the transformations being played out within Vermandero's castle.[18]

While audiences before the Restoration preferred the antics of the madhouse—its inmates dressed as birds and beasts (3.3.190), its antimasque-like dance (3.3.212)—and of Antonio, the disguised madman-playboy, the play's critical success in the last century has derived largely from the "psychological realism" of its main plot, centering on the relationship between Beatrice and De Flores.[19] Beatrice and De Flores begin the play possessed by complementary loathing and attraction, emotions whose physical intensity and seeming static quality individuate the two in ways indebted to the Jonsonian theatrical tradition of humoral comedy. Yet Beatrice and De Flores depart from this tradition through their discomfort with these emotions, which become occasions for self-scrutiny. Once Beatrice is coerced into a sexual relation with De Flores, loathing and attraction modulate into a surprising degree of mutual satisfaction based in part on mutual utility.

Despite the unusualness of these plot elements—especially Beatrice's affair with a servant—and the extreme shifts in emotion among the main characters, the play distinguishes itself in being, in the words of its editor, "conspicuous among Elizabethan plays for the naturalness of its characters, for its plausibility as an account of a particular human situation."[20] The effects of realism, depth, and plausibility popular with modern audiences and critics arise from Beatrice's and De Flores's extended discussions of their experiences of interiority, in particular of how they feel about each other. These discussions consist in large measure of their descriptions of struggle against and their confusion about those feelings. The effect of depth is, if anything, intensified by the monologic record of emotional confusion. The characters' interpretive efforts notwithstanding, affect in the play retains some Jonsonian flavor, possessing and fluctuating within its subjects as if by mechanistic quirk, from which Beatrice and De Flores weakly assert desires to be free while their passions are nonetheless experienced as compulsions.

The characters find the experience of all-consuming affect best expressed through metaphors of sickness, eccentricity, and confusion. In keeping with the Galenic model of affect that equated emotional intensity with humoral imbalance, Alsemero, later Beatrice's husband, initially makes the connection between affect and physical illness, describing his sudden, uncharacteristic infatuation with Beatrice to be like "some hidden malady / Within me, that I understand not" (1.1.24–25).[21] Trying to characterize the unstable and powerful emotions circulating between them, Beatrice and De Flores will echo Alsemero's terms of hidden sickness and hampered efforts at self-cognition. De Flores comments repeatedly on his feelings of compulsion with regard to Beatrice, which lead him to dog her despite her abrasive responses: "I know she hates me, / Yet cannot choose but love her" (1.1.230–31). Elsewhere, he employs Alsemero's sickness metaphor: "whatever ails me? Now a-late especially, / I can as well be hang'd as refrain seeing her / Some twenty times a day, nay, not so little, / . . . and I have small reason for't" (2.1.27–31). Like Alsemero, De Flores notes the irrationality of his impulses toward Beatrice. His longings are (at this stage) primarily visual and center on the exchange of glances: he cannot "refrain seeing her" and finds "excuses / To come into her sight" (2.1.30–31). Even so, he is unable to satisfy his visual appetite: "I must see her still!" (2.1.78).

For her part, as she explains to Alsemero, Beatrice's antipathy to De Flores similarly lacks rational cause, registers as a visual aversion, and is something of a personal foible:

> . . . 'tis my infirmity,
> Nor can I other reason render you,
> Than his or hers, of some particular thing
> They must abandon as a deadly poison,
> Which to a thousand other tastes were wholesome;
> Such to mine eyes is that same fellow there. (1.1.106–11)

Like Alsemero's and De Flores's infatuations and, for that matter, Tomazo's own repugnance for De Flores, Beatrice finds she can talk about her feelings without being able to reason with or about them: all emphasize that their experiences of affect not only arise from uncontrollable bodily predispositions but resist ratiocination.[22] The account of her hatred Beatrice gives reflects the paradoxical logic with which humoral theory distinguished the different needs, sympathies, and antipathies of different objects and people.[23] On the one hand, possessing an intense aversion, though she lacks "reason" for it and deems it a manifest "infirmity," places Beatrice within a generic, "his or hers" commonality rather than marking her as peculiar or idiopathic. (Apparently, such humoral extremes still seem reasonable, as is attested by critical satisfaction with her psychological "naturalness.") Yet at the same time, her account of antipathy is distinguished by the marked *individuality* of its subjects: each antipathy's object, experienced as poison, is "wholesome" "to a thousand other tastes." In this individual variability, as in her reluctance to attribute the causes of aversion to any particular quality of De Flores, Beatrice's account of her infirmity seems to resist the tendencies to generalize and to blame its object that we may associate with racialist logics. That is, in this description, Beatrice assumes neither that De Flores has any particular unsavory quality that motivates her distaste nor that others will share that distaste.

Alsemero responds to Beatrice politely with his own depiction of eccentric dislike:

This is a frequent frailty in our nature;
There's scarce a man amongst a thousand sound,
But hath his imperfection: one distastes
The scent of roses . . . one oil, the enemy of poison;
Another wine, the cheerer of the heart . . .
Indeed this fault (if so it be) is general,
There's scarce a thing but is both lov'd and loath'd.   (1.1.116–25)

Though Alsemero seconds Beatrice's claim that the "frailty" of loathing she claims to instantiate is a universal human characteristic, so "general" as to seem the less a flaw, his list of bêtes noires—including his own, "a cherry" (1.1.128)—presents loathings rather different from hers. Alsemero's understanding is that loathing typically centers on common, consumable objects, not people. That is, though the word "loathing," then as now, refers to any aversion—embodied hatred or disgust—Alsemero specifies it to its application in connection with literal or metaphorical foodstuffs (see *OED* "loathing" 4b). Two other qualities distinguish his account: first, the objects he names are far from harmful themselves, exaggerating the perversity of foible; and second, the vagaries and varieties of human loathing encompass virtually every object in an almost democratic fashion, reinforcing the impression, which all three give, that their impulses are *arbitrary* (hence irrational). Their descriptive consistency notwithstanding, we will have reason to counter this impression; before returning to consider the impact of Beatrice's and Alsemero's claims, a comparison with another, similar narrative of antipathy in *The Merchant of Venice* will clarify the diversionary tactics at work.

The Changeling is not the only play to posit aversion as a capricious, individualizing force; the terms of the exchange between Alsemero and Beatrice recall Shylock's defense of his antipathy for Antonio made in the trial scene in *The Merchant of Venice*. In that play, the Duke of Venice opens the trial proceedings by challenging the economic incoherence and gratuitous brutality of Shylock's persistence in his lawsuit against Antonio, incredulously interrogating Shylock's "strange apparent cruelty" (4.1.21). Shylock's response to the Duke echoes Alsemero's, Beatrice's, and De Flores's rhetoric of physical "frailty" and "malady" but transposes these terms more explicitly into the language of humors, which in his speech take on a resonance midway between quirk and compulsion:

> But say it is my humour,—is it answer'd? . . .
> Some men there are love not a gaping pig!
> Some that are mad if they behold a cat!
> And others when the bagpipe sings i'th'nose,
> Cannot contain their urine—for affection

Maisters of passion sways it to the mood
Of what it likes or loathes,—now for your answer:
As there is no firm reason to be rend'red
Why he cannot abide a gaping pig,
Why he a harmless, necessary cat,
Why he a woolen bagpipe, but of force
Must yield to such inevitable shame,
As to offend himself being offended:
So can I give no reason, nor will I not,
More than a lodg'd hate, and a certain loathing
I bear Antonio, that I follow thus
A losing suit against him!   (4.1.43–62)[24]

Shylock's terminology here—humor, affection, passion—emphasizes
the embodied, involuntary quality of human disposition toward
various objects.[25] Gesturing to the "facts" of his physical makeup,
the subject of humors defaults on responsibility for humors. As
Paster writes about the same speech, "he constructs his obduracy
as a natural antipathy of the sort common in humans and animals
both," calling it a "brilliant naturalization."[26] Shylock argues that
subject and object are linked by an emotive circuit (not unlike that
connecting De Flores and Beatrice): as the subject is "affected," so
his "affection" in turn constrains his responses and emanates from
him with occasionally shaming force, as in the reflex of urination in
response to bagpiping.[27] Urination in fact typifies the occasional liabilities of the uncontrollable humoral body. Paster notes that such
discourses of humoral incontinency were generally associated with
the disordered bodies of women.[28] However, Shylock recuperates
a leaky masculine shame itself in a rhetorical strategy; his image
of "offensive" expulsion of humoral superfluity further justifies his
triumphalist account of antipathy as "inevitable," involuntary, and
hardwired.

Like Beatrice and Alsemero, Shylock depends upon a notion of
individual fragility or "imperfection" to sustain what might be considered an unlikely analogy between an arbitrary "lodg'd" hatred

for a pig or a cat and the "certain loathing" he feels for Antonio. The analogy between objects and people (as objects of antipathy) is not the only element of his defense that suggests its application to evolving racist discourses. In addition, Shylock's materialist, humoral account of his hatred anticipates later uses of biology to naturalize a targeted antipathy, though (like Beatrice) he avoids relating that hatred to any causal impetus within Antonio himself. By emphasizing the involuntary, irrational ("there is no firm reason to be render'd") nature of this imperfection, Shylock and Beatrice refuse any account of the etiology or evolution of their antipathies. Their refusal can be seen as efficient and strategic, even exculpatory, since their explanations work to exonerate them from the charges that they hate unfairly or out of proportion and from the responsibilities of moderating their behavior—letting Antonio off the hook or being civil to De Flores.

What is most odd about these accounts, which bear substantial similarity, is that both plays provide abundant reasons and competing explanations for the sources and progress of their characters' loathing. In Shylock's first scene, he suggests that his "ancient grudge" (1.3.42) is based in both religious antipathy and religiously inflected economic resentment: "I hate him for he is a Christian: / But more, for that in low simplicity / He lends out money gratis, and brings down / The rate of usance" (1.3.37–40). Antonio admits that his own acts of (specially targeted) debt relief have exacerbated this grudge: "He seeks my life, *his reason well I know*; / I oft deliver'd from his forfeitures / Many that have at times made moan to me, / *Therefore* he hates me" (3.3.21–24; emphasis added). There is the matter of Antonio's oft-noted racist abuse of Shylock—spitting, kicking, name-calling (1.3.101–8) and extended attempts at economic sabotage (3.1.49–52)—for which, not so incidentally, a reason is also adduced: "and *what's his reason*? I am a Jew" (3.1.52; emphasis added). Such statements are couched in the language of rationality and causality; they depict a set of actions, provoked by prejudice and revenge, whose causes and results are clearly delineated. In other words, Shylock's speech before the court is fundamentally at odds with the rationales of his hatred depicted in the rest of the play. At the very moment he might offer a mitigating account of his actions, fully availing himself of the court's juridical authority and rumored need to accommodate strangers (3.3.26–31), Shylock is represented as choosing instead to mystify the bases of his loathing.[29] Significantly, an explanation centering on the interpersonal development of Antonio's and Shylock's entrenched, mutual religious antagonism is displaced in favor of one that recasts the hatred as individual, inexplicable, unalterable, and, ultimately, physical.

This sidestepping is also evident in *The Changeling*. For neither is Beatrice's dislike of De Flores as contingent as she would have Alsemero believe when she describes it as an irrational idiosyncrasy. Her references to De Flores dwell obsessively on her antipathy to his ugliness, ugliness she locates in his face. Thus, she describes him as "deadly poison" "to mine eyes"; elsewhere, her aversion to "this ominous ill-fac'd fellow" (2.1.53) is visually activated and so extreme as to be associated with presentiment: "I never see this fellow, but I think / Of some harm towards me, danger's in my mind still, / I scarce leave trembling of an hour after" (2.1.89–91). Such descriptions do not make her aversion seem either inexplicable or arbitrary, though they dwell on omen and presentiment to magnify a sense of mysterious causal force. De Flores is well aware of her superstitious associations with his face: "she . . . does profess herself / The cruellest enemy to my face in town, / At no hand can abide the sight of me, / As if danger or ill luck hung in my looks" (2.1.32–36). In fact, after he eagerly obeys her wish that he murder Alonzo de Piracquo, to whom she is initially betrothed, De Flores will claim a sexual reward from Beatrice and eventually kill her (and himself) when the affair is discovered. Just as De Flores's own name suggests the theatrical inevitability that he will achieve his sexual goal with Beatrice, the trajectory of the plot seems to validate the more baleful aspects of Beatrice's foreboding in narrative irony.[30] In this spirit, Bawcutt calls Beatrice's early loathing for De Flores "prophetic."[31]

When the role of De Flores's appearance in constituting Beatrice's aversion is ignored (in favor of an account of aversion as capricious), the play effectively supports the naturalization of an embodied and affective aesthetics in a highly overdetermined logic. By this logic, the same logic that reads her emotions as "prophetic," Beatrice's attitudes toward beauty or ugliness and toward the distance that class difference produces between species of "blood" are borne out by, rather than *directly responsible for,* her loathing. Similar assumptions govern the play's attitude toward the inevitability of De Flores's amorous responses to Beatrice's beauty. These assumptions take aesthetic impulses for truths and imperatives, disclosed by the body whose humors, after all, participate in a natural order. The logic is further buoyed by the play's denouement, in which both characters are killed and Beatrice describes herself as "defile[d]" (5.3.149) by her involvement with De Flores, just as Tomazo de Piracquo imagined De Flores's face and blood as so "deadly venomous" as to poison even the weapon used to attack him. Beatrice's fear of the "ominous, ill-fac'd fellow" becomes self-fulfilling prophecy.

Beatrice's correlation of ugliness, low rank, and immorality leads to her attempt to use De Flores in "kind" with his appearance, and ultimately to her own refiguration as racialized much in the way De Flores is. She will be described as diseased, "ugly," and dark because unchaste and murderous. When she finds herself in love with Alsemero though engaged to Alonzo de Piracquo, she rejects Alsemero's offer to challenge Piracquo to a duel out of fear of losing him and, she adds, because he is really too handsome for the act: "blood-guiltiness becomes [suits] a fouler visage" (2.2.40). Such aphorisms naturally suggest the object of her visual loathing to be the solution to her problem. Beatrice lights upon this solution in an analogy that equates De Flores's effect on her with her villainous need to do away with Piracquo, expressing the equation in a providentialist Paracelsan formula that stresses the beneficial and antithetical properties of poisons: "the ugliest creature / Creation fram'd for some use . . . / Why men of art make much of poison, / Keep one to expel another" (2.2.43–47). As Jonathan Gil Harris has argued, the popularity of the trope of the "poisonous pharmacy" derived from new models of the causation and treatment of contagions, models that proffered a folk homeopathy to combat pathology.[32]

The chain of substitutions Beatrice sets up, emphasizing the likeness of her personal ills, proves sufficient to incorporate her into its logic of moral and aesthetic corruption. An effort at feigning aesthetic approval of De Flores in order to manipulate him ("how lovely now dost thou appear to me" [2.2.138]) becomes, after the loss of her virginity to De Flores and in the light of their temporarily efficient collusion, something like provisional affection and acceptance: "How heartily he serves me! His face loathes one, / But look upon his care, who would not love him?" (5.1.70–71). When Alsemero witnesses evidence of this new affection, its reversal of the discourse of his and Beatrice's own courtship, in which they flirted over talk of her aversion to De Flores, is "enough for deep suspicion" (5.3.3). Alsemero and his companion Jasperino presume that Beatrice's emphatic yet false account (as they take it) of her loathing conceals a further unappealing truth. Their image for this truth?

> ALSEMERO: The black mask
> That so continually was worn upon't
> Condemns the face for ugly ere't be seen—
> Her despite to him, and so seeming-bottomless.
>
> JASPERINO: Touch it home then: 'tis not a shallow probe
> Can search this ulcer soundly, I fear you'll find it
> Full of corruption . . .   (5.3.3–9)

The deceit Beatrice used in maintaining the fiction of her aesthetic aversion to De Flores is emblematically depicted as a dark covering of an ugly, infected face. But this face is no longer De Flores's, though it looks like his and, like his, induces revulsion in Beatrice's husband. Suspicions of her chastity trade on the usual analogies between gender and race, as if Beatrice's former slogan, "blood guiltiness becomes a fouler visage," were reanimated to her own detriment. In this reprise of her former call to murderous arms, "blood" equivocates between meanings of murder and sexual desire, and "becomes" between meanings of "suits" and "transforms into."

When Alsemero immediately thereafter calls her a whore, Beatrice confirms the terminology of his conversation with Jasperino: "What a horrid sound it hath! / It blasts a beauty to deformity; / Upon what face soever that breath falls, / It strikes it ugly" (5.3.31–34).[33]

But rather than calling this transfer of terminology "prophetic," it seems important to contest the humoral epistemology governing the play's relentless associations of immorality with a contagious deformity, and its efforts to validate a dislike of difference by depicting dislike as subtle instinct for self-preservation, the body's "natural" or instinctive revulsion from debased, debasing matter. This epistemology has devastating effects. In *The Changeling*, the self-fulfilling prophecy threatens that to ignore such revulsion borders on self-destruction by contamination. The play represents Beatrice's sexual relationship with De Flores as one such contaminating mixture, which compromises the purity of her blood and beauty and causes her to absorb the deformity and poison associated with his face and blood. "Infected" by her acts of murder and corrupting patriarchal institutions with her lack of chastity, Beatrice mournfully figures her death at De Flores's hands as a purge, a bloodletting purifying her father's blood:

> Oh come not near me, sir, I shall defile you:
> I am that of your blood was taken from you
> For your better health; look no more upon't,
> But cast it to the ground regardlessly:
> Let the common sewer take it from distinction.   (5.3.149–53)

Like Tomazo de Piracquo's phobic intuition of the "contrariety" of De Flores's face and blood, which he imagined as so "deadly venomous" as to poison even the weapon used to attack De Flores, Beatrice's plea presents herself and her blood as physically dangerous to her father. Beatrice's blood now resembles De Flores's, and Beatrice wishes to have it removed from "distinction" (visibility; nobility) to the "common sewer"—even here, the aversion she imagines prompting is expressed through a pun that unites visual and class-based vocabulary.

Yet Beatrice's blood is substantially her father's. This avails her little: Paster notes that Beatrice's identification with her father's waste blood denies Beatrice "any claim to self-ownership while sustaining her full culpability."[34] In overriding filial agency with the material prerogatives of paternal blood, Beatrice's imagery recalls, perhaps, Brabantio's logic that Desdemona's "gross revolt" was a "treason of the blood." As with Desdemona, such treason and the resultant need for bloodletting suggest that all blood is vulnerable, corruptible, and, especially when housed in female frames, potentially unable to maintain its purity. Beatrice's self-figuration as not only wholly part of Vermandero but his waste expresses a desire both to be absorbed into and to erase kinship relations that are no longer possible because of her deformation. In this she echoes Jessica, Shylock, Lorenzo, Launcelot, and Salerio and Solanio—the characters in *The Merchant of Venice* who similarly seek to deny actual kinship relations when they betray an insufficient resemblance or unwanted difference. Alsemero intensifies this wish when he urges Vermandero to dissociate Beatrice from Vermandero's own name: "let it be blotted out, let your heart lose it" (5.3.182). Instead, offering "yet a son's duty living" (5.3.216), Alsemero volunteers himself as filial replacement. Earlier, Beatrice's humoral experiences of repulsion prompted her dismissal and ill-fated use of De Flores; now, the language of humoral regulation facilitates her abasement and figurative erasure as waste.

Both *The Changeling* and *The Merchant of Venice* depict longings for cultural discourses of materialism and objectivity that might confirm the naturalness—and thereby, perhaps, the desirability—of the plays' characters' private aversions. In these plays, the characters exploit a period notion of humoral antipathy in order to blur inclination and instinct. The two plays show that a notion of antipathy inhering in matter itself possesses a seductiveness beyond its pure explanatory force. A materialist theory of affect provides the enviable simplicity of a mechanistic explanation for human complexity and the still more enviable epistemological authority conveyed by

such an explanation. Though expressed here with a literary imprecision, the allure of a system of affect that might be ratified beyond
question nonetheless resonates with later developments in the history of racism (and the history of other systems of prejudice, as we
will shortly see).[35] *The Changeling* and *The Merchant of Venice* show
how closely the affective history of racism may be tied to the history
of the recruitment of biology for the production of racist data and
analyses.

The longing for certitude and validation revealed in these plays
will likely not seem foreign or antiquated to a modern reader. By
contrast, it may be hard for us to recover the vividness with which
humoralism's psychology and metaphysics imbued metaphors of purity, blood resemblance, attraction, contamination, infection, elimi-
nation, and repulsion with materialist and realist implications. Yet,
often expressed in different idioms, most of these humoral metaphors and self-understandings passed along with other early modern
racial discourses into the racialist repertoires of later eras with their
logics unchanged. The racial legacy of English Renaissance culture
would survive, reanimated in narratives of passing and infiltration,
fears and fantasies about miscegenation and conversion, shifts in
borders enclosing or excluding family and citizens, anxiety or ex-
hilaration at the hybridity or impurity of nations, and beliefs about
natural repulsions or affinities between groups and individuals. We
still feel the effects of early modern metaphors of race.

True Experiments

A final, related note on scientific epistemology, though it touches
only indirectly on race, will suggest further shortcomings inherent to *The Changeling*'s desire to site its moral in the objectivity of
truths read from the body and its passions. The play's investment in
the production of such truths is not only aligned with Beatrice's and
De Flores's meditations on their emotions. Instead, the play's most
explicit thematics of the explanatory satisfactions of science is closely
tied to its infidelity plot. For Alsemero himself is something of a

scientist, as Beatrice discovers to her dismay while raiding his closet. Reading matter there includes "The Book of Experiment, / Call'd Secrets in Nature" (4.1.24–25), and the closet is "set round with vials" (4.1.21), potions that serve as litmus tests to answer some of life's more vexing questions, such as "How to know whether a woman be with child or no" and "How to know whether a woman be a maid or not" (4.1.26, 41). The answer to the latter question—of great interest to the "undone" Beatrice—involves ingesting a spoonful of potion "M," after which "'twill make her incontinently gape, then fall into a sudden sneezing, last into a violent laughing; else dull, heavy, and lumpish" (4.1.48–50). The experiment's contrast between heavily and airily symptomatic women recapitulates period distinctions between "fair" virgins and more coarse, sexually active women. In a tone somewhere between lighthearted and threatening, the author of "The Book of Experiment" calls the test "a merry sleight, but true experiment" (4.1.45), corresponding to the virginity test's generic ambiguity, somewhere between comedy and tragedy.

Alsemero's test is designed to settle a burning question with certainty, and certainty is its greatest selling point, as he primly brags to Jasperino: "It has that secret virtue, it ne'er miss'd, sir, / Upon a virgin" (4.2.139–40). That is, a need for a rigorous epistemology generates and permeates the test; this need makes the test, despite the informality of its application, suggestive of the New Philosophical methodological reforms that were brewing. In this connection, the word "experiment" in the title of Alsemero's manual is also noteworthy, for it was to be the epistemological keyword for the Royal Society (twice mentioned in the minutes of the Society's first meeting in 1662, in calls "for the promoting of Physico-Mathematicall Experimentall Learning" and "of experimentall philosophy").[36] It is no accident that epistemological anxieties are mobilized around this particular question. Bawcutt notes the presence of various such tests—though none with quite these specified reactions—and Robert Burton expresses impatience with the lot: "to what end are all those Astrological questions, *an sit virgo, an sit casta, an sit mulier?* and such strange absurd trials . . . by stones, perfumes, to make them piss, and confess I know not what in their sleep; some jealous brain was the first founder of them."[37]

The "jealous brain" dictates the conditions of the virginity problematic and therefore the constraints on an epistemologically satisfactory response. First, as women are suspect given the nature of the question, their testimony cannot produce the certainty that would resolve epistemological anxiety; second, as the doubt itself presupposes male uncertainty, only nonsubjective evidence (such as a potion might provide) can generate proof. Once again, human insecurity produces a need for objective confirmation, preferably materialist and positivist. Juridical questioning of virginity ordinarily involved internal examinations conducted by female "juries" (as in the Frances Howard divorce scandal).[38] Alsemero's potion takes women and their testimony out of the equation, replacing the complexities of legal "proof" with scientific truth.[39] As Marjorie Garber puts it, in the case of Beatrice, "[Alsemero's] faith in her is tied to his faith in science." But, since proof of the potion "M" in turn requires independent, non-"M" confirmation, Garber continues: "and, indeed, [tied] to his own sexual expertise," which underlies his confidence, expressed to Jasperino, in the potion.[40] In other words, there is a certain circularity to the epistemology of certainty, introduced by the subjective observer who must ultimately corroborate that epistemology.

Once Beatrice has seen how the virginity symptoms should look, using her virginal servant Diaphanta as a control, she is able to fabricate them to Alsemero's satisfaction. She has appropriated the power he invests in scientific epistemology through her own "merry sleight," playing alchemical mountebank to his Robert Boyle. Because Beatrice is in fact lying about her chastity and because her plotting leads directly to her own disgrace and death, her finesse of Alsemero's scientific epistemology is neither an enduring victory nor one that will counteract misogynist assumptions about female sexual and moral integrity.[41] Still, Alsemero's science, which presumes its objects—women—will not participate in and distort the results as subjects, fails. Alsemero is doubly duped, for his "sexual expertise" is even inadequate to realize that his sexual partner is not Beatrice, after Beatrice sends Diaphanta to him on their wedding night as a final precaution.[42] Yet Alsemero's test satisfies him because it yields the answer he desires, producing the results he expected in the idiom predicted.[43] His desires that Beatrice be both sexually and scientifically naive, virtually a single desire in this instance, prevent him from correctly intuiting her ability to distort and disrupt the "secret virtue" of his vial. In short, Alsemero's beliefs about women undermine his ability to uncover truths about them. The very nature of his reliance on the epistemology of experiment is self-defeating.

In their history of "the nature and status of experimental practices," Steven Shapin and Simon Schaffer describe the mid-seventeenth-century development of conventions for standards of evidence deemed to be epistemologically sound by the scientific communities that produced them. Experimental "success" was only the first of these conventions: evidence further required that experiments be repeatable, public, and witnessed by colleagues who must be both knowledgeable and honorable.[44] Typically, the credible reports of actual witnesses had to compensate for lack of experimental replication, which was prone to failure, and for lack of public access to experiment, which was limited. Part of what made these new standards vulnerable to critique was their frequent failure; in response, experimentalists sought to consolidate their credibility by seeking out new spheres for scientific endeavor with which to broaden the field of experimental applicability, and they encouraged their culture to bring them new types of problems to solve.[45] Thus, the production of scientific knowledge depended upon changing social conventions for what constituted a scientific problem—as opposed, say, to a theological, economic, or moral one—what constituted a fact, and who was authorized to pronounce on the questions.

The significance of Shapin and Schaffer's analysis for the present argument lies in their careful exposition of the social circumscription of scientific knowledge production. Scientific need for cultural legitimacy cultivated experimental efforts to validate desired, but uncertain, cultural propositions: for example, "moralists could come to the natural historian if they wanted socially usable patterns of natural hierarchy, order, and the due submission of ranks."[46] In the service of making it more refined, rigorous, and authoritative, then, scientific epistemology was likely to be brought to bear on the social questions most in need of proof.[47] In this way, cultural prejudice was all too easily ratified by and structured into scientific fact and experiment. As Stephen Jay Gould shows at length in his work on the reification, ranking, and racialization of intelligence over centuries of testing, in questions of racial science, a priori prejudice leads without exception to the production of invidious problems to solve and predetermined results.[48]

Experimental confirmation of bias is an industry whose roots are revealed in part, I believe, in *The Changeling*. Burton makes the point himself with his jab at the "jealous brain" who was the "first founder" of virginity tests: what sorts of questions is that brain likely to ask? What answers will be convincing? The mutually constitutive analogies between race and gender that are pervasive during the Renaissance express both anxiety about and attraction to a natural order of differences. These emotions suffice to make prejudicial statements "of fact" about such differences both likely and persuasive, the more so when they appear to be confirmed by objective, empirical evidence. As Beatrice says while waiting for Diaphanta's virginity symptoms to manifest, "now if the experiment be true, 'twill praise itself" (4.1.105). Here Beatrice confuses the subjective validation of witnesses with the experiment's own voice. Our task is to separate those voices and to question the motives behind the praise, in the performances of the scientist and of the drama, whose insights and demonstrations—as much or more than those of the Royal Society—were witnessed by spectators, replicable, public, and persuasive.

Coda

❧❧

We have just seen the eagerness with which characters in *The Changeling* greet supposed objective confirmation of and material explanation for their personal prejudices. Such "conflation of natural with the social kinds"—a belief or will that purely human distinctions originate in nature—is identified by David Theo Goldberg as the key component of racialism. Both this conflation and the racialism it enables were therefore fully available to the culture of Shakespeare, Marlowe, Webster, and Middleton and Rowley.[1] In plays that vary plots of interracial desire, conversion, and disguise, these authors employ conflation of the natural and social to produce the substitutions and murky inferences that have drawn my attention throughout this book as characteristic Renaissance racial forms. By means of such conflation, Desdemona's adultery can be represented as physical darkening by Iago and Othello; familial discontent can be fantasized as a literal cancellation of lineal relationships (for example, Brabantio and Desdemona; Shylock and Jessica; Beatrice and Vermandero); and acts of cultural borrowing, as from Italians, can habituate an entire nation to imagining itself as members of a different nation, ethnicity, or race. Still more generally, the conflation of social and natural can, as we have seen, closely align the logics of gender and race or persuasively freight lineal relations themselves (with or among Moors, Jews, Italians, and gentility) with both privileged and derogatory symbolic associations.

Although these representations rely on fallacious beliefs about human groups, not all of their conflation of natural with social kinds is ethically suspect. In the simplest sense, such conflation is productive—of racism and antagonism, without doubt, but also of affection, empathy, and central individual and cultural fantasies, including those that feature appealing narratives of hybridity, adoption, and miscegenation. As the plays dramatize, and never more clearly than in the Beatrice–De Flores relationship in *The Changeling*, intense antagonism itself does not preclude desire and, more importantly, need not preclude eventual affection. Beliefs about human difference, even if inaccurate, also permeate and help structure fundamental human relationships and institutions: as *Othello* reveals, for this culture, one potent location of both xenophilia and xenophobia is marriage. Likewise, contradictory English beliefs about Italians lead to multiple forms of imitation and identification, enabling an extraordinary flowering of new ways to think, feel, and tell stories.

These narratives are at the heart of early modern England's understanding and experience of race and reveal to us the ways in which race exerted shaping pressure on other early modern categories of personal and corporate experience, such as gender, sexuality, nation, religion, and class. Yet even if, as I hope, the analyses in this book provide a clear account of how racial identities were produced and represented, they do not demonstrate racial identities as static, rule based, or governed by scientific fact. To the contrary, in early modern drama, beliefs about race are conveyed and racial identities depicted with a literary imprecision. These depictions express feelings and concerns about race that are by turns curious and anxious, punitive and expansive, playful and moralizing, and they do not aspire to the rigor of a considered argument or the clear agenda of a treatise. They are used in order to produce and resolve not only cultural tensions but dramatic ones. Are the conclusions we draw from this material therefore inconsequent, or further evidence that race was itself experienced at this time so inconsistently as to be inconsequent for us?

I would argue instead that the conflation of natural and social kinds in our own culture has grown so extreme as to blind us to the centrality of the imprecision, illogic, and inconsistency in our own views and narratives about race. In recovering the genealogy of race, we have unwisely given modern science pride of place as the origin and engine of racism. Work indeed remains to be done charting the earliest uses of science to satisfy cultural desires for (spurious) objective classification and evaluation of human groups.[2] But perhaps even more work remains in identifying—and taking seriously—the ways in which the early modern English labored both in and through the theater to generate and police boundaries between families and strangers, men and women, English and foreigners, natural and social kinds, while all along they blurred and crossed the boundaries themselves. This work will truly allow us to reassess the resonances of Renaissance racial logics with our own.

Notes

✧

Introduction

1. Salvini, *Leaves from the Autobiography of Tommaso Salvini*, 156. No translator is named in this edition or in the 1971 reprint by Benjamin Blom. Further citations are given parenthetically in the text.

2. See Honigmann's introduction to *Othello*, 92, 94.

3. The description is Furness's. See his New Variorum *Othello*, 250–51.

4. For convenience, at this point, I am assimilating Salvini's remarks about blood and climate into the categories of race and nation; all these categories will be given more careful and extended treatment.

5. Audience members might however follow along with dual-language playbooks, published in New York and London during Salvini's first tour (with the all-Italian cast) and reissued for the later tour with only Othello's lines in Italian. See Salvini, *Leaves*, 197; *Othello: A Tragedy in Five Acts;* and *Otello: Tragedia in Cinque Atti . . . come Rappresentata dal Signor Salvini.* I assume the translator (not named) is Giulio Carcano, whom Salvini preferred. Salvini, *Leaves*, 74, 92.

6. Fanny Kemble, "Salvini's Othello," *Temple Bar* 71 (July 1884): 376, cited in Rosenberg, *The Masks of Othello*, 102. Rosenberg provides an overview and excerpts of contemporary criticism of Salvini.

7. In addition to such claims, Salvini also details practices of extensive research and empirical modeling for his portrayal. It is noteworthy that in the context of audience debate about his performance, he prefers to heighten the spectacle of his Italianness, attributing his suitability for the role to origin rather than training. See *Leaves*, 80–81, 139–40.

8. James, "Tommaso Salvini," in James, *The Scenic Art*, 170. Originally published in the *Atlantic Monthly*, March 1883.

9. Ibid., 173–74, and James, "A Study of Salvini," in *The Scenic Art*, 189. Originally published anonymously in *Pall Mall Gazette*, March 27, 1884.

10. James, "Tommaso Salvini," 172.

11. Rosenberg provides numerous examples of critics who felt Salvini had overstepped in precisely this way, providing merely "lurid flashes of ferocity" (according to the review in the *Galaxy*). See Rosenberg, *The Masks of Othello*, 102–3, 106, 111–14. See also Towse, *Sixty Years of the Theatre*, 157–64.

12. James, "Tommaso Salvini," 175.

13. James, "A Study of Salvini," 188.

14. Ibid., 173. James also notes that Othello possesses "as little as possible of that intellectual iridescence which . . . is the sign of Shakespeare's hand, . . . [which] puts the character much more within Salvini's grasp than the study of Hamlet" (189).

15. Towse, *Sixty Years*, 160. Victorian audiences preferred a less confrontational approach to murder. Yet attitudes have not completely changed: writing of the standards of the age without apparent irony, E. A. J. Honigmann avers that "the smothering of Desdemona, if violence was emphasized, filled many . . . with indignation." See his introduction to *Othello*, 92.

16. The quarto and Folio titles are both *The Tragedy of Othello, the Moor of Venice*. We might imagine James's fantasy of Salvini alone amid the "Hottentots" as rounding out the catalog of mise-en-scènes of *Othello*.

17. For a brief exposition of the relevant associations, see Appiah, "Race," 276, 284–87.

18. Shakespeare, *Othello*, Arden edition, 3rd ser., 1.3.347. All quotations from *Othello* will hereafter be cited parenthetically in the text.

19. In the past, objections to that work likewise were both propelled and grounded by the perception of the "obviousness" of race's existence. See, for instance, Fromm, "The Hegemonic Form of Othering."

20. Race and racism are not, of course, the same—though the fallacies necessary for sustaining racialism (belief in different races and the evidence used to support this belief) often have their genealogy in racist motivation or instinct. In any case, each is often used to define the other.

21. Representative, canonical versions of the claim about biology and phenotype may be found in Todorov, "'Race,' Writing, and Culture," 370; and Gates, "Talkin' That Talk," 404: "It is the penchant to *generalize* based upon essences perceived as *biological* which defines 'racism'" (emphasis his).

In addition to those that will be discussed later, canonical versions of the periodization claim may be found in Hendricks and Parker's introduction to their *Women, "Race," and Writing in the Early Modern Period,* 2; and Hannaford, *Race.*

22. Within racialist systems, other fallacies coexist with fallacies of group membership—the systems are generally littered with them. However, group-based fallacies remain central and are insufficiently remarked.

23. This list includes discourses that imply the existence of discrete races, e.g., by differentiating groups. I discuss varying criteria of racial classification later in the Introduction.

24. Appiah is particularly cogent on this point. See his excellent "Racisms" and "The Uncompleted Argument," which help structure my thinking here.

25. Human evolution and situations of occasional reproductive isolation mean, of course, that people have changed slowly in response to their environment, and that individuals within certain populations will have likelihoods of possessing given phenotypes, abilities, or liabilities (such as the likelihood of manifesting particular diseases) different from the human race in aggregate. It is vital, however, to emphasize that these populations are subgroups and are not the same as the larger groups of individuals assigned membership in any particular social race in any particular time and place; that because of variable ancestry and genetic variability, not everyone in a given population will possess those phenotypes, abilities, or liabilities; that others outside of the population may well also possess them; and that determination of the membership of these populations is subject to the same logical difficulties as with other human groups. A special issue of *Nature Genetics* devoted to the existence of race provides representative clarification and elaboration of this point generally accessible to a lay reader. See *Nature Genetics* 36, no. 11S (2004): S1–S58. Richard Lewontin's classic work on the subject, now partly superseded by new results in genomics, is also useful. See Lewontin, "The Apportionment of Human Diversity," and *Not in Our Genes.*

26. See Werner Sollors's discussion of such strategies in "Ethnicity," and Fredrik Barth's introduction to *Ethnic Groups and Boundaries,* ed. Barth, 9–38, on which Sollors's remarks are partially based.

27. For exemplary discussion of the usual motives, methods, results, and fallacies of such orderings, see Gould, *The Mismeasure of Man;* and

Stepan, "Race and Gender" and *The Idea of Race in Science.* Analogous discussion of hierarchical gender orderings may be found in Fausto-Sterling, *Myths of Gender.*

28. As Gail Kern Paster has forcefully reminded us, the affect-substances involved in Renaissance humors were seen as fully materialist— melancholy was not an emotion in the casual modern sense but an actual fluid. However, humors explained behavior, predilections, capabilities, and the like, and therefore still connect material and immaterial human attributes. See Paster, *Humoring the Body,* esp. 1–9.

29. For the debate between Las Casas and Sepúlveda, see Hanke, *All Mankind Is One.* For Thomas Browne's theory that black skin color was transmitted through semen and his treatment of the thesis that blackness was caused by the sun, see his *Pseudodoxia Epidemica* in Browne, *Works,* 3: 231–55. Browne and the much-quoted George Best (who also explained blackness through semen) are excerpted in Walvin, *The Black Presence,* 37–47. For important critical discussions, see Boose, "'The Getting of a Lawful Race,'" 42–43; and Floyd-Wilson, *English Ethnicity,* 5–10, 79–83.

30. Barthelemy, *Black Face, Maligned Race,* 17.

31. Shapiro, *Shakespeare and the Jews.*

32. The Renaissance term that very roughly translates into our "class."

33. Floyd-Wilson, *English Ethnicity,* esp. 1–11, 48–66.

34. Shakespeare, *The Winter's Tale,* 5.1.155ff.

35. The separation was most famously argued by G. K. Hunter. See his *Dramatic Identities and Cultural Tradition,* 3–30, 60–102. See also Shapiro's discussion and critique of Hunter's sources and legacy, *Shakespeare and the Jews,* 83–88.

36. See, for instance, Barthelemy, *Black Face, Maligned Race;* Jones, *Othello's Countrymen;* Tokson, *The Popular Image of the Black Man in English Drama, 1550–1688;* Cowhig, "Blacks in English Renaissance Drama and the Role of Shakespeare's *Othello*"; D'Amico, *The Moor in English Renaissance Drama;* and Shapiro, *Shakespeare and the Jews.*

37. Compare Kujoory's more recent annotated critical bibliography, *Shakespeare and Minorities,* which is divided into separate chapters on "Blacks," "Jews," "Homosexuals," etc. Any comparative or synthetic work is then filed under "Others."

38. A typical formulation conveys the equivocations involved: "tempered by some virtue, they [good black female characters] nonetheless re-

main closer to the more notorious and more common type than distant from it," *Black Face, Maligned Race,* 136. See also x, 17, 47–48, 144–45.

39. Erickson, "The Moment of Race in Renaissance Studies," 33. Erickson rightly notes that Loomba's *Gender, Race, Renaissance Drama* anticipates developments in the field made by Hall and others; he also describes the complex relation of these developments to earlier feminist work (33–35).

40. The literature is far too vast to cite exhaustively, but Floyd-Wilson's *English Ethnicity* merits particular notice.

41. Hall, *Things of Darkness,* 6–7. A similar view is argued by Erickson, "The Moment of Race," 30.

42. *Things of Darkness,* 7.

43. This British usage is in flux. See note 68.

44. See Blackburn, *The Making of New World Slavery,* 8, 49–54, 79-82, 234–71; Matar, *Turks, Moors, and Englishmen in the Age of Discovery;* Colley, *Captives: Britain, Empire, and the World;* and Davis, *Christian Slaves, Muslim Masters.* See also Vitkus's collection of English captivity narratives, *Piracy, Slavery, and Redemption.*

45. Iyengar's fascinating account also details the fitful attempts of English judges to ban slavery in England before the mid-eighteenth century. See Iyengar, *Shades of Difference,* 200–219.

46. Floyd-Wilson, *English Ethnicity,* 5–19.

47. See Barbour, *Before Orientalism,* 2. I am indebted to the fine postcolonial criticism that has made analogous arguments, such as Vitkus's analysis of anachronistic critical accounts of colonialism in *Turning Turk,* 1–24, esp. 3–8. Bartels voices similar concerns in "*Othello* and Africa." Goldberg outlines the ideological power of such anachronism in "The History That Will Be."

48. Vitkus, *Turning Turk,* 22.

49. Ferguson, "Juggling the Categories of Race, Class, and Gender," 211.

50. Outlaw reaches a similar conclusion, noting that the referents of "race" and the divisions of human beings into "races" have changed significantly over time, so that a historical review of the shifts "should do much to dislodge the concept from its place as provider of access to a self-evident, obvious, even ontologically *given* characteristic of humankind." See his "Towards a Critical Theory of 'Race,' " 61. Gilroy argues for the same result in *Against Race.*

51. See Fields's important discussion, for instance, of the widely varying beliefs and programs comprehended by the slogan "White Supremacy" and of varying methods of classifying people as "black" in twentieth-century America, some dependent on region. "Ideology and Race in American History," 146, 155–57.

52. Schiesari, "The Face of Domestication," 57. Further citations of Schiesari will appear parenthetically in the text.

53. The notable exception is Loomba's *Shakespeare, Race, and Colonialism,* the best general treatment of race and Shakespeare. See esp. 2, 37–39.

54. See *English Ethnicity,* 106, 7, emphasis hers. See also 5, 12, 54, 106–8, 142, 157.

55. Boose, "The Getting of a Lawful Race," 35–54. Further citations of Boose will appear parenthetically in the text.

56. Note that Boose attributes cognitive agency to the century as a whole, rather than specifying a particular group or theory that makes the presumption she finds characteristic of racial discourse.

57. Shakespeare, *The Merchant of Venice,* 1.2 passim. All further citations of this play will appear parenthetically in the text.

58. See, for instance, Loomba, who, in a review essay on critical accounts of race in the early modern period, asserts that "over the last two centuries, skin colour has dominated racist ideologies" and, in her general history of race in the Renaissance, writes that "four centuries [after Shakespeare], skin colour and race have become virtually synonymous." See Loomba, "'Delicious Traffick,'" 204, and *Shakespeare, Race, and Colonialism,* 35. See also Iyengar, who accords skin color central status in her account of (post-Renaissance) racialism, which she defines in familiar terms as "a hierarchical ordering of human beings that depends upon skin color and labor, especially slavery"—a well-motivated definition that is nonetheless fairly exclusive (*Shades of Difference,* 13). Floyd-Wilson argues persuasively by contrast that until the seventeenth century, dark skin color, like other features identified with Southern geohumoralism, was seen as natural and a sign of temperance; Roxann Wheeler locates the origin of identification of race and skin color in the eighteenth century. See *English Ethnicity,* 5; Wheeler, *The Complexion of Race,* 2.

59. Especially with regard to groups such as the Irish, Italians, and Jews—groups Werner Sollors has pointed out have largely moved from being regarded as races, to being perceived as ethnicities (Sollors, "Ethnicity,"

289). This change represents an identity that may seem less intense or "real" (289) and more situational (Banton, *Racial Theories,* 159–60) than a racial identity. The fact that there is little American cultural memory of the racialization of the Irish and Italians indicates the speed with which new organizations of racial identity can come to seem natural and therefore even a long-standing part of the cultural tradition. All these groups, it need hardly be said, generate substantial racial discourse during the Renaissance (and up through the early twentieth century). For an account of the shifts in American Jewish racial identity during the twentieth century, see Sacks, "How Did Jews Become White Folks?" For the analogous impact of dizzying changes in categories of race and ethnicity appearing in the U.S. census, see Goldberg, *The Racial State,* 188–90. For the ascendance of ethnicity theories over race-based ones in twentieth-century sociology, see Omi and Winant, *Racial Formation in the United States,* 14–23. But for difficulties in distinguishing between ethnicity theory and race theory, see Banton, *The Idea of Race,* 8.

60. Hall, *Things of Darkness,* 255.

61. Ibid., 6.

62. I don't mean that science does not register and participate in social meaning but rather that scientific technique, on its own, does not motivate social hierarchies or behavior.

63. Even in articles contesting received notions of the history or "science" of race, the routinized association of racial classification with skin color is striking. For some examples, see note 58 above. Clearly, skin color distinctions have been hugely significant in many racial systems, though not all, and not for every racial classification within a system. One need only think of the racial tragedies of the twentieth century, from Nazi race theory and genocide to the genocide in Rwanda, to be reminded that the most extreme forms of racism do not require differences in skin color. Nonetheless, the virtual inability to dissociate racial taxonomy from skin color indicates a theoretical inflexibility with attendant repercussions of oversimplification and omission. For modern exceptions to racial classifications based on skin color, see Harris, "Race," 263–64; and Wagley's classic "On the Concept of Social Race in the Americas."

64. See Appiah's discussion of nineteenth-century racialism in "Race," esp. 276. See also Banton, *Racial Theories,* 5–7 and 44–80, and Banton and Harwood, *The Race Concept,* 26–35.

65. See Wagley, "On the Concept of Social Race," 537–43.

66. Consider, for instance, Martin Orkin's decision to use "racism" and "color prejudice" interchangeably in his discussion of racism in *Othello*. Like Boose, Orkin assumes that the latter term possesses more descriptive force for the Renaissance but that, in modern terms, the two are "not profitably to be distinguished." See Orkin, "Othello and the 'Plain Face' of Racism," 168n9.

67. Harris, "Race," 264. For an interesting account of racial misclassification made by police officers based on visual (i.e., phenotype) observations, in which misclassification of the profiles ranged from 34 to 70 percent, see Lowe, Urquhart, Foreman, and Evett, "Inferring Ethnic Origin by Means of an STR Profile."

68. All of which have happened in England or the United States. For Adam Gurowski's nineteenth-century trip to America, during which he "took every light-colored mulatto for a Jew," see Gilman, *The Jew's Body*, 174. For British reference to Arabs and South Asians as "blacks," see, among others, Lawrence, "Just Plain Common Sense," 60–61; and Lee, Mountain, and Koenig, "The Meanings of 'Race' in the New Genomics."

69. Harris, "Race," 263; also cited in Ferguson, "Juggling," 343n7, 12.

70. Ibid., 264.

71. Data were sought to fit preexisting hypotheses and altered or discarded as irrelevant when they did not; theories were argued circularly (ambiguous conclusions might be firmed by the very hypotheses supposedly being tested); and rankings were preserved at the cost of frequent contradictory interpretations of data (a given measurement might be said to indicate proof of environmental disadvantages for white or "Nordic" groups, but proof of inherited and unalterable defects in nonwhite groups). See Gould, *The Mismeasure of Man*.

72. Barth, "Introduction," *Ethnic Groups and Boundaries*, 9–38.

73. Ibid., 9, 10. Barth is thus especially interested in cultural narratives of conversion and assimilation that "cancel" a prior ethnic identification (which would have been perceived as an unalterable attribute until the transfer of identities). Such narratives will be taken up in chapter 2, but I wish to emphasize here that even where an individual's ethnic identity remains stable, Barth's theory shows that that stability depends less on "intrinsic" qualities of ethnic identification than on showy, possibly ad hoc contrasts with the identities of others.

74. Ibid., 15.

75. Similarly, Vitkus notes the analytic utility and interest of multi-valent dramatic representations: "they partake of both the xenophobic and the xenophilic tendencies in English culture" (*Turning Turk*, 22); Barbour also tracks the "tenacious dialogue" between "xenophobic and xenophilous impulses" in England (*Before Orientalism*, 102).

1. Desdemona's Blackness

1. Rymer dismisses the exchange as "a long rabble of Jack-pudden farce . . . trash below the patience of any countrey kitchin-maid." Rymer, *A Short View of Tragedy*, 110–11.

2. *Othello*, Arden edition, 2nd ser., ed. M. R. Ridley, 54. For E. A. J. Honigmann, the exchange shows that Desdemona "does not know when to stop." See *Othello*, Arden edition, 3rd ser., 43. All further citation of *Othello* will be to the Honigmann Arden edition.

3. Michael Neill notes that the play is "unique" in its "preoccupation with offstage action"—perhaps partly blurring critical obsessiveness (with the consummation of the marriage) with the play's own concerns. See Neill, "'Unproper Beds': Race, Adultery, and the Hideous in *Othello*," in his *Putting History to the Question*, 235–68, 250.

4. Audience and reader sympathy and indignation is slow to attract to Emilia despite her murder because she aids Iago in stealing the hand-kerchief, because she undermines the blanket value of marital chastity when she puts forth a claim for the right of abused wives to other men's atten-tions, and because she is not a gentlewoman (for some audience members, her theft and silence on the subject of Desdemona's abuse by Iago may be symptomatic of her position as servant). Compare Honigmann's bizarre musing on Emilia's death provoking less audience reaction—"perhaps be-cause less attractive women are less important?"—that suppresses the ways in which Emilia violates norms of femininity and class status (e.g., pre-eminent devotion to one's mistress) (Honigmann, introduction to *Othello*, 92). In an invidious fashion, Emilia is imagined to be at least partly to blame for her own murder. Just so, if Desdemona were imagined to be sleeping with Cassio, an audience presumably would be less upset at her murder. In other words, the intense frustration and pity that the tragedy inspires in the audience relies chiefly on Othello having been misled, that

is, on Desdemona's innocence of infidelity, not on the fact of his murder of his wife. Othello makes this point himself when he distinguishes "murder" from "sacrifice" (5.2.65), the distinction turning on Desdemona's guilt, which, to his understanding, makes him less culpable.

5. Ania Loomba observes that nearly all the racist imagery that accumulates around Othello in these early moments of the play is linked to descriptions of Desdemona's whiteness and of Othello's involvement with her. Loomba, *Gender, Race, Renaissance Drama*, 49. Loomba contrasts these descriptions of Othello with the treatment of Aaron in *Titus Andronicus*.

6. Neill, "Changing Places in *Othello*," in his *Putting History to the Question*, 207–36, 219.

7. Loomba, *Shakespeare, Race, and Colonialism*, 51. Loomba is referring to ideas about Africans appearing in early modern travel writing and anthropology. Mary Floyd-Wilson has recently argued that early modern geohumoral beliefs in fact emphasized the chaste temperament of Africans, and that exceptions to the geohumoral system have been read as normative by modern critics. Floyd-Wilson, *English Ethnicity*, 34, 44–47. Such exceptions may still be relevant to the characterization of specific Africans and Moors, such as Othello, who is described by Roderigo as "lascivious" (1.1.124)—perhaps shockingly so.

8. Here, for instance, in their sexual roles and color differences. Symmetrically invoked by Iago, the colors are elsewhere sharply distinguished. Jyotsna Singh has raised concerns that critics making overly simplistic links between oppression based on gender and on race do not acknowledge the specific history of racism—in effect sacrificing race to gender. See Singh, "Othello's Identity, Postcolonial Theory, and Contemporary African Rewritings of *Othello*," esp. 290–93. What I wish to point to here are the specific ways in which *Othello* reveals that on the early modern stage gender itself is racialized, and racial experience is both strongly gendered and precipitated out of sexual and gender discourse. I believe this is the best way *not* to elide racism's specific history.

9. Numerous critics helpfully identify the ways in which Othello's representation is linked to contemporary beliefs about Turks, Moors, and Muslims as well as Africans. See especially Loomba, *Shakespeare, Race, and Colonialism*, 91–97, 102–7; and Vitkus, *Turning Turk*, 77–106. Nonetheless, at the play's start, Othello is identified with Venetian interests and presented as Venice's only defense against the Ottoman military threat.

10. But note the Duke's diplomatic claim to Brabantio not to have noticed him (1.3.50).

11. Michael Neill traces a still less appealing twentieth-century critical tradition marking a similar trajectory for Othello, in which the play is read "as the study of an assimilated savage who relapses into primitivism under stress." Neill, "'Unproper Beds,'" 247.

12. Roderigo's familiarity is inappropriate in the strictly hierarchized Renaissance social order, whether Venetian or Jacobean.

13. The *OED* indicates American coinage in 1864. (The word, invented by Confederate spies posing in the North as Yankee advocates of a miscegenistic Union, replaced the previous term, "amalgamation," which dates most likely from the beginning of the nineteenth century.) For Hall's defense of the anachronistic term, see Hall, "Guess Who's Coming to Dinner?" 106n1.

14. I imagine similar problems obtain in the present, since "miscegenation" is imprecise or metaphorical at best, referring to *individuals* who marry (or, Webster adds, cohabit) as a unit, a mixture—however, without implying procreation (but see *OED* "miscegenated"). The word was created to express fantasies of interracial sexual acts and the "mixing" of "bloods" or racial temperament such acts might entail, but its typical application sidesteps sexual acts to dwell instead on legal or illegal unions. In addition, there is some disagreement, reflecting the whiteness-obsessed history of the word's use, over whether miscegenation can take place when neither of the couple is white: compare the *OED* and Webster definitions.

15. Fiedler, *The Stranger in Shakespeare*, 172. The virtues of Fiedler's textured, often breathtaking readings are compromised by his (prolix) reluctance to see race as a concern for Shakespeare, even as his study is motivated by Shakespeare's representation of Othello's alienation.

16. Newman, *Fashioning Femininity*, 74, 75.

17. See ibid., 78–88. For similar links between race, gender, monstrosity, and the spectacular, see Parker, "Fantasies of 'Race' and 'Gender.'" For doubts about the currency of Renaissance views of African hypersexuality, see Floyd-Wilson, *English Ethnicity*, 34, 44–47.

18. Florizel is attempting to cover up Perdita's (as he believes) humble origins: here race stands in for class difference (and whatever class difference would be taken to imply visually, for instance, the darkening of skin

from tanning). See also my discussion of color and gender difference later in this chapter.

19. See Barthelemy, *Black Face, Maligned Race;* Cowhig, "Blacks in English Renaissance Drama"; D'Amico, *The Moor in English Renaissance Drama;* and Jones, *Othello's Countrymen.*

20. Rymer, *A Short View of Tragedy,* 89; also cited by Newman, *Fashioning Femininity,* 86.

21. For discussion of this tradition, see Barthelemy, *Black Face, Maligned Race,* 2–6; Hunter, *Dramatic Identities,* 35–39; and Jones, *The Elizabethan Idea of Africa,* 48.

22. As Hunter famously does.

23. See Eve Sedgwick's discussion of cuckoldry ("by definition a sexual act, performed on a man, by another man") that helps structure my sense of Iago's threat against Brabantio in her *Between Men,* 49–66, esp. 49–55.

24. Othello had once been enslaved, according to his seductively deployed autobiography (1.3.139), a point perhaps suggesting that, for Shakespeare and his audience, the conversion of African people to chattel existed as a perennial possibility—though Brabantio and Iago may also be thinking of Othello's past in particular in making this leap. It is significant that Othello, awash in self-chastisement for his role in the tragedy when it is revealed, adopts Brabantio's terminology: "O cursed, cursed slave!" (5.2.274). But for problems with assuming the relevance here of race-based slavery, see my Introduction.

25. Jonathan Goldberg discusses the similar agreement between Caliban and Prospero that Caliban's rape of Miranda would have "peopled" the island "with Calibans" (*The Tempest,* 1.2.353–54), connecting the logic to a reading of race as "unremovable taint." See Goldberg, "The Print of Goodness," 247.

26. The Folio speech prefixes for Edmond often baldly make this equation in referring to the character as, simply, "Bastard." See also the discussion between Kent and Gloucester that opens the play.

27. Compare Marvin Harris's observation that the child of parents of different races is generally identified with "the racial group of the lower-ranking parent." Harris, "Race," 264.

28. Hall, *Things of Darkness,* 9.

29. Because the chromatic predicates of racial language (white/black/etc.) are already highly metonymic, it is not possible for women to be de-

scribed with "literal" color imagery. Cf. Gates's analysis of race as a "trope," not an "objective term of classification," in "Writing 'Race' and the Difference It Makes," 5.

30. See Boose, "'The Getting of a Lawful Race.'"

31. Jonathan Crewe suggests that such a mystification occurs when we habitually "genteelly speak of Shakespeare's Dark Lady sonnets" instead of "bring[ing] ourselves to call them the Black Woman sonnets." See his *Trials of Authorship*, 120. The point is not to literalize such a locution according to our modern racial constructions but to reanimate the ambiguities and disruptions such an anti-Petrarchan ideal occasioned for the Shakespearean reader in the domains of skin tone, skin color, humoral theory, genealogical theory, and codes of conduct—to engage the word "black" rather than eliding it in euphemism.

32. See Orgel, *Impersonations*. This perspective highlights *Othello*'s structural and thematic affinities with comedy; see, for instance, Snyder, *The Comic Matrix of Shakespeare's Tragedies*.

33. Orgel, *Impersonations*, 13.

34. In Gayle Rubin's familiar words. See Rubin, "The Traffic in Women."

35. In fact, the convention of men and women being distinguishable by differential color when juxtaposed persists today, as images of male-female embraces on movie posters and the covers of romance novels illustrate.

36. For metatheatrical implications of the practice for concepts of nation, race, and gender, see chapter 3 and Callaghan, *Shakespeare without Women*, 80–86.

37. See *Two Gentlemen* (4.4.147–54). Compare Pisanio's counsel that Innogen allow herself to tan in order to disguise herself as a boy in *Cymbeline* (3.4.159–63). Similar beliefs about the differential darkness of those of lower degree underlie Celia's strategy of "smirch[ing]" her face "with a kind of umber" to pass as an unremarkable, "mean" peasant in *As You Like It* (1.3.105–6). The relevance of such darkening to Renaissance dramatic narratives of female cross-dressing bears investigation.

38. For a detailed examination of the racially coded, coextensive blushes of virtue and desire, see Crewe, "Out of the Matrix," esp. 17–21.

39. Compare Michael Neill's argument that the seventeenth century saw adultery as literally adulteration, marriage made unnatural (Neill, "'Unproper Beds,'" 264). Here, I would argue, marriage itself is seen as partly unnatural (when nature is conceived as preferring to match like

substances). My reading extends arguments about the play's systemic fears or indictments of marriage and heterosexual desire to be found, for instance, in Edward Snow's Freudian analysis, "Sexual Anxiety and the Male Order of Things in *Othello*" and Stephen Greenblatt's account of how contemporary Christian doctrine leads to "Othello's buried perception of his own sexual relations with Desdemona as adulterous," in *Renaissance Self-Fashioning*, 232–54, 233. For the period's attraction to homonormativity (and its consequent valuation of same-sex friendship over marriage), see Shannon, *Sovereign Amity*, esp. 54–68.

40. I follow Honigmann in preserving the second quarto's "Her" as opposed to the Folio's "My" in line 389, so that Othello is talking about Desdemona and not himself. However, the Folio reading also contrasts virginal female whiteness with a shamed darkness (emphasizing the masculine color difference); the contrasting sexual shame in that case is cuckoldry.

41. Compare the play's ironic name for the camp follower, Bianca, mocked for her erotic agency in pursuing Cassio. Bianca's "white" is intended as its own parody through the same associations that punish Desdemona. Joyce Green MacDonald argues that the play's discourse of "sexualized contempt" for Bianca is used primarily to attempt to preserve canons of appropriate female behavior that Desdemona's choices have blurred (and therefore to redeem Desdemona); but, like me, she sees "a broadly racialized connection" between the two characters. See MacDonald, "Black Ram, White Ewe," 195, 196.

42. In an argument about the patriarchal logics of place, Lena Cowen Orlin similarly connects Desdemona's agency (particularly in leaving the home) to Brabantio's disavowal of her compromised "perfection." See "Desdemona's Disposition," 176.

43. One core narrative, it goes without saying, of Shakespeare's *Sonnets*.

44. A myth of intense significance in later racist theories as well, as noted by Etienne Balibar: "Most racist philosophies present themselves as inversions of the theme of progress, in terms of decadence, degeneration, degradation of race, culture, identity, and national integrity" (trans. Michael Edwards). See Balibar, "Racisme et nationalisme," 79. In *Othello*, degeneration operates independently of Darwinist theory, with which most myths of racial degeneration of the last two centuries are associated. For other reflections on literary uses of the degeneration trope, see Coetzee,

"Blood, Taint, Flaw, Degeneration: The Novels of Sarah Gertrude Millin," in his *White Writing*, 136–62.

45. Compare his simultaneously self-congratulatory and self-exculpatory (since he seems to describe a general dynamic in society) remarks later: "My medicine, work! / . . . And many worthy and chaste dames, even thus, /All guiltless, meet reproach" (4.1.45–47).

46. For the "fairness" of virtue, see the Duke's bland attempt to comfort Brabantio: "If virtue no delighted beauty lack, / Your son-in-law is far more fair than black" (1.3.290–91).

47. Compare also Othello's further equation of surface darkening and misogynist labeling: "was this fair paper, this most goodly book / Made to write 'whore' upon?" (4.2.72–73).

48. Gail Kern Paster reminds us that such spiritual transformations were seen as actually material and not metaphorical. She traces similar imagery of darkening and thickening of Othello's "collied" (blackened) "judgment" (2.3.202) and "puddled" "spirit" (3.4.144). Paster is insistent that these transformations, potentially experienced by anyone, are not specific to Othello's racialization; I would argue that in this context their racializing is the more potent for its materiality. See Paster, *Humoring the Body*, 60–76.

49. See also 3.3.407; 5.2.310.

50. For reflections on the early modern analogy between household and state, and the accompanying implications for and distortions of the operations of power in both, see Jordan, "The Household and the State," and Amussen, "Gender, Family, and the Social Order, 1560–1725."

51. Foucault, *The History of Sexuality*, 147.

52. His conclusion is of course arbitrary: Brabantio's gender ideology could be used, instead, to argue that Desdemona should only marry a woman (indeed, in its wholesale indictment of contact with men, it comes within a hair's breadth of that solution) or a sibling; depending on which set of values is felt most at risk, gender ideology can serve the interests of class hierarchy using precisely the same logic.

53. Coetzee, "Blood, Taint, Flaw, Degeneration," 140. Othello's blood is cited as overwhelming his judgment at 2.3.201–3 and 4.1.275–76.

54. Emilia's imagery adds force to the adulterous threat in Iago's claim to Othello that he saw Cassio "wipe his beard" with the missing handkerchief (3.3.442).

55. Compare his desire to consume Cassio in revenge: "had all his hairs been lives / My great revenge had stomach for them all" (5.2.73–74).

56. The transition is prefigured at 5.2.4–5.

57. I am indebted to Fiedler's account of Iago's racial vilification at the play's close, which he sees as pointing to Iago's "archetypal" Judaism. However, I do not agree with Fiedler that this identification essentially reverses or absorbs the pernicious energies previously associated with Othello, showing the characters' "true colors" at the play's end, since Othello's status, as I have argued, is never reversed but reinforced, even if Iago is ultimately also seen as a "slave." See Fiedler, *The Stranger in Shakespeare*, 191–95.

2. Exemplary Jews and the Logic of Gentility

1. The first volume in the Casebook Series devoted to criticism of what it calls Shakespeare's "Jewish" play provides a useful anthology of critical attitudes toward Shylock from the eighteenth century through the mid-twentieth, while the New Casebooks Series sequel self-consciously moves beyond such character criticism "divided fairly evenly between those who see [Shylock] as a tragic figure and those who see him as a monster." See Wilders, ed., *Shakespeare: The Merchant of Venice*, 11; and Coyle, ed., *The Merchant of Venice*, 2. The stage history discussed by Toby Lelyveld reminds us that the question of "Shakespeare's" anti-Semitism is resolved in a variety of ways by actual performance. See Lelyveld, *Shylock on the Stage*. Katharine Eisaman Maus begins her undergraduate-directed introduction to the play in *The Norton Shakespeare* by drawing student attention to the question of anti-Semitism: "*Jew. Jew. Jew.* The word echoes through *The Merchant of Venice* . . . Is [the play] anti-Semitic? Does it criticize anti-Semitism?" See Maus, introduction to *The Merchant of Venice*, in Greenblatt et al., eds., *The Norton Shakespeare*, 1081. Jonathan Gil Harris notes a critical need for an "absolute assessment as to whether [Shylock] is an evil villain or a sympathetic, tragic victim" in *Foreign Bodies and the Body Politic*, 163n5.

2. For an indictment of Shakespeare's anti-Semitism, see Cohen, "The Jew and Shylock." Defenses of Shakespeare's portrayal of Shylock traditionally center on his mistreatment and his "Hath not a Jew" speech. For a conflicted example, see Cartelli, "Shakespeare's *Merchant*, Marlowe's *Jew*." Martin D. Yaffe argues that Shylock refuses a common Judeo-

Christian ethics and is therefore to be faulted and deservedly punished: "Shakespeare . . . indicat[es] how Shylock might have avoided his legal catastrophe by simply sticking to the moral teachings of his own religion . . . the teaching of mercy that it shares with Christianity" (164). See Yaffe, *Shylock and the Jewish Question*, 4–8, 74–77, 163–65. In its assumption that the play thereby interrogates actual contemporary theological beliefs (that is, including Jewish ones), Yaffe's argument resembles Maus's curiously pro-Christian assertion that Shylock's "Hath not" speech is "effective because it uses a Christian argument about the unique value of human life." See Maus, introduction, 1086. For C. L. Barber, however, the speech reveals Shylock's inability to imagine or figure nonmaterial aspects of humanness, hence, his ultimate "menace." See Barber, *Shakespeare's Festive Comedy*, 182.

3. Ragussis, *Figures of Conversion*, 58; emphasis added. That Ragussis is speaking of Shylock in particular emerges in his discussion, in which Shylock and *Merchant* are said to alike "invade" English fiction and Shylock to "perennially mediate, regulate, and displace Jewish identity for the English mind"; see *Figures of Conversion*, 58–64.

4. Shylock is frequently referred to as "the Jew" in the play, for instance by Salerio and Solanio in 2.8, and Portia in 3.2. He is often so "named" by the play itself when his lines are designated by the speech prefix "Iew" or "Iewe" (rather than by "Shy," "Shyl," or "Shylocke") in both the play's quartos and Folio. In all three texts, he is increasingly designated as Jew rather than by name during the trial scene, when his juridical and moral difference from Christian Venetians is perhaps most insistently represented.

5. Stage histories such as Lelyveld's help to document changes (and their literary and material effects) in these attitudes.

6. Shakespeare, *The Merchant of Venice*, ed. John Russell Brown, Arden edition. All further citations of *Merchant* will follow this edition except where otherwise specified.

7. *The Jew of Malta* was performed thirty-six times by Henslowe's companies, taking in consistently high receipts, making it one of the most popular plays of the 1590s. See Marlowe, *The Jew of Malta*, ed. Richard W. Van Fossen, xii. Marlowe's play's general popularity and particular importance to Shakespeare in *Merchant* and elsewhere underlies my identification of its protagonist with Shylock's name "Barabas." However, "Barabas" would also be familiar to an Elizabethan audience as the name of the Jewish

thief released in Jesus' stead in Mark 15, doomed in folk legend to wander the earth—Marlowe's own source for the name.

8. For a full and careful consideration of these, see Shapiro, *Shakespeare and the Jews.*

9. Scandalously, Marlowe's prologue is spoken by "Machevil"—a suggestively spelled Machiavelli—who claims that Barabas "favors me," i.e., both "endorses" and "resembles" (prologue, l. 35). Since Isaac Reed's 1780 edition of Marlowe's play, editors have regularized the speaker's name as "Machiavel" to conform more closely to modern orthographic expectations of "Machiavelli," and thereby suppress a means by which the reader might access the quasi-superstitious and quasi-religious connotations Machiavelli possessed for the early modern English.

10. Barabas the "Wandering Jew" was, like the Flying Dutchman, doomed in folk legend to seek a redemptive lover; thus, he, too, would lack offspring.

11. Shapiro, *Shakespeare and the Jews,* 5.

12. Merchant may not be the expected early modern "Jewish" profession for a modern reader. However, only Barabas himself elides his profession of merchant, by way of Jewishness, with that of usurer. See his boastful list of "Jewish" villainy, 2.3.191–99.

13. See also 1.1.112–16; 1.2.144–45; 1.2.160–61.

14. See also 1.1.63; 1.2.185–89; and 5.3.27–31.

15. One might include Barabas's own remarkably performative, controlled death in this category: "die, life! fly, soul! tongue, curse thy fill and die!" (5.5.88).

16. Along these lines, Matthew Biberman argues that Shakespeare's play facilitates the transformation of hypermasculine "Jew-Devil" (Barabas) into "Jew-Sissy" in the service of refiguration on a grand scale of gendered values associated with Christianity and Jewishness. See *Masculinity, Anti-Semitism,* 18–25, 32–37.

17. See chapter 1. The repetition of the familial problematic from *Malta* to *Othello* is significant. "Brabantio" itself may be a barbarously playful anagram for "Barabas."

18. The first quarto, printed by James Roberts, is dated 1600. The play was reprinted in quarto in 1619 and subsequently in the 1623 Folio. See Brown, introduction to *Merchant,* xi, xviii–xix. Brown is unusual in representing the original text: Jay Halio's Oxford edition and *The Norton*

Shakespeare give the less arresting "gentile." Halio sees Gratiano as making use of a "pun" (2.6.51n), which, like Brown's note, implies the two words are distinct in meaning. David Bevington's Chicago edition gives "gentle."

19. The example of Barabas's daughter Abigail in *Malta* is less elaborated. Still, Abigail's character arc provides a trifecta of mooted Jewishness: in addition to falling in love with a Christian and, prevented in this by her father's murder of her suitor, professing vows as a nun, Abigail later dies (poisoned by her father).

20. See, for instance, Barthelemy's discussion of dramatic Moors "of the Nonvillainous Type," in *Black Face, Maligned Race,* 147–81. Such transformations, as we will see, generally spur anxieties about the instability of identity and the corruption of the Christian community or polity. For a useful recent account of these anxieties, see Vitkus, *Turning Turk,* esp. 77–162.

21. The plots of the English drama do not mimic these events of the Iberian Peninsula, only rarely (as with Shylock) motivating conversion with threats of death or banishment. For the presence of Marranos in England, see Shapiro, *Shakespeare and the Jews,* 62–76, and Lucien Wolf's groundbreaking essays, "Jews in Elizabethan England" and "Jews in Tudor England."

22. Paranoia was reinforced by and structured perceptions of events such as the attempted poisoning of the queen by the Portuguese Marrano Roderigo Lopez, her physician, in 1594: Lopez's Jewishness became most suspect when his connections to Phillip II were revealed. The rampant fears that linked Marrano double consciousness—outward Christian, inward Jew—to secret treason are amply illustrated by the outraged public incredulity to Lopez's avowal, on the scaffold, "that he loved the Queen as well as he loved Jesus Christ." For the paranoid logic of suspicions of Marranos, see Shapiro, *Shakespeare and the Jews,* 18–24, esp. Florio's involuted definition of "Marrano" at 18 and the Lopez anecdote at 73. For a full account of the Lopez affair, see Katz, *The Jews in the History of England,* 49–106. For Lopez's speech, see Samuel, "Dr. Roderigo Lopes' Last Speech from the Scaffold at Tyburn."

23. Marlowe and Shakespeare's dramatic conversions, set in Malta and Italy, do not wholly skirt this anxiety, however, since Abigail's and Jessica's conversions are perforce Catholic ones (Abigail enters a nunnery). While Shakespeare evidently values Venetian Catholicism over Judaism, Marlowe

satirizes the Catholic institutions of Malta, where nuns are pregnant by the friars, the clerics in general are as greedy as Barabas, and Spain's interest in defending Malta from the Turks is clearly imperialist.

24. See most recently Janet Adelman's fine "Her Father's Blood." Adelman's argument about the limits of Jessica's convertibility often parallels mine, though she is less concerned with the play's construction of gentility. See also Metzger, "'Now by my Hood, a Gentle and no Jew'"; Boehrer, "Shylock and the Rise of the Household Pet"; Hall, "Guess Who's Coming to Dinner"; Shapiro, *Shakespeare and the Jews,* 120, 157–58; and Tambling, "Abigail's Party."

25. Shapiro, *Shakespeare and the Jews,* 120. Shapiro offers numerous examples of English interest in circumcision. Still, circumcision's marking of the male Jewish body is typically more likely to be inferred or discursive than embodied or observed as a feature of Jewish difference. Understanding of the practice varied (for instance, in frequent conflation of circumcision and castration), with experts needed to verify its presence. Circumcision did not, therefore, represent a marker of Jewish difference somehow clearer or more real than purely textual or otherwise symbolic markers. Its absence in *Merchant* makes Jessica's body less textually differentiated from her father's than in those contemporary representations of Jews that stress alternative gendering of Jews (male menstruation along with circumcision).

26. For instance, Shapiro writes that "it was also clear to Christian theologians that for the Jews . . . the Covenant could only be transmitted through men." Shapiro, *Shakespeare and the Jews,* 120. For female fluidity, see also Boose, "The Getting of a Lawful Race," which argues that female difference is always "convertible" (41).

27. It is characteristic of the satiric and hypercritical bent of the Portia courtship plotline that her English suitor is endowed with stereotyped English shortcomings from a compulsively "Italian" point of view. (For ways in which this compulsive exteriorizing of the play's point of view may facilitate English national identifications, see chapter 3.)

28. See also Abigail's conversion in *The Jew of Malta.* Impromptu conversions are also featured in plays with virtuous Muslim characters. See Barthelemy, *Black Face, Maligned Race,* 168–69; and Philip Massinger, *The Renegado,* 4.3.134–58; 5.3.45–133: "then thus I spit at Mahomet."

29. See, for example, Shapiro, *Shakespeare and the Jews,* 120; and Hall, "Guess Who's Coming to Dinner."

30. Metzger, "'Now by my Hood,'" 60n3.

31. Ibid., 53, 57. Metzger echoes Shapiro's reading of circumcision. Her conclusion is seemingly incompatible with Shylock's forced conversion (discussed later).

32. Shylock is forced to convert as part of his desperate plea for life and subsistence when the laws of Venice are turned against him, though he is never referred to as a Christian. Instead, he is twice referred to as "the Jew" (and never by name) after the trial (4.2.1; 5.1.292). Cf. Michael Ragussis's intuition of conversion's ominous, yet implicit, goal: "Here [conversion's] deepest ideological meaning is revealed: conversion is nothing more than a masked form of banishment so radical that death is its clearest analogue." Ragussis, *Figures of Conversion*, 42.

33. Karen Newman provides a careful account of the agency encoded in Portia's "gift." See her "Portia's Ring."

34. Salerio's comparisons, however, tend to undermine their own oppositions by suggesting that Shylock is also formed of valuable material.

35. Adelman is particularly acute on the ways in which the play's repeated flirtation with a possibility of Jessica's nonlineal relation to Shylock both limits her ability for successful conversion and insists on racial definitions of Jewishness. See "Her Father's Blood," 5–8, 13.

36. Boehrer, "Shylock," 158; Metzger, "'Now by my Hood,'" 52. See also Hall, "Guess Who's Coming to Dinner," 92–116, which notes both Launcelot's anxiety and Jessica's money.

37. Nerissa does not endorse either subjective or objective construction here (in which Portia will properly love the correctly choosing suitor, or he will properly love her). As Andrew Mattison has pointed out to me, her indifference recalls Stanley Cavell's treatment of a similar construction in *Coriolanus*. Here, however, we have not two complexly linked, symmetrical actions but a theory of singular propriety of affect: there is only one "right love" in Belmont. See Cavell, *Disowning Knowledge in Six Plays of Shakespeare*, 150–52.

38. The principle often holds true even when temporarily diverted: at the end of *Othello*, Lodovico announces that Othello's (and Brabantio's) estate will revert to Gratiano, a relative of Brabantio and a Venetian nobleman. Likewise, as will be discussed later, *Merchant*'s punch line has the Jewish wealth feathering Christian nests, a reward that reorients Jessica's elopement plot as Christian wish fulfillment.

39. These values are complicated, however, by their selective application, because the test's penalty of enforced abstinence suggests that procreative heterosexuality is less a universal value in Belmont than a privilege from which undesirables are to be prevented.

40. My argument here parallels Newman's fine reading of Portia as an "unruly woman," unsettling the homosocial traffic in women. See Newman, "Portia's Ring," 24–28.

41. Among other reasons for assuming Belmont to be imagined as an Italian locale is the casual remark of Portia's servant that the "four strangers" among her suitors are leaving, which seems to name the French, German, Scottish, and English suitors, and not the Neapolitan or County Palatine (1.2.117).

42. For Portia's song, which may guide Bassanio through its rhymes with "lead," and other suspicious features of the test, see, most interestingly, Berger, "Merchants and Mercifixion," in his *Making Trifles of Terrors,* 1–9, 2.

43. Freud, "The Theme of the Three Caskets."

44. Extracts from History 32 of *Gesta Romanorum,* translated by R. Robinson (1595), in *The Merchant of Venice,* ed. John Russell Brown, 172–74.

45. This inconsistent use of "pale" presumably motivates Theobald's proposed emendation of "plainness" for "paleness" in l. 106.

46. The irony of "Indian beauty" may derive not only from reference to a woman deemed unattractively dark or inharmoniously featured but also from allusion to the tropical climes from which so many of the ingredients of cosmetics were obtained. See Hall, *Things of Darkness,* 85–90.

47. The unlikelihood of fairness unmediated by ornament is hinted at in Bassanio's ecphrasis of the lead casket's portrait of Portia, expressed as an extremely traditional Petrarchan *blazon,* in which he describes her hair as "a golden mesh t'entrap the hearts of men" (3.2.122), closely resembling the prosthetic wig he abhors. Bassanio refers to the portrait itself as "fair Portia's counterfeit" (3.2.115).

48. See also Bassanio's analogy of shooting a second arrow after a first in order to recover it: "by adventuring both, / I oft found both" (1.1.140–52). For readings of the play's mercantilism, see, for instance, Holmer, *The Merchant of Venice,* and Moisan, "'Which Is the Merchant Here? and Which the Jew?'"

49. Quoting, respectively, from the opening speeches of Barabas and Portia: *Malta* 1.1.36–37 and *Merchant* 1.2.1.

50. Morocco in effect augments his aristocratic claim to Portia-worthiness with what Gail Kern Paster (and the humoral theorists she invokes) would call "laudable blood." See Paster's discussion of Paré and Crooke in her *The Body Embarrassed*, 64–84, esp. 71.

51. While not strictly identical to "gentle," a "citizen," possessed of full rights and freedoms of his city, would normally be of middling or high degree. See *OED* 1.

52. For instance, in *The Jew of Malta*, it permits Ferneze, the governor of Malta, selectively to target Jews in order to raise funds for a delinquent tribute to the Turks. Ferneze initially presents the nonce tax as compensation for the Maltese accommodation of "alien" Jewish residency: "have strangers leave with us to get their wealth? / Then let them with us contribute" (1.2.60–61).

3. The English Italian

1. Shakespeare, *The Merchant of Venice*, ed. John Russell Brown. The possibility that Balthazar is African has not been suggested before (because Portia chooses the name later?), though Portia evidently has Moorish servants, since Launcelot is accused by Lorenzo of impregnating one (3.5.35–36). For a brief but thought-provoking account of the chief conventions for visual representations of Africans in the Renaissance, see Erickson, "Representations of Blacks and Blackness in the Renaissance," esp. 505–15. As Erickson reports, the two most common roles for black figures are Balthazar the Magus and servants or attendants. See also Kaplan, *The Rise of the Black Magus in Western Art*.

2. As I discussed in chapter 1, men in Renaissance England were imagined to be darker-skinned than women, and aristocratic women habitually wore gloves and masks to preserve this color differential against tanning. This belief was supported by the material practices of embodying gender difference on the stage, in which boy actors wore whiteface and rouge to simulate femininity. See Callaghan, *Shakespeare without Women*, 80–86.

3. A vast critical literature has specified and correlated these associations with varying intensities by city/republic. Thus, for example, Venice centralized English associations of Italy with trade, sexual promiscuity, and

republicanism, while Florence connoted the vices of sodomy and atheism and the virtues of humanism. However, as Manfred Pfister points out in a useful review of this material, in contextualizing the realities of Baroque Italian city-states, criticism can obscure the discretionary and imaginative use by plays of Italian stereotypes: "the paradigms . . . do not sufficiently take into account the *constructedness* of the stereotypes. What is at stake is not simply images of Italy, reflecting Italian reality, but constructions of Italy reflecting at least as much the interests, needs and anxieties of the English themselves." Pfister, "Shakespeare and Italy," 299; emphasis his.

4. For discussion of the figural and color diversity that comprised painterly *varietà,* see Alberti, *On Painting,* 75–76, 84–85; and Baxandall, *Painting and Experience in Fifteenth-Century Italy,* 133–35.

5. Roughly one quarter of Shakespeare's plays contain scenes in Italy; virtually all the comedies, tragedies, and romances are set outside England. The ratio of Jacobean-era tragedies (by Middleton, Marston, Webster, et al.) set in Italy and elsewhere is far higher.

6. James Shapiro notes that "aliens" or "strangers" made up some 4 or 5 percent of London's population, between five and ten thousand people, while phobic contemporary rumor periodically inflated that number tenfold, to forty or fifty thousand. See Shapiro, *Shakespeare and the Jews,* 181–82, and Scouloudi, *Returns of Strangers in the Metropolis,* 76. Nabil Matar makes related points about Muslims in England in *Turks, Moors, and Englishmen in the Age of Discovery,* 3–6, and *Islam in Britain, 1558–1685.*

7. Birth, race, and nation may alike be conveyed by Latin *natio,* from which English "nation" derives. For a brief recapitulation of the development of the word, see Greenfeld, *Nationalism,* 4–5.

8. Anderson, *Imagined Communities.*

9. Howard, "An English Lass amid the Moors," 101.

10. A relationship between the emergence of racial and national identity is also a familiar component of later racialist theories from Gobineau onward. For a clear presentation of this intersection, see Goldberg, *Racist Culture,* 78–80.

11. Mary Floyd-Wilson masterfully explains early modern connections between climate, ethnicity, nation, and character, or geohumoralism, in *English Ethnicity.* See also Paster, *The Body Embarrassed,* 9–10, 78. For Thomas Browne, climatic influence was the most unchanging factor in "fasten[ing] a material or temperamental propriety upon any nation; there

being scarce any condition (but what depends upon clime) which is not exhausted or obscured from the commixture of introvenient nations either by commerce or conquest." *Pseudodoxia Epidemica,* 1: 325.

12. In an argument that dovetails with mine and whose conclusions could be applied to the early modern period, Kwame Anthony Appiah contends that "nation is the key middle term in understanding the relations between the concept of race and the idea of literature." See Appiah, "Race," 282.

13. Helgerson, *Forms of Nationhood,* esp. 6–14, 25–40, 7.

14. McEachern, *The Poetics of English Nationhood, 1590–1612,* 3.

15. As Richmond Barbour puts it in a slightly different context, "constructions of otherness . . . recombine promiscuously." *Before Orientalism,* 15.

16. Bate, "The Elizabethans in Italy," 71.

17. For important work on the effect of these overlapping fields of literary endeavor, see Greene, *The Light in Troy,* and Crewe's discussions of Wyatt and Surrey in *Trials of Authorship,* 23–78.

18. These tropes were not simply employed in drama. Roger Ascham's *Scholemaster* and Thomas Nashe's *Unfortunate Traveler* illustrate most of them in contexts emphasizing the deleterious effects of Italianness on the English and the mingling of poetic form and more xenophobic stereotypes.

19. See, for instance, Hunter, *Dramatic Identities and Cultural Tradition,* 113–14; and Loughrey and Taylor, who write that "the fictional Italian courts of Jacobean tragedy are never far away from the perceived Court of King James," in their introduction to Thomas Middleton, *Five Plays,* xiv.

20. Peter A. Parolin provides a rare critical consideration of the "necessarily hybridize[d]" forms of English identification with Rome and Italy in *Cymbeline.* See "Anachronistic Italy," 189.

21. The Italian language of the sonnets also performs a gesture of self-awareness of English literary history in representing the Italian origins of the English sonnet.

22. Like Milton himself and according to the English convention, I represent the incorporation of foreign language into English with the typeface known as italic. Quotations of these poems are from the Oxford Authors edition, *John Milton,* ed. Orgel and Goldberg, 31. Here and elsewhere I have modified their translation of the poems.

23. See Milton, *Complete Poems and Major Prose,* ed. Hughes, 54; Orgel and Goldberg, *John Milton,* 750n.

24. For personifications of England, see Helgerson, *Forms of Nationhood,* 107–47.

25. See French, ed., *The Life Records of John Milton,* vol. 1, *1608–1639,* esp. 98–99, 104–5, 341–42, 345–47.

26. It is not surprising that one of the beloved's admirable qualities is her "*Parole adorna di lingua piu d'una* [speech adorned by more than one language]" (Sonnet 4.10).

27. Diodati's father was actually born in Geneva, where the family settled after being forced to leave their native Lucca. For the Diodati family history, see Masson, *The Life of John Milton,* vol. 1, *1608–1639,* 98–102; and Fletcher, *The Intellectual Development of John Milton,* vol. 1, *The Institution to 1625,* 416–18. Fletcher provides a useful treatment of the documentary evidence of the Diodatis.

28. Making *The White Devil* one of her proof texts, Dympna Callaghan argues for the centrality of female agency and transgression to notions of Jacobean tragedy. See *Women and Gender in Renaissance Tragedy,* esp. 50–68, 140–46.

29. For the significance of accumulated references to Italian "topography, climate and national character," argued to present an autonomous and realist Italian nationhood on stage, see Hoenselaars, "Italy Staged in English Renaissance Drama," 31.

30. A corresponding oxymoronic paradox that shares terminology with Webster's title is registered in Ascham's proverb, cited as the epigraph to this chapter, which both deplores and strikes an Italianate pose: "Inglese italianato e un diavolo incarnato."

31. Webster, *The White Devil,* ed. John Russell Brown. Further citations follow this edition, though I have retained the quarto's spelling of "Brachiano" in homage to Random Cloud's brilliant critique of inconsistent, post-Renaissance, neo-Italianating Anglicist textual editing. See Cloud, "Shakspear Babel," esp. 36–41.

32. I am thinking here of arguments such as appear in Redmond, "'I have read them all.'" Redmond focuses on English criticism of Italianate vice to argue that "domestic texts that failed to provide the requisite condemnations of Italian culture would be received unfavorably" (134). However, such condemnations could draw attention to (or even generate) opportunities for a reader's Italianate titillation, as in Ben Jonson's own satiric references to English interest in the "obscene" Aretino in *Volpone*

(130), which trades on the charge of Aretino's recognizability. Even without Aretino's explicit pornography, Italian excesses were an increasing draw on the Jacobean stage.

33. As I have discussed, Anthony Gerard Barthelemy argues that Moorish characters are often seen to occupy multiple positions in period racial taxonomies. See *Black Face, Maligned Race,* 17. Ann Rosalind Jones argues that the play represents the Irish as the paradigmatic savage English "other" in "Italians and Others."

34. Cited in Jones, "Italians and Others," 113. Camillo and Francisco are also compared to the "wild" Irish at moments of weakness and passion (1.2.30–32; 4.1.137–38). The vulnerability of these characters to being represented as the ever-demonized and ever-racialized Irish underscores the proximity of Italian to other racialized categories for the English.

35. The Turkish "pretext" was a familiar English ploy. In the context of competition between Western European empires, as Lisa Jardine and Jerry Brotten remind us, a rhetoric of hostility against the Turks, used by England and others, was often compatible with economic and even political cooperation with the Ottoman Empire throughout the sixteenth century. Though Webster's play is performed under Jacobean rule, its subtle depiction of the internecine Italians' use of the Turks would still be relevant to England's own cultural memory (especially in its echoes of Marlowe and Shakespeare). See Jardine and Brotten, *Global Interests,* esp. 58–62, 87–88, 113–14.

36. Of course, these "possibilities" resemble contemporary political realities.

37. This use of the English Ambassador (as well as his presence in an international cluster) recalls the satire directed against Portia's English suitor in *The Merchant of Venice.* In both plays, an English identity is represented as one nationality among many equivalent ones (a trick that might be thought to do much to advance the abstract notion of nationality itself). The display of multiple national identities amassed onstage provides at once an exciting theatrical spectacle, a link of satiric sophistication between text and audience, and a disturbing check on the unique value of Englishness.

38. Flamineo's critique points to English notions of Italian physical darkness. Yet the anti-Petrarchan Petrarchan beauty was itself an English standby (most familiarly in Shakespeare's *Sonnets*). For a rich consideration of the rhetorical power of an authorial position that bestows "fairness" on unworthy objects, see Hall, *Things of Darkness,* 62–122.

39. Here, as elsewhere, a quasi-anthropological discourse designates tokens of cultural variety to be evidence of reprehensible alien impulse and custom. The play's references to putative Irish behaviors facilitate similar colonialist urges. For an account of similar "mirror effects," in which European divisions are figured as distressing "native" customs, see Goldberg, *Sodometries*, 183–88.

40. Present in Petrarch as a minor trope (see, for instance, poems 46, 127, 131, 146, 157), female red and white beauty will become commonplace in English Petrarchism. Petrarch depicts his own cosmetic shifts with far greater frequency. See *Petrarch's Lyric Poems.*

41. As in Webster's *The Devil's Law-Case,* when Romelio scolds his grieving sister: "that pale face / Will make men think you us'd some art before, / Some odious painting" (3.3.2–4).

42. Crewe, "Out of the Matrix," 17–22, 19.

43. The English discourse of red and white as incitement to desire is preponderantly, but not exclusively, gendered female, while the liability posed by emotive transparency may be shared by men, as when Flamineo guards against revealing more than he wishes by drinking to prevent further reddening: "this face of mine / I'll arm and fortify with lusty wine / 'Gainst shame and blushing (1.2.330–32).

44. For the relative infrequency of depictions of Moorish or African women, see Hall, *Things of Darkness,* 9 ff., and Boose, "The Getting of a Lawful Race," 35–54.

45. Jones, "Italians and Others,"115.

46. Zanche echoes Aaron's famous sentiments in *Titus Andronicus,* similarly praising the stability of blackness: "Coal-black is better than another hue / In that it scorns to bear another hue. / For all the water in the ocean / Can never turn the swan's black legs to white" (4.2.101–4).

47. Callaghan, *Shakespeare without Women,* 80–81.

48. *The Two Gentlemen of Verona,* 4.4.150–54.

4. Race, Science, and Aversion

1. Goldberg, "The Social Formation of Racist Discourse," 298. For similar chronologies that associate "real" race with the emergence of classification-directed, "rationalist" science, see Gates, "Critical Remarks," 319–21; Stepan, "Race and Gender," 39; Appiah, "Race," 274–76; Hannaford, *Race;* Kidd, *British Identities before Nationalism,* 23–24.

2. Goldberg, *Racist Culture*, 74, 63.

3. Ibid., 246n5.

4. Compare Kim Hall's crucial observation that the opposition between "dark" and "fair" emerges only in the 1550s. Hall, *Things of Darkness*, 3.

5. The retrospective nature of periodization risks distorting both the specificity and diffusion of past experiences and trends. New Philosophical reforms were not always, or always perceived to be, quite as rigorous as their proponents believed; moreover, these reforms had their roots in experimental practices, such as alchemy, from which proponents attempted to differentiate them. Steven Shapin and Simon Schaffer have provided important revisionist accounts of Robert Boyle's epistemology and its critics in *Leviathan and the Air-Pump;* see esp. 3–15, 49–79, 110–54. Recent accounts detailing the emergence of concepts of empiricism and objectivity out of discourses such as law have been many and productive. Richard Serjeantson provides a concise summary of this field in his "Testimony and Proof in Early-Modern England," 195–99.

6. For the materialism sustaining humoral theory, see Paster, *Humoring the Body*, 1–9; Siraisi, *Medieval and Early Renaissance Medicine*, 104–6; and Cook, "The New Philosophy and Medicine in Seventeenth-Century England."

7. See Paster, *The Body Embarrassed*, 6–13, and *Humoring the Body;* Paster, Rowe, and Floyd-Wilson, eds., *Reading the Early Modern Passions;* and Schoenfeldt, *Bodies and Selves in Early Modern England.*

8. This can strike readers differently. Paster expects readers to find humoral vocabulary variously "quaint . . . bizarre . . . no longer possible for us," while Schoenfeldt enthuses over the transhistorical force and vividness of humoral evocations of bodily phenomena. Paster, *The Body Embarrassed,* 13; Schoenfeldt, *Bodies and Selves,* 6–7.

9. Ben Jonson's Asper emphasizes this inflexibility when he presents a theory of humors in the Induction to *Every Man Out of His Humor*: "when some one peculiar quality / Doth so possess a man, that it doth draw / All his affects, his spirits, and his powers, / In their confluctions, to run one way, / This may be truly said to be a humour." Jonson, *Every Man Out of His Humor,* 62.

10. Paster, *The Body Embarrassed,* 16.

11. For the materialist mechanics of reactions of sympathy and antipathy, proceeding by rule according to the specific humoral makeup of individual and type, see Paster, *Humoring the Body*, 13, 17, 145.

12. Middleton and Rowley, *The Changeling*. Though he is most interested in the castle's structural and allegorical correspondences to the play's psychological plot, Michael Neill notes that "this castle is imagined with a density and particularity unmatched in any play before the advent of the illusionistic proscenium stage." Neill, "'Hidden Malady,'"101.

13. As when De Flores uses the narrowness of a downward passage (presumably designed to slow invaders) to disarm, trap, murder, and conceal the corpse of the castle's guest, Alonzo de Piracquo, who is betrothed to Beatrice.

14. In keeping with a reading that focuses on the play's emphasis on the dangers of *internal* subversion, one might point out that despite occasional piracy and abductions, North Africa was far less a threat to the English than was Spain and occasioned a less fearful or hateful reflexive response. In fact, in the 1570s, Elizabeth had traded cannonballs and bullets for Moroccan saltpeter, munitions the English and Moroccans would use against the Spanish and Portuguese, respectively. See D'Amico, *The Moor in English Renaissance Drama,* 14–25; Jones, *The Elizabethan Image of Africa,* 35–37.

15. Neill, "Hidden Malady," 96. The phrase is evidently used without irony.

16. Ibid., 117n1. Neill imagines that the casting thereby registered *Othello* as intertext; however, I suspect that the production was rather figuring *The Changeling*'s own concerns in its apt casting choices.

17. Thomas Middleton and William Rowley, *The Changeling,* Sheafer Theater, Duke University, April 2001.

18. Associations made explicit and belabored in the play's final speeches.

19. Neill, "Hidden Malady," esp. 96–97, 101, 110; Bawcutt, introduction to *The Changeling,* xxvi, xxxii, xliv–xlv, lx–lxi; Loughrey and Taylor, introduction to Middleton, *Five Plays,* xxi. The phrase "psychological realism" appears in Neill and Loughrey and Taylor.

20. Bawcutt, introduction, lx. Affairs between male servants and aristocratic women are relatively rare; Webster's *The Duchess of Malfi* is an obvious example, containing its own racial effects: Bosola sardonically praises the Duchess's raising Antonio "by that curious engine, your white hand" and suggests that her marriage will inspire "Turks and Moors" to convert to Christianity and serve her (3.2.288–93), while rumors persistently circulate that Antonio is a hermaphrodite or a Jew (3.2.214–222; 5.2.136).

21. For a closely contemporary version of the humoral relationship between emotional intensity and psychosomatic disturbance, see Robert Burton's *The Anatomy of Melancholy*, pt. 1, sec. 2, memb. 3.1.

22. De Flores is aware of this element of the system: "must I be enjoin'd / To follow still whilst she flies from me? . . . / She knows no cause for't, but a peevish will" (1.1.101–7).

23. I am grateful for helpful clarifications of this point made by Gail Kern Paster and Rebecca Totaro.

24. I preserve the quarto and Folio's "Maisters" to allow for the possibilities of the ambiguous "Mistress"/ "Masters" [noun or verb].

25. Etymologically, both "affection" and "passion," meaning something like "acted upon" and "passive," likewise emphasize the physical passivity of their subjects.

26. *Humoring the Body*, 205, 207. Paster provides a fascinating account of the period's views of such antipathies in animals and others, 145–55.

27. In his notes to this speech, John Russell Brown offers evidence that these humors, if not quite proverbial, were nonetheless established oddities. He cites a further reference to the bagpipe phenomenon in Jonson's *Every Man in His Humor* (4.1.40); similar references exist for pigs. See *Merchant*, 4.1.49n.

28. Paster, *The Body Embarrassed*, 23–63.

29. This choice does not work to Shylock's advantage and, as I am suggesting, it represents him less sympathetically than does the more organic account of his feud with Antonio. If it signals the play's desire to validate racial antipathy, it may simultaneously participate in the play's equal desire to vilify Shylock. Paster disagrees, seeing Shylock's speech as a knowing, daring attempt to evade the anti-Semitic workings of state power *(Humoring the Body*, 205–6). In any case, the attempt is unsuccessful.

30. This logic, however, is itself contingent. In Middleton's and Rowley's source, John Reynolds's *The Triumphs of God's Revenge against Murther*, from which the name "De Flores" is taken, the character does not, in fact, "deflower" Beatrice. Bawcutt, introduction, xxxi.

31. Ibid., lix.

32. Harris, *Foreign Bodies and the Body Politic*, 50–57. The ontological view of pathogens favored by Paracelsus and his iatrochemical followers differed from Galenic theories of humoral imbalance as causing disease (20–25); therefore, here Beatrice departs somewhat from her previous

humoral model of disturbance. Harris provides a useful account of the enduring medico-political association of pathogens with foreign invaders, against whom the internal damage of the poisonous cure could be marshaled. The resemblance of internal to external breach and corruption resonates with many of the logics I have been describing.

33. See also Alsemero's links between vocabulary of Beatrice's beauty, unlawful blood, and deformity at 5.3.72–77.

34. Paster, *The Body Embarrassed,* 89.

35. In a fascinating parallel, current research on disgust (one of the emotions aroused by De Flores) continues to weigh whether reactions of disgust originate in an objective, natural mechanism for self-protection or even for moral awareness. For a useful review of theories of disgust, see Miller, *Disgust,* 1–22. For a provocative, important early account of disgust's moral utility, see Kolnai, *On Disgust,* 62–72, 80–90; for a critique of disgust's reliability, see Nussbaum, "'Secret Sewers of Vice.'"

36. *The Record of the Royal Society,* 4th ed. (London: 1940), 289, 312, quoted in Hall, *Promoting Experimental Learning,* 9. Hall notes both the centrality of experiment to the Society and that such experimental emphasis is original to the Society and to England (9).

37. Middleton and Rowley, *The Changeling,* 4.1.25n; Burton, *Anatomy of Melancholy,* pt. 3, sec. 3, memb. 2, 844–45, also cited by Bawcutt.

38. When Beatrice questions Diaphanta about her virginity, the servant worries about just such an internal examination from her mistress: "she will not search me, will she, / Like the forewoman of a female jury?" (4.1.100–101). Fisting frisson aside, such juries hardly represented an alternative to the misogynist epistemology in whose service they performed their examinations, though they occasionally were suspected of corruption and protecting the interests of the accused (as was alleged during the Howard trial, when Howard evidently attempted a bed trick of her own, sending in a veiled substitute to be examined).

39. It may be that only the sex of the witnesses and administrators of virginity tests concerns Alsemero. Law and science were not necessarily sharply distinguished in the world outside the play. Changing standards of scientific truth were in fact indebted to standards of the legal testimony of witnesses, standards increasingly shaped to facilitate epistemological rigor. For connections between legal and scientific epistemologies, see Shapiro, "The Concept 'Fact,'" revised and expanded in her *A Culture of Fact.* For

period interest in the epistemology of testimony itself, see Serjeantson, "Testimony and Proof in Early-Modern England."

40. Garber, "The Insincerity of Women," 27.

41. Cf. Garber, who reads Beatrice's mimicry of orgasm as feminist triumph ("she is . . . in control") and suggests that "a woman's pleasure is her secret—and her power[.] Can she fake it?" "The Insincerity of Women," 28–29.

42. It is one of the play's ironies that Beatrice can fake the symptoms of potion "M," symptoms that, as Garber points out, bear more than a passing resemblance to orgasm, but inexplicably does not trust herself to fake the responses of a virgin to actual sex. On the experiment and orgasm, see Garber, "The Insincerity of Women," 22–25.

43. Ibid., 22. Compare Barbara Shapiro's argument that in seventeenth-century England, a "fact" (as explicitly distinct from logic) was that which was worthy of belief. Shapiro, *A Culture of Fact*, 46.

44. Shapin and Schaffer, *Leviathan and the Air-Pump*, 3, 55–60, 111–15. These criteria for evidentiary reliability are of course much remarked. Further discussion may be found in Shapiro, *A Culture of Fact*. In *A Social History of Truth*, Shapin elaborates on the criteria for reliable witnesses. While he does not dispute the importance of empiricist principles to the Royal Society, William T. Lynch argues that a more dispersed set of methodological and epistemological determinants characterized their work. See *Solomon's Child*, esp. 1–33.

45. Shapin and Schaffer, *Leviathan and the Air-Pump*, 339–41.

46. Ibid., 340.

47. Compare the Royal Society's interest in experimental confirmation of witchcraft and of Christianity: Shapiro, *A Culture of Fact*, 170–81. Compare too Robert Markley's careful argument that theology was the interpretive lens through which the experimenters of the Royal Society (including Boyle and Newton) made sense of the results of their findings. See his *Fallen Languages*, esp. 1–33. It is interesting to note in this context that, as part of his early work on behalf of experimentalism and the Royal Society, Robert Boyle conducted research on the nature of differences in skin color, published as part of his *The Beginning of an Experimental History of Colours* (1664).

48. Gould, *The Mismeasure of Man*, esp. 47–50, 54–60.

Coda

1. Goldberg, *Racist Culture,* 63.

2. A good start can be seen in Malcolmson, "'The Explication of Whiteness and Blackness,'" and in Floyd-Wilson's seminal work on geo-humoralism, *English Ethnicity and Race in Early Modern Drama.*

Bibliography

Adelman, Janet. "Her Father's Blood: Race, Conversion, and Nation in *The Merchant of Venice*." *Representations* 81 (2003): 4–30.

Alberti, Leon Battista. *On Painting*. Translated by John R. Spencer. New Haven, Conn.: Yale University Press, 1956.

Alexander, Catherine M. S., and Stanley Wells, eds. *Shakespeare and Race*. Oxford: Oxford University Press, 2000.

Amussen, S. D. "Gender, Family, and the Social Order, 1560–1725." In *Order and Disorder in Early Modern England*, edited by Anthony Fletcher and John Stevenson, 196–217. Cambridge: Cambridge University Press, 1985.

Anderson, Benedict. *Imagined Communities: Reflections on the Origin and Spread of Nationalism*. London: Verso, 1991 (1983).

Appiah, Kwame Anthony. "Race." In *Critical Terms for Literary Study*, edited by Frank Lentricchia and Thomas McLaughlin, 274–87. Chicago: University of Chicago Press, 1990.

———. "Racisms." In *Anatomy of Racism*, edited by David Theo Goldberg, 3–17. Minneapolis: University of Minnesota Press, 1990.

———. "The Uncompleted Argument: Du Bois and the Illusion of Race." In *"Race," Writing, and Difference*, edited by Henry Louis Gates Jr., 21–37. Chicago: University of Chicago Press, 1985.

Balibar, Etienne. "Racisme et nationalisme." In *Race, Nation, Classe*, edited by Etienne Balibar and Immanuel Wallerstein. Paris: Editions la decouverte, 1990.

Banton, Michael. *The Idea of Race*. Boulder, Colo.: Westview Press, 1977.

———. *Racial Theories*, 2nd ed. Cambridge: Cambridge University Press 1998.

Banton, Michael, and Jonathan Harwood. *The Race Concept*. New York: Praeger, 1975.

Barber, C. L. *Shakespeare's Festive Comedy.* Princeton, N.J.: Princeton University Press, 1959.

Barbour, Richmond. *Before Orientalism: London's Theatre of the East, 1576–1626.* Cambridge: Cambridge University Press, 2003.

Bartels, Emily C. "*Othello* and Africa: Postcolonialism Reconsidered." *William and Mary Quarterly* 54 (1997): 45–64.

Barth, Fredrik, ed. *Ethnic Groups and Boundaries: The Social Organization of Culture Difference.* Boston: Little, Brown and Company, 1969.

Barthelemy, Anthony Gerard. *Black Face, Maligned Race: The Representation of Blacks in English Drama from Shakespeare to Southerne.* Baton Rouge: Louisiana State University Press, 1987.

Bate, Jonathan. "The Elizabethans in Italy." In *Travel and Drama in Shakespeare's Time,* edited by Jean-Pierre Maquerlot and Michele Willems, 55–74. Cambridge: Cambridge University Press, 1996.

Bawcutt, N. W., ed. Introduction to *The Changling,* by Thomas Middleton and William Rowley. Revels Plays. London: Methuen, 1958.

Baxandall, Michael. *Painting and Experience in Fifteenth-Century Italy: A Primer in the Social History of Pictorial Style.* Oxford: Oxford University Press, 1972.

Berger, Harry. *Making Trifles of Terrors: Redistributing Complicities in Shakespeare,* edited by Peter Erickson. Stanford, Calif.: Stanford University Press, 1997.

Biberman, Matthew. *Masculinity, Anti-Semitism, and Early Modern English Literature: From the Satanic to the Effeminate Jew.* Aldershot, Hampshire, England: Ashgate Publishing, 2004.

Blackburn, Robin. *The Making of New World Slavery: From the Baroque to the Modern, 1492–1800.* London: Verso, 1997.

Boehrer, Bruce. "Shylock and the Rise of the Household Pet: Thinking Social Exclusion in *The Merchant of Venice.*" *Shakespeare Quarterly* 50 (1999): 152–70.

Boose, Lynda. "'The Getting of a Lawful Race': Racial Discourse in Early Modern England and the Unrepresentable Black Woman." In *Women, "Race," and Writing in the Early Modern Period,* edited by Margo Hendricks and Patricia Parker, 35–54. London: Routledge, 1994.

Browne, Thomas. *Pseudodoxia Epidemica.* 2 vols. Edited by Robin Robbins. Oxford: Clarendon Press, 1981.

——. *Works.* 6 vols. Edited by Geoffrey Keynes. London: Faber and Gwyer, 1928.

Burton, Robert. *The Anatomy of Melancholy.* New York: New York Review Books Classics, 2001.

Callaghan, Dympna. *Shakespeare without Women: Representing Gender and Race on the Renaissance Stage.* London: Routledge, 2000.

——. *Women and Gender in Renaissance Tragedy.* London: Harvester Wheatsheaf, 1989.

Cartelli, Thomas. "Shakespeare's *Merchant,* Marlowe's *Jew:* The Problem of Cultural Difference." *Shakespeare Studies* 20 (1988): 255–60.

Cavell, Stanley. *Disowning Knowledge in Six Plays of Shakespeare.* Cambridge: Cambridge University Press, 1987.

Cloud, Random. "Shakspear Babel." In *Reading Readings: Essays on Shakespeare Editing in the Eighteenth Century,* edited by Joanna Gondris, 1–70. Madison, N.J.: Fairleigh Dickinson University Press, 1998.

Coetzee, J. M. *White Writing: On the Culture of Letters in South Africa.* New Haven, Conn.: Yale University Press, 1988.

Cohen, D. M. "The Jew and Shylock." *Shakespeare Quarterly* 31 (1980): 53–63.

Colley, Linda. *Captives: Britain, Empire, and the World, 1600–1850.* London: J. Cape, 2002.

Cook, Harold J. "The New Philosophy and Medicine in Seventeenth-Century England." In *Reappraisals of the Scientific Revolution,* edited by David C. Lindberg and Robert S. Westman, 405–11. Cambridge: Cambridge University Press, 1990.

Cowhig, Ruth. "Blacks in English Renaissance Drama and the Role of Shakespeare's *Othello.*" In *The Black Presence in English Literature,* edited by David Dabydeen, 1–25. Manchester: Manchester University Press, 1985.

Coyle, Martin, ed. *The Merchant of Venice.* New Casebooks. New York: St. Martin's Press, 1998.

Crewe, Jonathan. "Out of the Matrix: Shakespeare and Race-Writing." *Yale Journal of Criticism* 8 (1995): 13–29.

——. *Trials of Authorship: Anterior Forms and Poetic Reconstruction from Wyatt to Shakespeare.* Berkeley: University of California Press, 1990.

D'Amico, Jack. *The Moor in English Renaissance Drama.* Tampa: University of South Florida Press, 1991.

Davis, Robert C. *Christian Slaves, Muslim Masters: White Slavery in the*

Mediterranean, the Barbary Coast, and Italy, 1500–1800. Houndsmills, England: Palgrave Macmillan, 2003.

Erickson, Peter. "The Moment of Race in Renaissance Studies." *Shakespeare Studies* 26 (1998): 27–36.

———. "Representations of Blacks and Blackness in the Renaissance." *Criticism* 35 (1993): 499–527.

Fausto-Sterling, Anne. *Myths of Gender.* 2nd ed. New York: Basic Books, 1985.

Ferguson, Margaret. "Juggling the Categories of Race, Class, and Gender: Aphra Behn's *Oroonoko.*" In *Women, "Race," and Writing in the Early Modern Period,* edited by Margo Hendricks and Patricia Parker, 209–24. London: Routledge, 1994.

Fiedler, Leslie A. *The Stranger in Shakespeare.* New York: Stein and Day, 1972.

Fields, Barbara. "Ideology and Race in American History." In *Region, Race, and Reconstruction,* edited by J. Morgan Kousser and James M. McPherson, 143–78. New York: Oxford University Press, 1982.

Fletcher, Harris Francis. *The Intellectual Development of John Milton.* 2 vols. Vol. 1, *The Institution to 1625: From the Beginnings through Grammar School.* Urbana: University of Illinois Press, 1956.

Floyd-Wilson, Mary. *English Ethnicity and Race in Early Modern Drama.* Cambridge: Cambridge University Press, 2003.

———. "Temperature, Temperance, and Racial Difference in Ben Jonson's *The Masque of Blackness.*" *English Literary Renaissance* 28 (1998): 183–209.

Foucault, Michel. *The History of Sexuality: An Introduction.* Translated by Robert Hurley. 1976. Reprint, New York: Vintage Books, 1978.

Freeman, Arthur. "Marlowe, Kyd, and the Dutch Church Libel." *English Literary Renaissance* 3 (1973): 44–52.

French, J. Milton, ed. *The Life Records of John Milton.* 5 vols. Vol. 1, *1608–1639.* New Brunswick, N.J.: Rutgers University Press, 1949.

Freud, Sigmund. "The Theme of the Three Caskets." Translated by James Strachey. *Standard Edition* 17: 291–301.

Fromm, Harold. "The Hegemonic Form of Othering; or, The Academic's Burden." In *"Race," Writing, and Difference,* edited by Henry Louis Gates Jr., 396–99. Chicago: University of Chicago Press, 1985.

Garber, Marjorie. "The Insincerity of Women." In *Desire in the Renaissance:*

Psychoanalysis and Literature, edited by Valeria Finucci and Regina
Schwartz, 19–38. Princeton, N.J.: Princeton University Press, 1994.

Gates, Henry Louis Jr. "Critical Remarks." In *Anatomy of Racism,* edited
by David Theo Goldberg, 319–29. Minneapolis: University of Minnesota
Press, 1990.

———. "Talkin' That Talk." In *"Race," Writing, and Difference,* edited by
Henry Louis Gates Jr., 402–9. Chicago: University of Chicago Press,
1986.

———. "Writing 'Race' and the Difference It Makes." In *"Race," Writing,
and Difference,* edited by Henry Louis Gates Jr., 1–20. Chicago:
University of Chicago Press, 1985.

Gilman, Sander. *The Jew's Body.* New York: Routledge, 1991.

Gilroy, Paul. *Against Race: Imagining Political Culture beyond the Color Line.*
Cambridge, Mass.: Harvard University Press, Belknap Press, 2000.

Goldberg, David Theo. *The Racial State.* Oxford: Blackwell, 2002.

———. *Racist Culture: Philosophy and the Politics of Meaning.* Cambridge,
Mass.: Blackwell, 1993.

———. "The Social Formation of Racist Discourse." In *Anatomy of Racism,*
edited by David Theo Goldberg, 295–318. Minneapolis: University of
Minnesota Press, 1990.

Goldberg, Jonathan. "The History That Will Be." *GLQ: A Journal of Lesbian
and Gay Studies* 1 (1995): 385–403.

———. "The Print of Goodness." In *The Culture of Capital: Property, Cities,
and Knowledge in Early Modern England,* edited by Henry S. Turner,
231–54. New York: Routledge, 2002.

———. *Sodometries: Renaissance Texts, Modern Sexualities.* Stanford, Calif.:
Stanford University Press, 1992.

Gould, Stephen Jay. *The Mismeasure of Man.* New York: Norton, 1981.

Greenblatt, Stephen. *Renaissance Self-Fashioning.* Chicago: University of
Chicago Press, 1980.

Greenblatt, Stephen, Walter Cohen, Jean E. Howard, and Katharine
Eisaman Maus, eds. *The Norton Shakespeare.* New York: W. W. Norton,
1997.

Greene, Thomas M. *The Light in Troy: Imitation and Discovery in Renaissance
Poetry.* New Haven, Conn.: Yale University Press, 1982.

Greenfeld, Leah. *Nationalism: Five Roads to Modernity.* Cambridge, Mass.:
Harvard University Press, 1992.

Hall, Kim F. "Guess Who's Coming to Dinner? Colonization and Miscegenation in *The Merchant of Venice*." *Renaissance Drama* 23 (1992): 87–111.

———. *Things of Darkness: Economies of Race and Gender in Early Modern England*. Ithaca, N.Y.: Cornell University Press, 1995.

Hall, Marie Boas. *Promoting Experimental Learning: Experiment and the Royal Society, 1660–1727*. Cambridge: Cambridge University Press, 1991.

Hanke, Lewis. *All Mankind Is One: A Study of the Disputation between Bartolomé de Las Casas and Juan Ginés de Sepúlveda in 1550 on the Intellectual and Religious Capacity of the American Indians*. Dekalb: Northern Illinois University Press, 1974.

Hannaford, Ivan. *Race: The History of an Idea in the West*. Washington, D.C.: Woodrow Wilson Center Press, 1996.

Harris, Jonathan Gil. *Foreign Bodies and the Body Politic: Discourses of Social Pathology in Early Modern England*. Cambridge: Cambridge University Press, 1998.

Harris, Marvin. "Race." In *International Encyclopedia of the Social Sciences*, edited by David L. Sills. 19 vols. 13: 263–69. New York: Macmillan Company and Free Press, 1968–91.

Helgerson, Richard. *Forms of Nationhood: The Elizabethan Writing of England*. Chicago: University of Chicago Press, 1992.

Hendricks, Margo, and Patricia Parker, eds. *Women, "Race," and Writing in the Early Modern Period*. London: Routledge, 1994.

Hoenselaars, A. J. "Italy Staged in English Renaissance Drama." In *Shakespeare's Italy: Functions of Italian Locations in Renaissance Drama*, edited by Michele Marrapodi, A. J. Hoenselaars, Marcello Cappuzzo, and L. Falzon Santucci, 30–48. Manchester: Manchester University Press, 1993.

Holmer, Joan Ozark. *The Merchant of Venice: Choice, Hazard, and Consequence*. New York: St. Martin's Press, 1995.

Howard, Jean E. "An English Lass amid the Moors: Gender, Race, Sexuality, and National Identity in Heywood's *The Fair Maid of the West*." In *Women, "Race," and Writing in the Early Modern Period*, edited by Margo Hendricks and Patricia Parker, 101–17. London: Routledge, 1994.

Hunter, G. K. *Dramatic Identities and Cultural Tradition: Studies in Shakespeare and His Contemporaries*. New York: Barnes and Noble Books, 1978.

Iyengar, Sujata. *Shades of Difference: Mythologies of Skin Color in Early Modern England.* Philadelphia: University of Pennsylvania Press, 2005.
James, Henry. *The Scenic Art: Notes on Acting and the Drama, 1872–1901.* Edited by Allan Wade. New Brunswick, N.J.: Rutgers University Press, 1948.
Jardine, Lisa, and Jerry Brotten. *Global Interests: Renaissance Art between East and West.* Ithaca, N.Y.: Cornell University Press, 2000.
Jones, Ann Rosalind. "Italians and Others: Venice and the Irish in *Coryat's Crudities* and *The White Devil.*" *Renaissance Drama* 18 (1987): 101–19.
Jones, Eldred. *The Elizabethan Image of Africa.* Charlottesville: University of Virginia Press for the Folger Shakespeare Library, 1971.
———. *Othello's Countrymen: The African in English Renaissance Drama.* London: Oxford University Press, 1965.
Jonson, Ben. *Every Man Out of His Humor.* In *The Complete Plays of Ben Jonson,* vol. 1. Edited by Felix E. Schelling. Everyman Library. London: J. M. Dent, 1940.
Jordan, Constance. "The Household and the State: Transformations in the Representation of an Analogy from Aristotle to James I." *Modern Language Quarterly* 54, no. 3 (1993): 307–26.
Kaplan, Paul H. D. *The Rise of the Black Magus in Western Art.* Ann Arbor: University of Michigan Press, 1985.
Katz, David. *The Jews in the History of England.* Oxford: Oxford University Press, 1994.
———. *Philo-Semitism and the Readmission of the Jews to England, 1603–1655.* Oxford: Oxford University Press, 1982.
Kidd, Colin. *British Identities before Nationalism: Ethnicity and Nationhood in the Atlantic World, 1600–1800.* Cambridge: Cambridge University Press, 1999.
Kolnai, Aurel. *On Disgust.* Translated by Elizabeth Kolnai and Barry Smith. Edited by Barry Smith and Carolyn Korsmeyer. Chicago: Carus, 2004.
Kujoory, Parvin. *Shakespeare and Minorities: An Annotated Bibliography, 1970–2000.* Lanham, Md.: Scarecrow Press, 2001.
Lawrence, Errol. "Just Plain Common Sense: The 'Roots' of Racism." In *The Empire Strikes Back: Race and Racism in 70s Britain,* edited by the Center for Contemporary Cultural Studies, 95–142. London: Hutchinson, 1982.
Lee, S., J. Mountain, and B. Koenig. "The Meanings of 'Race' in the New

Genomics: Implications for Health Disparities Research." *Yale Journal of Health Policy Law Ethics* 1 (2001): 33–75.

Lelyveld, Toby. *Shylock on the Stage*. Cleveland: Western Reserve University Press, 1960.

Levin, Harry. "Shakespeare's Italians." In *Shakespeare's Italy: Functions of Italian Locations in Renaissance Drama,* edited by Michele Marrapodi, A. J. Hoenselaars, Marcello Cappuzzo, and L. Falzon Santucci, 17–29. Manchester: Manchester University Press, 1993.

Lewontin, Richard. "The Apportionment of Human Diversity." *Evolutionary Biology* 6 (1972): 381–98.

———. *Not in Our Genes.* New York: Pantheon, 1984.

Loomba, Ania. "'Delicious Traffick': Racial and Religious Difference on Early Modern Stages." In *Shakespeare and Race,* edited by Catherine M. S. Alexander and Stanley Wells, 203–24. Oxford: Oxford University Press, 2000.

———. *Gender, Race, Renaissance Drama.* Delhi: Oxford University Press, 1992.

———. *Shakespeare, Race, and Colonialism.* Oxford: Oxford University Press, 2002.

Lowe, A., A. Urquhart, L. Foreman, and I. Evett. "Inferring Ethnic Origin by Means of an STR Profile." *Forensic Science International* 119 (2001): 17–22.

Lynch, William T. *Solomon's Child: Method in the Early Royal Society of London.* Stanford, Calif.: Stanford University Press, 2001.

MacDonald, Joyce Green. "Black Ram, White Ewe: Shakespeare, Race, and Women." In *A Feminist Companion to Shakespeare,* edited by Dympna Callaghan, 188–206. Oxford: Blackwell, 2000.

Malcolmson, Cristina. "'The Explication of Whiteness and Blackness': Skin Color and the Physics of Color in the Works of Robert Boyle and Margaret Cavendish." In *Fault Lines and Controversies in the Study of Seventeenth-Century English Literature,* edited by Claude J. Summers and Ted-Larry Pebworth, 187–203. Columbia: University of Missouri Press, 2002.

Markley, Robert. *Fallen Languages: Crises of Representation in Newtonian England, 1660–1740.* Ithaca, N.Y.: Cornell University Press, 1993.

Marlowe, Christopher. *The Jew of Malta.* Edited by Richard W. Van

Fossen. Regents Renaissance Drama. Lincoln: University of Nebraska Press, 1964.

Marrapodi, Michele, A. J. Hoenselaars, Marcello Cappuzzo, and L. Falzon Santucci, eds. *Shakespeare's Italy: Functions of Italian Locations in Renaissance Drama.* Manchester: Manchester University Press, 1993.

Massinger, Philip. *The Renegado.* In *Three Turk Plays from Early Modern England,* edited by Daniel J. Vitkus. New York: Columbia University Press, 2000.

Masson, David. *The Life of John Milton.* 3 vols. Vol. 1, *1608–1639.* London: Macmillan, 1881.

Matar, Nabil. *Islam in Britain, 1558–1685.* Cambridge: Cambridge University Press, 1998.

———. *Turks, Moors, and Englishmen in the Age of Discovery.* New York: Columbia University Press, 1999.

Maus, Katharine Eisaman. Introduction to *The Merchant of Venice,* by William Shakespeare. In *The Norton Shakespeare,* edited by Stephen Greenblatt, Walter Cohen, Jean E. Howard, and Katharine Eisaman Maus, 1081–88. New York: W. W. Norton, 1997.

McEachern, Claire. *The Poetics of English Nationhood, 1590–1612.* Cambridge: Cambridge University Press, 1996.

Metzger, Mary Janell. "'Now by my Hood, a Gentle and no Jew': Jessica, *The Merchant of Venice,* and the Discourse of Early Modern English Identity." *PMLA* 113 (1998): 52–63.

Middleton, Thomas. *Five Plays.* Edited by Bryan Loughrey and Neil Taylor. London: Penguin Books, 1988.

Middleton, Thomas, and William Rowley. *The Changeling.* Edited by N. W. Bawcutt. Revels Plays. London: Methuen, 1958.

Miller, Susan B. *Disgust: The Gatekeeper Emotion.* Hillsdale, N.J.: Analytic Press, 2004.

Milton, John. *Complete Poems and Major Prose.* Edited by Merritt Y. Hughes. Englewood Cliffs, N.J.: Macmillan, 1957.

———. *John Milton.* Edited by Stephen Orgel and Jonathan Goldberg. Oxford Authors. Oxford: Oxford University Press, 1991.

Moisan, Thomas. "'Which Is the Merchant Here? And Which the Jew?' Subversion and Recuperation in *The Merchant of Venice.*" In *Shakespeare Reproduced: The Text in History and Ideology,* edited by Jean E. Howard and Marion F. O'Connor, 188–206. New York: Methuen, 1987.

Neill, Michael. "'Hidden Malady': Death, Discovery, and Indistinction in *The Changeling*." *Renaissance Drama* 22 (1991): 95–121.

———. *Putting History to the Question: Power, Politics, and Society in English Renaissance Drama*. New York: Columbia University Press, 2000.

Newman, Karen. *Fashioning Femininity and English Renaissance Drama*. Chicago: University of Chicago Press, 1991.

———. "Portia's Ring: Unruly Women and Structures of Exchange in *The Merchant of Venice*." *Shakespeare Quarterly* 38 (1987): 19–33.

Nussbaum, Martha. "'Secret Sewers of Vice': Disgust, Bodies, and the Law." In *The Passions of Law,* edited by Susan Bandes, 19–62. New York: New York University Press, 1999.

Omi, Michael, and Howard Winant. *Racial Formation in the United States.* 2nd ed. New York: Routledge, 1994.

Orgel, Stephen. *Impersonations: The Performance of Gender in Shakespeare's England*. Cambridge: Cambridge University Press, 1996.

Orkin, Martin. "Othello and the 'Plain Face' of Racism." *Shakespeare Quarterly* 38 (1987): 166–88.

Orlin, Lena Cowan. "Desdemona's Disposition." In *Shakespearean Tragedy and Gender,* edited by Shirley Nelson Garner and Madelon Sprengnether, 171–92. Bloomington: Indiana University Press, 1996.

Outlaw, Lucius. "Towards a Critical Theory of 'Race.'" In *Anatomy of Racism,* edited by David Theo Goldberg, 58–82. Minneapolis: University of Minnesota Press, 1990.

Parker, Patricia. "Fantasies of 'Race' and 'Gender': Africa, *Othello,* and Bringing to Light." In *Women, "Race," and Writing,* edited by Margo Hendricks and Patricia Parker, 84–100. London: Routledge, 1994.

Parolin, Peter A. "Anachronistic Italy: Cultural Alliances and National Identity in *Cymbeline*." *Shakespeare Studies* 30 (2002): 188–215.

Paster, Gail Kern. *The Body Embarrassed: Drama and the Disciplines of Shame in Early Modern England*. Ithaca, N.Y.: Cornell University Press, 1993.

———. *Humoring the Body: Emotions and the Shakespearean Stage*. Chicago: University of Chicago Press, 2004.

Paster, Gail Kern, Katherine Rowe, and Mary Floyd-Wilson, eds. *Reading the Early Modern Passions: Essays in the Cultural History of Emotion*. Philadelphia: University of Pennsylvania Press, 2004.

Petrarch. *Petrarch's Lyric Poems*. Translated and edited by Robert M. Durling. Cambridge, Mass.: Harvard University Press, 1976.

Pfister, Manfred. "Shakespeare and Italy, or the Law of Diminishing Returns." In *Shakespeare's Italy: Functions of Italian Locations in Renaissance Drama*, edited by Michele Marrapodi, A. J. Hoenselaars, Marcello Cappuzzo, and L. Falzon Santucci, 295–303. Manchester: Manchester University Press, 1993.

Ragussis, Michael. *Figures of Conversion: "The Jewish Question" and English National Identity*. Durham, N.C.: Duke University Press, 1995.

Redmond, Michael J. "'I have read them all': Jonson's *Volpone* and the Discourse of the Italianate Englishman." In *The Italian World of English Renaissance Drama: Cultural Exchange and Intertextuality*, edited by Michele Marrapodi, 122–40. Newark: University of Delaware Press, 1998.

Rosenberg, Marvin. *The Masks of Othello*. Berkeley: University of California Press, 1961.

Rubin, Gayle. "The Traffic in Women: Notes on the 'Political Economy' of Sex." In *Toward an Anthropology of Women*, edited by Rayna Reiter, 157–210. New York: Monthly Review Press, 1973.

Rymer, Thomas. *A Short View of Tragedy*. London, 1693.

Sacks, Karen Brodkin. "How Did Jews Become White Folks?" In *Race*, edited by Steven Gregory and Roger Sanjek, 78–102. New Brunswick, N.J.: Rutgers University Press, 1994.

Salvini, Tommaso. *Leaves from the Autobiography of Tommaso Salvini*. No translator named. New York: Benjamin Blom, 1971.

Samuel, Edgar R. "Dr. Roderigo Lopes' Last Speech from the Scaffold at Tyburn." *Transactions of the Jewish Historical Society of England* 30 (1989): 51–53.

Schiesari, Juliana. "The Face of Domestication: Physiognomy, Gender Politics, and Humanism's Others." In *Women, "Race," and Writing in the Early Modern Period*, edited by Margo Hendricks and Patricia Parker, 55–70. London: Routledge, 1994.

Schoenfeldt, Michael C. *Bodies and Selves in Early Modern England: Physiology and Inwardness in Spenser, Shakespeare, Herbert, and Milton*. Cambridge: Cambridge University Press, 1999.

Scouloudi, Irene. *Returns of Strangers in the Metropolis: 1593, 1627, 1635, 1639: A Study of an Active Minority*. Quarto Series, vol. 57. London: Huguenot Society, 1985.

Sedgwick, Eve Kosovsky. *Between Men: English Literature and Male Homo-social Desire*. New York: Columbia University Press, 1985.

Serjeantson, Richard. "Testimony and Proof in Early-Modern England." *Studies in History and Philosophy of Science* 30, no. 2 (1999): 195–236.

Shakespeare, William. *The Merchant of Venice*. Edited by John Russell Brown. Arden edition, 2nd ser. London: Methuen, 1955.

———. *The Merchant of Venice*. Edited by Jay L. Halio. The Oxford Shakespeare. Oxford: Oxford University Press, 1993.

———. *Otello: Tragedia in Cinque Atti . . . come Rappresentata dal Signor Salvini*. London: Clayton and Co., 1876.

———. *Othello*. Edited by Horace Howard Furness. New Variorum edition. Philadelphia: J. B. Lippincott Company, 1886.

———. *Othello*. Edited by C. D. Koppel. New York, 1889.

———. *Othello*. Edited by J. J. Little. New York, 1883, 1886.

———. *Othello*. Edited by M. R. Ridley. Arden edition, 2nd ser. London: Methuen, 1958.

———. *Othello*. Edited by E. A. J. Honigmann. Arden edition, 3rd ser. Walton-on-Thames, Surrey: Thomas Nelson and Sons, 1997.

———. *Othello: A Tragedy in Five Acts*. New York: G. F. Nesbitt, 1873.

———. *Titus Andronicus*. Edited by Jonathan Bate. Arden edition, 3rd ser. London: Routledge, 1995. Reprint, London: Thomson Learning, 2000.

———. *The Two Gentlemen of Verona*. Edited by Clifford Leech. Arden edition, 2nd ser. London: Methuen, 1969.

———. *The Winter's Tale*. Edited by J. H. P. Pafford. Arden edition, 2nd ser. London: Routledge, 1966.

Shannon, Laurie. *Sovereign Amity: Figures of Friendship in Shakespearean Contexts*. Chicago: University of Chicago Press, 2002.

Shapin, Steven. *A Social History of Truth: Civility and Science in Seventeenth-Century England*. Chicago: University of Chicago Press, 1994.

Shapin, Steven, and Simon Schaffer. *Leviathan and the Air-Pump: Hobbes, Boyle, and the Experimental Life*. Princeton, N.J.: Princeton University Press, 1985.

Shapiro, Barbara. "The Concept 'Fact': Legal Origins and Cultural Diffusion." *Albion* 26 (1994): 227–52.

———. *A Culture of Fact: England, 1550–1720*. Ithaca, N.Y.: Cornell University Press, 2000.

Shapiro, James. *Shakespeare and the Jews.* New York: Columbia University Press, 1996.

Singh, Jyotsna. "Othello's Identity, Postcolonial Theory, and Contemporary African Rewritings of *Othello.*" In *Women, "Race," and Writing,* edited by Margo Hendricks and Patricia Parker, 287–99. London: Routledge, 1994.

Siraisi, Nancy. *Medieval and Early Renaissance Medicine: An Introduction to Knowledge and Practice.* Chicago: University of Chicago Press, 1990.

Snow, Edward. "Sexual Anxiety and the Male Order of Things in *Othello.*" *English Literary Renaissance* 10 (1980): 384–412.

Snyder, Susan. *The Comic Matrix of Shakespeare's Tragedies: "Romeo and Juliet," "Hamlet," "Othello," and "King Lear."* Princeton, N.J.: Princeton University Press, 1979.

Sollors, Werner. "Ethnicity." In *Critical Terms for Literary Study,* edited by Frank Lentricchia and Thomas McLaughlin, 288–305. Chicago: University of Chicago Press, 1990.

Stepan, Nancy. *The Idea of Race in Science: Great Britain, 1800–1960.* London: Macmillan, 1982.

———. "Race and Gender: The Role of Analogy in Science." In *Anatomy of Racism,* edited by David Theo Goldberg, 38–57. Minneapolis: University of Minnesota Press, 1990.

Tambling, Jeremy. "Abigail's Party: 'The Difference of Things' in *The Jew of Malta.*" In *In Another Country: Feminist Perspectives on Renaissance Drama,* edited by Dorothea Kehler and Susan Baker, 95–112. Metuchen, N.J.: Scarecrow, 1991.

Todorov, Tzvetan. "'Race,' Writing, and Culture." In *"Race," Writing, and Difference,* edited by Henry Louis Gates Jr., 370–80. Chicago: University of Chicago Press, 1985.

Tokson, Elliot H. *The Popular Image of the Black Man in English Drama, 1550–1688.* Boston: G. K. Hall, 1982.

Towse, J. R. *Sixty Years of the Theatre.* New York: Funk and Wagnalls, 1916.

Vitkus, Daniel, ed. *Piracy, Slavery, and Redemption: Barbary Captivity Narratives from Early Modern England.* New York: Columbia University Press, 2001.

———. *Turning Turk: English Theater and the Multicultural Mediterranean, 1570–1630.* New York: Palgrave, 2003.

Wagley, Charles. "On the Concept of Social Race in the Americas." In *Contemporary Cultures and Societies of Latin America,* edited by Dwight B. Heath and Richard N. Adams, 531–45. New York: Random House, 1965.

Walvin, James. *The Black Presence: A Documentary History of the Negro in England, 1555–1860.* New York: Schocken Books, 1971.

Webster, John. *The Devil's Law-Case.* Edited by Frances A. Shirley. Regents Renaissance Drama. Lincoln: University of Nebraska Press, 1972.

———. *The Duchess of Malfi.* In *Three Plays,* edited by D. C. Gunby. London: Penguin Books, 1972.

———. *The White Devil.* Edited by John Russell Brown. Revels Plays. Cambridge, Mass.: Harvard University Press, 1960.

Wheeler, Roxann. *The Complexion of Race: Categories of Difference in Eighteenth- Century British Culture.* Philadelphia: University of Pennsylvania Press, 2000.

Wilders, John, ed. *Shakespeare: The Merchant of Venice.* Casebook Series. London: Macmillan, 1969.

Wolf, Lucien. "Jews in Elizabethan England." *Transactions of the Jewish Historical Society of England* 11 (1928): 1–91.

———. "Jews in Tudor England." In *Essays in Jewish History,* edited by Cecil Roth. London: Jewish Historical Society of England, 1934.

Yaffe, Martin D. *Shylock and the Jewish Question.* Baltimore: Johns Hopkins University Press, 1997.

Index

LARA BOVILSKY is assistant professor of English at the University of Oregon.